accounting

study guide

Stephen C. Schaefer
Contra Costa College

accounting

CHAPTERS 1 – 13
fourth edition

Charles T.
Horngren | Walter T.
Harrison | Linda Smith
Bamber

Prentice Hall, Upper Saddle River, NJ 07458

Acquisitions editor: Debbie Emry
Associate editor: Natacha St.Hill Moore
Project editor: Richard Bretan
Printer: Banta Book Group

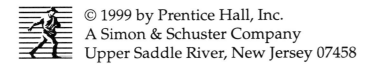 © 1999 by Prentice Hall, Inc.
A Simon & Schuster Company
Upper Saddle River, New Jersey 07458

Printed in the United States of America

10 9 8 7 6 5 4 3 2

ISBN 0-13-080765-6

Prentice-Hall International (UK) Limited, *London*
Prentice-Hall of Australia Pty. Limited, *Sydney*
Prentice-Hall Canada Inc., *Toronto*
Prentice-Hall Hispanoamericana, S.A., *Mexico*
Prentice-Hall of India Private Limited, *New Delhi*
Prentice-Hall of Japan, Inc., *Tokyo*
Simon & Schuster Asia Pte. Ltd., *Singapore*
Editora Prentice-Hall do Brasil, Ltda., *Rio de Janeiro*

Contents

Preface

This Study Guide will assist you in mastering ACCOUNTING, Fourth Edition, by Horngren, Harrison, and Bamber. The 13 chapters in the first volume of this Study Guide correspond to the first 13 chapters in the textbook. Each chapter of this Study Guide contains three sections: Chapter Review, Test Yourself, and Demonstration Problems.

Chapter Review. The Chapter Review parallels the chapter in you textbook. It is organized by learning objective and provides a concise summary of the major elements in each objective. Emphasis is given to new terms and concepts, particularly in the earlier chapters where it is essential for the student to be conversant with accounting terminology. A Chapter Overview links each chapter to previous or subsequent topics.

Test Yourself. The test yourself section is divided into six parts: matching, multiple choice, completion, daily exercises, exercises, and beyond the numbers. Answers are provided for each section along with explanations, when appropriate. The six sections provide a comprehensive review of the material in each chapter and should be used after you have read each chapter thoroughly to determine which topics you understand and those requiring further study.

Demonstration Problems. Two demonstration problems are provided for each chapter. These problems attempt to incorporate as many of the topics in the chapter as possible. For some chapters, the first demonstration problem must be completed before the second one is attempted. For those chapters, complete the first one, check your answers, make any necessary corrections, then go on to the second problem. The solutions to the demonstration problems provide explanations as well.

THIS STUDY GUIDE IS NOT A SUBSTITUTE FOR YOUR TEXTBOOK. It is designed as an additional support tool to assist you in succeeding in your accounting course.

Comments about the Study Guide are encouraged and should be sent to me in care of the publisher.

Stephen C. Schaefer
Contra Costa College

Acknowledgments

Thanks to Loc Huynh, a former student and graduate of the Walter A. Haas School of Business at the University of California-Berkeley, for his invaluable assistance in the preparation of this Study Guide. Loc did all the word processing and his comments and suggestions were always thought provoking and worthwhile. Thanks also to Joseph Marshman, a current student at the Walter A. Haas School of Business, for his help with proofreading and error checking. Thanks to current and former students who are a constant source of inspiration and challenge.

Chapter 1—Accounting and its Environment

CHAPTER OVERVIEW

Chapter One introduces you to accounting. Some of the topics covered in this chapter are the types of business organization, the basic accounting equation, analyzing business transactions, and preparing financial statements. Like many disciplines, accounting has its own vocabulary. An understanding of accounting terminology and the other topics covered in this chapter will give you a good foundation towards mastering the topics in upcoming chapters. The learning objectives for this chapter are to

1. Use an accounting vocabulary for decision-making.
2. Apply accounting concepts and principles to business situations.
3. Use the accounting equation to describe an organization's financial position.
4. Use the accounting equation to analyze business transactions.
5. Prepare and use the financial statements.
6. Evaluate the performance of a business.

CHAPTER REVIEW

Objective 1 - Use an accounting vocabulary for decision-making.

Accounting is a system that measures business activities, processes that information into reports, and communicates the results to decision makers.

There are many users of accounting information. Individuals use accounting information to make decisions about purchases and investments and to manage their bank accounts. Businesses use accounting information to set goals for their businesses and to evaluate progress toward achieving those goals. Investors use accounting information to evaluate the prospect of future returns on their investments. Creditors use accounting information to evaluate a borrower's ability to meet scheduled repayments of money loaned. Accounting information is also used by government regulatory agencies, taxing authorities, nonprofit organizations, and others, such as employee and consumer groups.

The **Financial Accounting Standards Board** (FASB), the **Securities and Exchange Commission** (SEC), the **American Institute of Certified Public Accountants** (AICPA) and the **Institute of Management Accountants** (IMA) are four groups that influence the practice of accounting in the United States. **Generally Accepted Accounting Principles** (GAAP) are the rules governing accounting. In addition, accountants are expected to maintain high ethical standards. (Helpful hint: Review Exhibit 1-2 in your text.)

The three forms of business organization are:

proprietorship - a business owned by one person
partnership - a business owned by two or more individuals
corporation - a business owned by shareholders whose liability for business debts is limited to the amount the stockholders invested in the corporation.

In the United States, proprietorships are the largest form of business numerically, whereas corporations are the dominant form in terms of total assets, income, and number of employees. (Helpful hint: Review Exhibit 1-3 in the textbook.)

Objective 2 - Apply accounting concepts and principles to business situations.

The rules governing accounting practice are called **Generally Accepted Accounting Principles (GAAP)**, which include five important standards, or rules: 1) the **entity concept**, 2) the **reliability (or objectivity) principle**, 3) the **cost principle**, 4) the **going-concern principle**, and 5) the **stable-monetary-unit concept**.

The **entity concept** states that the records of a business entity should be separate from the personal records of the owner. For example, if a business owner borrows money to remodel her home, the loan is a personal debt, not a debt to the business.

The **reliability (or objectivity) principle** states that accountants should attempt to provide reliable, accurate records and financial statements. All data that the accountant use should be verifiable by an independent observer. Ideally, accounting records should be determined by objective evidence. For example, the most objective and reliable measure of the value of supplies is the price paid for the supplies. The objective evidence documenting the price is the bill from the supplier.

The **cost principle** states that the assets and services should be recorded at their actual (historical) cost. For example, if a firm pays $10,000 for land, then $10,000 is the value recorded in the books, even if an independent appraiser states that the land is worth $12,000.

The **going-concern concept** holds that the entity will remain in operation for the foreseeable future. Therefore, the relevant measure of the entity's assets is historical cost. If the entity were going out of business, the relevant measure of its assets would be market value.

The **stable-monetary-unit** concept holds that the purchasing power of the dollar is relatively stable. Therefore, accountants may add and subtract dollar amounts as though each dollar had the same purchasing power.

Objective 3 - Use the accounting equation to describe an organization's financial position.

The **accounting equation** is expressed as:

$$ASSETS = LIABILITIES + OWNER'S EQUITY$$

Assets are a firm's resources that are expected to provide future benefits. Liabilities are claims by outsiders (creditors) to those resources. Claims by insiders (owners) are called owner's equity or capital.

Examples of assets are cash, accounts receivable, notes receivable, supplies, land, and buildings. A receivable and notes receivable both arise when the firm makes sales to customers for cr payment is expected at a later date. Accounts receivable are promises of payment. Notes written promises of payment.

...ples of **liabilities** are accounts payable and notes payable, which arise when the business makes ...ases on credit. Liabilities represent claims on assets by outsiders.

...er's equity is what is left of the assets after subtracting the liabilities:

ASSETS - LIABILITIES = OWNER'S EQUITY

...ective 4 - Use the accounting equation to analyze business transactions.

...ry transaction will have a dual effect on the accounting equation. Therefore, the equation always ...ins in balance. Study carefully the eleven business transactions analyzed in the text, and reinforce your ...standing by following the demonstration problem and explanations in this chapter of the Study Guide. ...u must have a thorough knowledge of how transactions affect the accounting equation in order to ...ceed further in this course.

...e Exhibit 1-6 in the text. Transactions affecting owner's equity are owner investment, owner withdrawal, ...nue, and expense transactions. Owner investment occurs when the owner places assets in the business; ...versely, owner withdrawal results from the owner taking assets out of the business. **Revenues** increase ...ner's equity by bringing cash or other assets into the business in the form of earnings made by delivering ...ds or services to customers. **Expenses** are decreases in owner's equity that occur in the course of ...ning revenue. Examples of expenses include rent, utilities, and employees' salaries.

...ective 5 - Prepare and use the financial statements.

...countants summarize the results of business activity in four primary financial statements: 1) the **income statement** 2) the **statement of owner's equity** 3) the **balance sheet**, and 4) the **statement of cash flows**.

...e **income statement** presents a summary of the firm's revenues and expenses for some period of time, ...ch as a month, and reports **net income** if total revenues exceed total expenses. A **net loss** occurs if total ...expenses are greater than total revenues.

...e **statement of owner's equity** presents a summary of changes in owner's equity during the same period ...s the income statement. Owner's equity increases with owner's investment and net income, and decreases ...ith owner's withdrawals and net losses.

...e **balance sheet** reports all assets, liabilities, and owner's equity, as of a specific date. That date will be ...e same date as the last day of the period for which activities are summarized in the income statement and ...he statement of owner's equity. Note that the term balance sheet comes from the fact that the report ...balances; that is, total assets equal total liabilities plus total owner's equity.

...e **statement cash flows** shows the cash inflows and outflows, organized into three areas—operating ...ctivities, investing activities, and financing activities. This financial statement is covered in detail in ...Chapter 17.

Objective 6 - Evaluate the performance of a business.

All financial statements begin with three line headings, as follows:

Company Name
Statement Name
Appropriate Date

The income statement is prepared first, listing the revenues and expenses for the period. The result is either net income (when revenues are greater than expenses) or net loss (when revenues are less than expenses). This result is carried forward to the next statement.

The statement owner's equity is prepared after the income statement. It details the amounts and sources of changes in capital during the period, as follows:

Beginning Capital
+ Net Income (or - Net Loss)
- Withdrawals
Ending Capital

Ending capital is carried forward to the next financial statement.

The balance sheet is a formal listing of the accounting equation as of the last day in the financial period. The individual assets are added together to equal total assets. The liabilities are totaled and added to ending capital.

The statement of cash flows reports cash flows (receipts and payments) for the same period covered by the other financial statements, and groups these into three types of business activities—operating, investing, and financing. The amount of net cash increase (or decrease) will, when added to the beginning cash balance, agree with the ending cash balance reported on the balance sheet.

Study Tip: The statement order is important to remember.
1. Income Statement
2. Statement Owner's Equity
3. Balance Sheet
4. Statement of Cash Flows

TEST YOURSELF

All the self-testing materials in this chapter focus on information and procedures that your instructor is likely to test in quizzes and examinations.

I. Matching   *Match each numbered term with its lettered definition.*

_____	1.	AICPA	_____	9.	IMA
_____	2.	Assets	_____	10.	Partnership
_____	3.	Corporation	_____	11.	Proprietorship
_____	4.	Expenses	_____	12.	Revenues
_____	5.	FASB	_____	13.	SEC
_____	6.	GAAP	_____	14.	Statement of Cash Flows
_____	7.	Income Statement	_____	15.	Statement of Owner's Equity
_____	8.	Liabilities	_____	16.	Balance Sheet

A. A summary of revenues and expenses for a period.
B. A business owned by one person.
C. A professional organization of Certified Public Accountants.
D. A financial statement summarizing changes in capital.
E. A legal entity, owned by stockholders, which conducts its business in its own name.
F. The body that formulates GAAP.
G. Resources expected to provide future benefit.
H. The "rules" of accounting.
I. Claims on assets by outsiders.
J. Inflows of assets from the sale of a product or service.
K. A business co-owned by two or more individuals.
L. A federal agency with the legal power to set and enforce accounting and auditing standards.
M. Costs incurred to generate revenue.
N. A professional organization of management accountants.
O. Details the net change in cash from one period to the next.
P. Lists an entity's assets, liabilities, and owner's equity as of a specific date.

II. Multiple Choice   *Circle the best answer.*

1. An example of a liability is:

   A. Fees Earned
   B. Supplies

   C. Note payable
   D. Investments by the owner

2. When cash is received on an accounts receivable:

   A. Total assets increase
   B. Total assets decrease

   C. Total assets are unchanged
   D. Cannot be determined

3. A receivable is recorded when a business makes:

   A. Sales on account
   B. Purchases on account

   C. Sales for cash
   D. Purchases for cash

4. An investment of equipment by the owner will result in:

   A. An increase in both assets and liabilities
   B. An increase in both liabilities and owner's equity

   C. An increase in both assets and owner's equity
   D. No change in assets or owner's equity

5. If the date on a financial statement is June 30, 19X9, then the financial statements must be:

   A. The income statement
   B. The statement of owner's equity

   C. The balance sheet
   D. The statement of cash flows

6. If the financial statement is dated For the Month Ended June 30, 19X9, then the financial statement must be:

   A. The income statement
   B. The statement of owner's equity

   C. The statement of cash flows
   D. All of the above

7. Net income equals:

   A. Assets - Liabilities
   B. Liabilities + Owner's equity

   C. Revenues + Expenses
   D. Revenues – Expenses

8. If total assets equals three times liabilities, and owner's equity is $40,000, what are total assets?

   A. $40,000
   B. $50,000

   C. $60,000
   D. $80,000

9. If the beginning balance in owner's equity was $100, the ending balance is $144, net income for the month was $172, and there were no investments by the owner, how much did the owner withdraw during the month?

   A. $42
   B. $106

   C. $148
   D. $128

10. On January 1, 2000, David Designs had assets of $250,000 and owner's equity of $150,000. During the year, assets increased by $50,000 and owner's equity decreased by $24,000. What were the liabilities on December 31, 2000?

   A. $100,000
   B. $174,000

   C. $74,000
   D. $126,000

II. Completion   *Complete each of the following statements.*

The four primary financial statements are: 1) _Income statement_
2) _Statement of owners equity_, 3) _Balance Sheet_
and 4) _statement of cash flows_.

Keeping accounting records for a business separate from the owner's personal accounting records follows from the _entity_ concept.

Revenues are _amounts earned by delivering goods or services to customers_

Expenses are the costs incurred in operating a business.

Outsider claims against assets are called _liabilities_ and insider claims are called _owners equity_.

What is the accounting equation?
assets = Liabilities + Owner's Equity.

When assets are purchased by a firm, they are recorded at _cost_.

Bookkeeping is the clerical recording of the data used in an accounting system.

All financial statements begin with a three line heading listing:
Company name
Statement name
Appropriate Date

10. Assuming the purchasing power of the dollar remains relatively stable over time underlies the _Stable-monetary-unit_ concept.

IV. Daily Exercises

1. For each of the following questions, indicate the financial statement where the answer can be found?

Question	Financial Statement
a. Where did all the money go?	Statement of cash flows
b. How much is the business worth?	Balance Sheet
✓ c. How much do I owe?	Balance Sheet
d. Is the business profitable?	Income Statement
e. Is my investment in the business more or less than last period?	Statement of owner's equity

2. At the beginning of the year, a business purchased a building for $100,000, paying $25,000 cash and signing a promissory note for $75,000. By the end of the first year, the amount due on the note had been reduced to $70,000, and real estate values had increased by 20% in the area. At what amount should the building be listed on the balance sheet? Which decision guideline supports your answer?

$100,000   Cost principle

3. At the end of its first month of operations, a business had total revenues of $3,700, cash receipts from customers of $2,300, total expenses of $2,500, and an owner's withdrawal of $1,200. Was the business profitable during its first month of operations?

4. Refer to question #3 above. Assuming the owner made no additional investments during the month, did the value of the business increase or decrease during the period?

3,700 - 2,300 = 1,400   owner's investment

V. Exercises

1,400 - 1,200 = 200

the value of the business increase by $200.

1. Tabitha Taylor operates a hair styling service. During the first month of operation the following events occurred:

   A. Tabitha invested $15,000 in the business.
   B. She paid rent of $750.
   C. She purchased $4,000 of equipment on account.
   D. She purchased $85 of supplies for cash.
   E. She performed services on account, $1,275.
   F. She paid $600 on the equipment purchased in C.
   G. She received $400 from a customer on her account.
   H. She sold supplies (which cost $27) to a friend for $27.

   Prepare an analysis of transactions showing the effects of each event on the accounting equation. (Hint: You may want to refer to Exhibit 1-6 in your text.)

	ASSETS				=	LIABILITIES	+	OWNER'S EQUITY
	Cash +	Accounts Receivable +	Supplies +	Equipment	=	Accounts Payable	+	Capital
A.	15,000							15,000
B.	-750				=	~~750~~		-750
C.	14,250 ~~4,000~~			4,000				14,250
D.	~~14,250~~ -85 14,250		85	4,000	=			14,250
E.	10,165	1275	85	4,000	=			14,250 1,275
F.								
G.								
H.								

2. Presented below are the balances in the assets, liabilities, revenues, and expenses for Smitty's Service on November 30, 19X9.

Accounts Payable	$ 25
Accounts Receivable	20
Cash	12
Smitty, Capital	?
Equipment	16
Service Revenues	22
Supplies	7

Prepare a balance sheet for Smitty's Service for November 30, 19X9.

Smitty's Service
Balance Sheet
November 30, 19X9

Assets:		Liabilities:	
Cash		Accounts Payable	
Accounts Receivable	_____	Total Liabilities	_____
Supplies	_____	Owner's Equity:	
Equipment	_____	Smitty, Capital	_____
	_____	Total Liabilities	
Total Assets		and Owner's Equity	
	=======		=======

3. The following are the balances in the accounts of Pat's Packaging Service on August 31, 19X9.

Accounts Receivable	$ 22
Accounts Payable	26
Equipment	298
Notes Receivable	13
Salary Payable	24
Salary Expense	50
Service Revenue	321
Supplies	18
Supplies Expense	28
Telephone Expense	27
Pat, Capital	116
Truck Rental Expense	50

Prepare an income statement for Pat's Packaging Service for the month of August, 19X9.

Pat's Packaging Service
Income Statement
For the Month Ended August 31, 19X9

Service revenue		$_____
Expenses:		
Salaries	$_____	
Truck Rental	_____	
Supplies	_____	
Telephone	_____	_____
Net income		$_____

VI. Beyond the Numbers

Can a profitable business (one where revenues consistently exceed expenses) become insolvent (unable to pay their bills)? Conversely, can an unprofitable business remain solvent?

_____

_____

_____

_____

VII. Demonstration Problems

Demonstration Problem #1

Nick Russel, CMA (Certified Management Accountant) opened a consulting practice in Midtown, USA. The business, which is named Russel Consulting, is owned solely by Russel. During the month of March, 19X9 (the first month of operation), the following transactions occurred.

3/1	Russel invested $25,000 of personal funds to start the business and deposited the funds in a checking account in the name of the business.
3/1	An office was located in town and rent of $1,250 was paid for the first month.
3/3	Office equipment were purchased for cash at a cost of $2,100.
3/5	A computer and a laser printer to be used in the business were purchased on account for $3,200.
3/8	Office supplies costing $200 were purchased on account.
3/10	Services of $1,500 were provided on account to a client.
3/15	Additional consulting fees totaling $2,300 collected from clients during the first 15 days of the month were deposited in the business checking account.
3/16	Cash of $1,300 was received for the services rendered on 3/10.
3/18	Paid for the office supplies purchased on 3/8.
3/21	Russel withdrew $3,000 from the business for personal use.
3/31	Consulting fees totaling $4,100 were collected from clients during the second half of the month. These fees were deposited in the business checking account.

Required:

1. Prepare an analysis of transactions of Russel Consulting. Use Exhibit 1-6 and the Summary Problem in Chapter 1 of the text as a guide and the format on page 12 for your answers.

2. Prepare the income statement, the statement of owner's equity, and balance sheet of the business after recording the March transactions. Use the formats on pages 12 and 13.

Requirement 1 (Analysis of transactions)

	ASSETS			=	LIABILITIES	+	OWNER'S EQUITY
Cash +	Accounts Receivable +	Supplies +	Equipment	=	Accounts Payable	+	Capital

Requirement 2 (Income Statement, Statement of Owner's Equity, and Balance Sheet)

Income Statement

Statement of Owner's Equity

Balance Sheet

Demonstration Problem #2

Mildred Mann Amis is an artist living in Northern California. Her business is called Mann Made. From the following information, prepare an Income Statement, Statement of Owner's Equity, and Balance Sheet for Mann Made for the month of May, 19X9.

Accounts Payable	$	700
Accounts Receivable		1,800
Advertising Expense		500
Building		55,000
Cash		8,200
Commissions Earned		12,000
Equipment		6,600
Interest Expense		200
Interest Receivable		100
Mildred Amis, Capital 5/1/19X9		59,325
Mildred Amis, Withdrawals		2,000
Notes Payable		14,000
Notes Receivable		1,000
Salaries Expense		1,750
Salaries Payable		250
Supplies		2,325
Supplies Expense		2,900
Utilities Expense		100
Vehicle		3,800

Balance Sheet

Statement of Owner's Equity

Income Statement

SOLUTIONS

I. Matching

1. C	5. F	9. N	13. L
2. G	6. H	10. K	14. O
3. E	7. A	11. B	15. D
4. M	8. I	12. J	16. P

II. Multiple Choice

1. C Of the choices given, only "Notes Payable" meets the definition of a liability. Fees Earned is revenue, supplies are assets, and investments by the owner are increases in equity.

2. C When cash is received on an account receivable, two assets are affected: cash is increased and accounts receivable is decreased. Since the increase in cash is equal to the decrease in accounts receivable, total assets are unchanged.

3. A Only sales on account causes a receivable to be recorded. Purchases on account cause a payable to be recorded, sales for cash and purchases for cash do not affect receivables.

4. C The owner's investment of equipment in the business causes an increase in the assets of the business. Since the owner has a claim to those assets he or she invested in the business, there is also an increase in owner's equity.

5. C The balance sheet lists all the assets, liabilities, and owner's equity as of a specific date. The income statement, statement of owner's equity, and statement of cash flows cover a specific time period.

6. D The income statement, statement of owner's equity, and statement of cash flows cover a specific period of time. The balance sheet lists all the assets, liabilities, and owner's equity as of a specific date.

7. D Revenues minus expenses equals net income. Assets minus liabilities equals owner's equity. Liabilities plus owner's equity equals assets. Revenues plus expenses has no meaning.

8. C Let "L" stand for liabilities. Given that total assets equals $3L$ and that owner's equity equals $40,000, then according to the accounting equation:

$$3L = L + \$40,000$$

Subtract L from both sides of the equation.

$$2L = \$40,000, \text{ therefore } L = \$20,000$$
$$\text{Total Assets} = \$20,000 + \$40,000$$
$$\text{Total Assets} = \$60,000$$

Study Tip: Memorizing and understanding the basic accounting equation is important and will be helpful in future chapters.

9. D

Beginning balance in owner's equity	$100
+ Net income	172
Subtotal	272
- Withdrawals	128
Ending balance in owner's equity	$144

Study Tip: There is an important concept in this problem that you can use over and over throughout your accounting course. In general terms the concept can be stated:

Beginning balance + Additions - Reductions = Ending balance.

10. B

	Assets	=	Liabilities	+	Owner's Equity	
Jan. 1	$250,000	=	$100,000	+	$150,000	
	+50,000				-24,000	
Dec. 31	$300,000	=	$174,000	+	$126,000	Dec. 31

III. Completion

1. Income Statement, Statement of Owner's Equity, Balance Sheet, and Statement of Cash Flows
2. entity (The most basic concept in accounting is that each entity has sharp boundaries between it and every other entity.)
3. _____ amounts earned by delivering goods and services to customers
4. _____ expenses
5. _____ liabilities, owner's equity
6. _____ Assets = Liabilities + Owner's equity
7. _____ cost
8. _____ Bookkeeping
9. _____ company name, statement name, date
10. _____ Stable Monetary Unit

IV. Daily Exercises

1.
a. The statement of cash flows lists the cash inflows and outflows (i.e., receipts and payments) for the period and would, therefore, answer the question.
b. The balance sheet indicates the financial position of the business on any particular date.
c. The balance sheet includes a list of all liabilities (amounts owed to creditors) on any particular date.
d. Profitability is determined by comparing revenues with expenses and is reported on the income statement.
e. The statement of owner's equity starts with beginning capital and calculates ending capital by adding net income and additional investment for the period then deducting any owner withdrawals.

2. The building should be listed on the balance sheet at $100,000. This amount is supported by the cost principle, which answers the question 'how much to record for assets and liabilities?'

3. Yes. A business is profitable when revenues exceed expenses (net income) and is not profitable when expenses exceed revenues (net loss). Therefore, net income was $1,200 ($3,700 - $2,500). Cash receipts from customers and owner's draw are irrelevant.

4. The value of the business to the owner did not change during the period. Net income of $1,200 was offset by the $1,200 the owner withdrew during the period. Therefore, beginning capital and ending capital were the same amount.

V. Exercises

1.

	Cash	+	Accounts Receivable	+	Supplies	+	Equipment	=	Accounts Payable	+	Capital
A.	$15,000							=			$15,000
B.	-750							=			-750
	$ 14,250							=			$14,250
C.							$4,000	=	$4,000		
	$ 14,250					+	$4,000	=	$4,000	+	$14,250
D.	-85			+	$ 85			=			
	$ 14,165			+	$ 85	+	$4,000	=	$4,000	+	$14,250
E.			$1,275					=			$ 1,275
	$ 14,165	+	$1,275	+	$ 85	+	$4,000	=	$4,000	+	$15,525
F.	-600							=	- 600		
	$ 13,565	+	$1,275	+	$ 85	+	$4,000	=	$3,400	+	$15,525
G.	400		-400					=			
	$ 13,965	+	$ 875	+	$ 85	+	$4,000	=	$3,400	+	$15,525
H.	27				-27			=			
	$ 13,992	+	$ 875	+	$ 58	+	$4,000	=	$3,400	+	$15,525

2.

Smitty's Service
Balance Sheet
November 30, 19X9

Assets:			Liabilities:		
Cash	$	12	Accounts Payable	$	25
Accounts Receivable		20	Total Liabilities		25
Supplies		7	Owner's Equity:		
Equipment		16	Smitty, Capital		30
			Total Liabilities		
Total Assets	$	55	and Stockholders' Equity	$	55

3.

Pat's Packaging Service
Income Statement
For the Month Ended August 31, 19X9

Service revenue			$321
Expenses:			
Salaries	$	50	
Truck Rental		50	
Supplies		28	
Telephone		27	155
Net income			$166

VI. Beyond the Numbers

The answer to both questions is yes. How is this possible? Profitability is presented on the Income Statement and occurs when revenues exceed expenses. Solvency is analyzed by examining the Balance Sheet and comparing assets (specifically cash and receivables) with liabilities. A business is solvent when there are sufficient assets on hand to pay the debt as the debt becomes due. Remember, however, there is a third financial statement—the Statement of Owner's Equity—which links the Income Statement to the Balance Sheet. A profitable business will become insolvent if, over time, the owner withdraws assets in excess of net income. Conversely, an unprofitable business can remain solvent over time if the owner is able to contribute personal assets in excess of the net losses.

VII. Demonstration Problems

Demonstration Problem #1 Solved and Explained

Requirement 1 (Analysis of transactions)

3/1 Russel's investment of $25,000 increased his equity in the business by the same amount. Thus:

Assets	=	Liabilities	+	Owner's Equity
Cash				Russel, Capital
+25,000		no change		+25,000

3/1 Monthly rent of $1,250 was paid, so Cash decreased by $1,250. In return for the rent, Russel's business received the right to use the office space. However, Russel still owns no part of the office; his right to use the office cannot be considered an asset. Since he has paid $1,250 cash but has not received an asset in return, nor paid a liability, his equity in the business has decreased by $1,250.

Assets	=	Liabilities	+	Owner's Equity
Cash				Russel, Capital
-1,250		no change		-1,250

3/3 $2,100 was paid for office equipment. In return for the cash, Russel's business received ownership of the office equipment. When a business owns a resource to be used in the business, that resource is an asset. Since the $2,100 cash was exchanged for $2,100 worth of asset, owner's equity was not affected. Remember: When cash is exchanged for an asset, owner's equity is unaffected.

Assets		=	Liabilities	+	Owner's Equity
Cash	Office Equipment				
-2,100	+2,100		no change		no change

3/5 A computer and laser printer were purchased for $3,200 on account. Russel's business now owns the equipment, which is an asset. However, payment was not made, but promised. The promise of payment is a debt, a liability. By promising the computer sales company $3,200, Russel has added $3,200 to his company's liabilities, which until this point were zero.

Assets	=	Liabilities	+	Owner's Equity
Computer				
+3,200		+3,200		no change

3/8   Office supplies costing $200 were purchased on account. As we saw in the 3/5 debt transaction, when a business incurs a debt in exchange for an asset, the business has added the asset but it has also added a corresponding liability.

Assets	=	Liabilities	+	Owner's Equity
Supplies		Accounts Payable		
+200		+200		no change

3/10   Consulting services of $1,500 were provided on account to a client. When a client promises to pay for services rendered, the promise represents an asset to the business. A business earns revenue when it performs a service, whether it receives cash immediately or expects to collect the cash later. Revenue transactions cause the business to grow, as shown by the increase in total assets and equities. Note that both the assets and the owner's equity in the business have increased.

Assets	=	Liabilities	+	Owner's Equity
Accounts Receivable				Russel, Capital
+1,500				+1,500

3/15   Fees totaling $2,300 were earned and collected. When services are rendered and cash is collected, the asset cash increases by the amount collected and the owner's interest (equity) in the business increases as well.

Assets	=	Liabilities	+	Owner's Equity
Cash				Russel, Capital
+2,300		no change		+2,300

3/16   Collected $1,300 cash on the account receivable created on 3/10. The asset Cash is increased and the asset Accounts Receivable is decreased by the same amount. Note that revenue is unaffected by the actual receipt of the cash since the firm already recorded the revenue when it was earned on 3/10.

Assets		=	Liabilities	+	Owner's Equity
Cash	Accounts Receivable				
+1,300	-1,300		no change		no change

3/18   Paid for the supplies purchased on 3/8. The payment of cash on account does not affect the asset Office Supplies because the payment does not increase or decrease the supplies available to the business. The effect on the accounting equation is a decrease in the asset Cash and a decrease in the liability Accounts Payable.

	Assets	=	Liabilities	+	Owner's Equity
	Cash		Accounts Payable		
	-200		-200		no change

3/21 The owner withdrew $3,000 for personal use. The withdrawal of cash decreases the asset Cash and reduces the owner's equity in the business. Note that the withdrawal does not represent a business expense.

	Assets	=	Liabilities	+	Owner's Equity
	Cash				Russel, Capital
	-3,000		no change		-3,000

3/31 Fees totaling $4,100 were collected. When services are rendered and immediately collected, the asset Cash increases by the amount received, and the owner's interest in the assets of the business increases as well.

	Assets	=	Liabilities	+	Owner's Equity
	Cash				Russel, Capital
	+4,100				+4,100

RUSSEL CONSULTING

		ASSETS					LIABILITIES +	OWNER'S EQUITY	
	Cash +	Office Supplies +	Accounts Receivable +	Equipment	=		Accounts Payable +	Russel, Capital	Type of owner's equity transaction
3/1	+25,000							+25,000	Owner investment
3/1	-1,250							-1,250	Rent expense
3/3	-2,100			+2,100					
3/5				+3,200			+3,200		
3/8		+200					+200		
3/10			+1,500					+1,500	Service income
3/15	+2,300							+2,300	Service income
3/16	+1,500		-1,300						
3/18	-200						-200		
3/21	-3,000							-3,000	Owner withdrawal
3/31	+4,100							+4,100	Service income
	$26,150	$200	$200	$5,300			$3,200	$28,650	
	$31,850						$31,850		

Requirement 2 (Income Statement, Statement of Owner's Equity, and Balance Sheet)

Russel Consulting
Income Statement
For the Month Ended March 31, 19X9

Service Income	$7,900
Less: Expenses	
Rent	1,250
Net Income	$6,650

Russel Consulting
Statement of Owner's Equity
For the Month Ended March 31, 19X9

Russel, Capital 3/1/X9		$25,000
Add: Net Income	6,650	
Less: Withdrawals	3,000	3,650
Russel, Capital 3/31/X9		$28,650

Russel Consulting
Balance Sheet
March 31, 19X9

ASSETS		**LIABILITIES**	
Cash	$26,150	Accounts Payable	$ 3,200
Accounts Receivable	200		
Office Supplies	200		
Equipment	5,300	**OWNER'S EQUITY**	
		Russel, Capital 3/31/X9	28,650
Total Assets	$31,850	Total Liabilities & Owner's Equity	$31,850

Demonstration Problem #2 Solved

Mann Made, Inc.
Income Statement
Month Ended May 31, 19X9

Commissions Earned		$12,000
Less: Expenses		
Advertising	500	
Interest	200	
Salaries	1750	
Supplies	2900	
Utilities	100	
Total Expenses		5,450
Net Income		$ 6,550

Mann Made, Inc.
Statement of Owner's Equity
Month Ended May 31, 19X9

Mildred Amis, Capital 5/1/X9		$59,325
Add: Net Income	6,550	
Less: Withdrawals	2,000	4,550
Mildred Amis, Capital 5/31/X9		$63,875

Mann Made, Inc.
Balance Sheet
May 31, 19X9

ASSETS		LIABILITIES	
Cash	$ 8,200	Accounts Payable	$ 700
Accounts Receivable	1,800	Notes Payable	14,000
Notes Receivable	1,000	Salaries Payable	250
Interest Receivable	100	Total Liabilities	$14,950
Supplies	2,325		
Equipment	6,600		
Vehicle	3,800	**OWNER'S EQUITY**	
Building	55,000	Mildred Amis, Capital 5/31/X9	63,875
Total Assets	$78,825	Total Liabilities and Owner's Equity	$78,825

Chapter 2—Recording Business Transactions

CHAPTER OVERVIEW

Chapter Two uses the foundation established in the previous chapter and expands the discussion of recording business transactions. A thorough understanding of this process is vital to your success in mastering topics in future chapters. The learning objectives for this chapter are to

1. Define and use key accounting terms: *account, ledger, debit,* and *credit.*
2. Apply the rules of debit and credit.
3. Record transactions in the journal.
4. Post from the journal to the ledger.
5. Prepare and use a trial balance.
6. Set up a chart of accounts for a business.
7. Analyze transactions without a journal.

CHAPTER REVIEW

Objective 1 - Define and use key accounting terms: account, ledger, debit, and credit.

The terms used in accounting sometimes have meanings that differ from ordinary usage. You must learn the accounting meaning of terms now. Key terms to remember are: account, ledger, assets, liabilities, owner's equity, capital, withdrawals, revenues, expenses, double-entry bookkeeping, T-account, debit, and credit.

An **account** is the basic summary device used to record changes that occur in a particular asset, liability, or owner's equity.

All accounts grouped together form the **ledger**. The order of the accounts in the ledger is assets first, then liabilities, and finally owner's equity (i.e., the order in which the accounts are listed in the accounting equation).

Assets are those economic resources that will benefit the business in the future. Examples of asset accounts are Cash, Notes Receivable, Accounts Receivable, Prepaid Expenses, Land, Buildings, Equipment, Furniture, and Fixtures.

Liabilities are obligations that the business owes. Examples of liability accounts include Notes Payable and Accounts Payable.

Owner's equity is the claim that the owner has on the assets of the business. Examples of owner's equity accounts are **capital**, which is the owner's claim on the assets; **withdrawals**, which are assets that the owner removes for personal use; revenues, such as Service Revenue; and expenses such as Rent Expense.

Accounting is based on **double-entry** bookkeeping. Each transaction affects two accounts. **T-accounts** illustrate the dual effects of a transaction. The left side of the T-account is the **debit** side. The right side is the **credit** side. Remember: debit = left side and credit = right side.

Objective 2 - Apply the rules of debit and credit.

The account type determines how debits and credits are recorded. A debit increases the balance of an asset and a credit decreases the balance. A credit increases the balance of a liability or owner's equity, and a debit decreases the balance.

Assets		=	Liabilities		+	Owner's equity	
debit for increase	credit for decrease		debit for decrease	credit for increase		debit for decrease	credit for increase

To illustrate, suppose that Bob Bush, proprietor of Bob's Appliance Repairs, buys on credit office equipment of $5,000 for his appliance repair business. What debits and credits should be recorded? Debit Office Equipment, an asset, for $5,000. (Assets are increased by a debit.) Credit a liability, for $5,000. (Liabilities are increased by a credit.)

> **Study Tip**: Refer to the basic accounting equation to understand the debit/credit rules. Increases in items on the *left side* of the equation are placed on the *left side* (debit) of the account. Increases in the items on the *right side* of the equation are placed on the *right side* (credit) of the account.

Objective 3 - Record transactions in the journal.

A **journal** is a chronological record of a firm's transactions. It is the first place where a transaction is recorded. To record a transaction in the journal, follow these four steps:

1. Identify the transaction from the source documents.
2. Specify each account affected and determine whether it is an asset, a liability, or an owner's equity account.
3. Determine whether each account balance is increased or decreased, and whether to debit or credit the account.
4. Enter the transaction in the journal: first the debit, then the credit, and finally a brief explanation.

To illustrate, suppose that Bob Bush, borrows $10,000 from the bank to expand the business. What is the journal entry for this transaction?

1. The source documents are a deposit slip for $10,000 and a loan agreement with the bank, both of which are dated January 10, 19X9.
2. The accounts affected are Cash (an Asset) and Notes Payable (a Liability).
3. Both accounts will increase by $10,000. Debit Cash for $10,000 to increase Cash, and Credit Notes Payable for $10,000 to increase Notes Payable.
4. Record the journal entry:

Date		Debit	Credit
Jan. 10	Cash	10,000	
	Notes Payable		10,000
	Bank loan for business expansion.		

> **Study Tip**: If one of the accounts affected is Cash, first determine whether Cash increases or decreases.

Examples of some typical journal entries are:

Cash	25,000	
Smith, Capital		25,000
Owner invests money into the business.		
Prepaid Insurance	3,000	
Cash		3,000
Purchased a three-year insurance policy.		
Supplies	1,500	
Accounts Payable		1,500
Purchased supplies on account.		
Accounts Receivable	2,200	
Commissions Earned		2,200
Billed clients for services rendered.		
Salary Expense	800	
Cash		800
Paid salaries.		
Cash	1,400	
Accounts Receivable		1,400
Received payments from clients previously billed.		

Objective 4 - Post from the journal to the ledger.

Posting means transferring amounts from the journal to the appropriate accounts in the ledger. The journal entry for the bank loan in the previous example would be posted this way:

Cash		Notes Payable	
10,000			10,000

Review Exhibit 2-8 in your text for a detailed illustration of journalizing and posting.

Objective 5 - Prepare and use a trial balance.

The **trial balance** is a list of all accounts with their balances. It tests whether the total debits equal the total credits. If total debits do not equal the total credits, an error has been made.

However, some errors may not be detected by a trial balance. One example is the posting of a transaction to the wrong account. Another is a transaction recorded at the wrong amount.

Objective 6 - Set up a chart of account.

A **chart of accounts** consists of a list of all the accounts used in the business. Each account is assigned a unique number (this account number is used as a reference in the posting process). The order of the accounts in this list parallels the accounting equation. In other words, assets are listed first, followed by liability accounts, and lastly, owner's equity. Owner's equity is subdivided into capital, withdrawals, revenue and expense accounts. The numbers are assigned in ascending order so assets are assigned the lowest numbers while expenses carry the highest numbers.

The term **normal balance** refers to the type of balance (debit or credit) the account usually carries. The normal balance for any account is always the side of the account where increases are recorded. Therefore, the normal balances are:

Account	Normal Balance
Assets	debit
Liabilities	credit
Capital	credit
Withdrawals	debit
Revenues	credit
Expenses	debit

Study Tip: Spend some time reading and thinking about the decision guidelines in your text. These should help you place the recording process in the proper context.

Objective 7 - Analyze transactions without a journal.

In general, the ledger is more useful than the journal in providing an overall model of a business. Therefore, when time is of the essence, decision makers frequently skip the journal and go directly to the ledger in order to compress transaction analysis, journalizing, and posting into a single step.

TEST YOURSELF

All the self-testing materials in this chapter focus on information and procedures that your instructor is likely to test in quizzes and examinations.

I. Matching   *Match each numbered term with its lettered definition.*

_____ 1.   Account
_____ 2.   Capital
_____ 3.   Chart of accounts
_____ 4.   Compound entry
_____ 5.   Credit
_____ 6.   Debit
_____ 7.   Double-entry system
_____ 8.   Journal

_____ 9.   Ledger
_____ 10.   Normal balance
_____ 11.   Posting
_____ 12.   Post reference
_____ 13.   Prepaid expenses
_____ 14.   Trial balance
_____ 15.   Withdrawals

A. Detailed record of changes in a particular asset, liability, or owner's equity during a period of time.
B. Costs recorded before being used.
C. A way of tracing amounts between the journal and ledger.
D. Left side of an account.
E. List of all the accounts and their account numbers.
F. Transferring information from the journal to the ledger.
G. A list of all the accounts with their balances which tests whether total debits equals total credits.
H. The book of accounts.
I. Right side of an account.
J. Chronological record of an entity's transactions.
K. The type of balance an account usually carries.
L. The owner's claim to the business assets.
M. The removal of assets by the owner.
N. When three or more accounts are affected by a transaction.
O. Recording the dual effects of transactions.

II. Multiple Choice   *Circle the best answer.*

1. An attorney performs services for which he receives cash. The correct entry for this transaction is:

   A. Debit Service Revenue and credit Accounts Payable
   B. Debit Service Revenue and credit Cash
   C. Debit Accounts Receivable and credit Service Revenue
   D. Debit Cash and credit Service Revenue

2. An accountant debited Insurance Expense $600 and credited Cash $600 in error. The correct entry should have been to debit Prepaid Insurance for $600 and credit Cash for $600. As a result of this error:

   A. Assets are overstated by $600
   B. Expenses are understated by $600

   C. The trial balance will not balance
   D. Expenses are overstated by $600

3. Accounts Receivable had total debits for the month of $2,500 and total credits for the month of $1,700. If the beginning balance in Accounts Receivable was $2,200, what was the net change in Accounts Receivable?

A. A decrease of $800
B. An increase of $3,200

C. An increase of $800
D. A decrease of $3,200

4. Accounts Payable had a balance of $3,000 on April 1. During April, $1,750 of equipment was purchased on account. The April 30 balance was a credit of $2,850. How much were payments on Accounts Payable during April?

A. $ 1,100
B. $ 2,250

C. $ 1,900
D. $ 4,600

5. Income statement accounts are:

A. Assets and liabilities
B. Revenues and withdrawals

C. Revenues and expenses
D. Assets and withdrawals

6. The posting reference in the ledger tells:

A. The page of the ledger that the account is on
B. The explanation of the transaction

C. Whether it is a debit or a credit entry
D. The page of the journal where the entry can be found

7. The list of accounts and their account numbers is called the:

A. Chart of accounts
B. Trial balance

C. Ledger
D. Accountants Reference

8. The revenue earned by lending money is called:

A. Advertising expense
B. Loan revenue

C. Interest revenue
D. Debit to Withdrawals

9. When the owner of a business withdraws cash, the journal entry should include a:

A. Debit to Accounts Payable
B. Credit to Capital

C. Debit to Cash
D. Debit to Withdrawals

10. When cash was received in payment for services rendered on account, the accountant debited Cash and credited Service Revenue. As a result there was:

A. An overstatement of Cash and Service Revenue
B. An understatement of assets and overstatement of revenues
C. An overstatement of assets and liabilities
D. An overstatement of assets and an overstatement of revenues

III. Completion   *Complete each of the following statements.*

1. Put the following in proper sequence by numbering them from 1 to 4.

   _____ A. Journal entry
   _____ B. Post to ledger
   _____ C. Source document
   _____ D. Trial balance

2. Indicate whether debits increase or decrease each of the following accounts.

	Increase	**Decrease**
A. Land	_____	_____
B. Capital	_____	_____
C. Prepaid Insurance	_____	_____
D. Interest Payable	_____	_____
E. Commission Earned	_____	_____
F. Rent Expense	_____	_____
G. Interest Revenue	_____	_____
H. Accounts Payable	_____	_____
I. Withdrawals	_____	_____
J. Advertising Expense	_____	_____

3. Indicate the normal balance for each of the following.

	Debit	**Credit**
A. Notes Receivable	_____	_____
B. Accounts Payable	_____	_____
C. Prepaid Advertising	_____	_____
D. Building	_____	_____
E. Capital	_____	_____
F. Accounts Receivable	_____	_____
G. Rent Expense	_____	_____
H. Interest Revenue	_____	_____
I. Land	_____	_____
J. Withdrawals	_____	_____

IV. Daily Exercises

1. Classify each of the following accounts as asset, liability, capital, revenue, or expense.

Account	Classification
a. Salaries Payable	_____
b. Supplies	_____
c. Fees Receivable	_____
d. Machinery	_____
e. Fees Earned	_____
f. Rent Expense	_____

2. Review the list of accounts in #1 above and indicate which side of the account (debit or credit) is used to reflect an increase.

a. _____

b. _____

c. _____

d. _____

e. _____

f. _____

3. Analyze the following errors and indicate which will cause the trial balance to be out of balance.

a. A payment of $235 for advertising was recorded as a debit of $235 to Advertising Expense and a credit of $235 to Accounts Payable.

b. When billing a client for $400 the bookkeeper forgot to record the transaction.

c. The withdrawal of $100 by the owner was recorded as a debit to Withdrawals for $10 and a credit to Cash for $10.

4. Prepare a trial balance from the following list of accounts and balances. List the accounts in their proper order.

Accounts Payable	$ 630
Accounts Receivable	850
Capital	2,200
Cash	1,150
Fees Earned	3,500
Furniture and Fixtures	4,600
Insurance Expense	300
Notes Payable	1,500
Rent Expense	750
Supplies	180

Accounts	Debit	Credit

V. Exercises

1. John Collins opened a financial planning firm on July 1, 2000. During the first month of operations, the following transactions occurred:

   7/1   John invested $5,000 cash in the business.
   7/2   Purchased used office equipment for $2,000. He made a $600 cash down payment and gave the seller a note payable due in 120 days.
   7/3   Paid $425 for a month's rent.
   7/15   Collected $4,000 in cash for services rendered during the first 15 days of July.
   7/17   Withdrew $1,100 to pay the rent on his apartment.
   7/19   Purchased $350 of supplies on account.
   7/19   Paid the phone bill for the month, $169.
   7/21   Received but did not pay the $187 utility bill for July.
   7/25   Paid his secretary a salary of $1,750.
   7/28   Paid for the supplies purchased on 7/19.
   7/31   Performed $7,500 in services for the last half of July. Clients paid for $4,000 of these services.

   Prepare the journal entries for each of these transactions.

Date	Accounts	PR	Debit	Credit

2. The following are normal balances for the accounts of Grant's Dog Grooming Service on May 31, 19X9.

Accounts payable	$1,250
Accounts receivable	2,075
Advertising expense	115
Cash	5,380
Food expense	975
Grooming supplies	605
Rent expense	640
Prepaid insurance	90
Salary expense	2,755
Salaries payable	215
Grant, capital	3,625
Grooming	7,545

Prepare a trial balance based on the account balances above.

	Debit	Credit
Cash	_____	_____
Accounts receivable	_____	_____
Grooming supplies	_____	_____
Prepaid insurance	_____	_____
Accounts payable	_____	_____
Salaries payable	_____	_____
Grant, capital	_____	_____
Grooming revenue	_____	_____
Advertising expense	_____	_____
Rent expense	_____	_____
Grooming expense	_____	_____
Salary expense	_____	_____
Total	=========	=========

3. Anthony's Answering Service had the following trial balance on April 30, 19X9.

Cash	$ 36,000	
Accounts receivable	18,000	
Notes receivable	6,000	
Land	40,000	
Accounts payable		$ 8,400
Anthony, capital		70,000
Service revenue		24,000
Salary expense		7,000
Insurance expense	3,000	
	$103,000	$ 109,400

The following errors caused the trial balance not to balance:

A. Anthony recorded a $2,000 note payable as a note receivable.
B. He posted a $4,000 credit to Accounts Payable as $400.
C. He recorded Prepaid Insurance of $3,000 as Insurance Expense.
D. He recorded a cash revenue transaction by debiting Cash for $6,000 and crediting Accounts Receivable for $6,000.

Prepare a corrected trial balance as of April 30, 19X9.

Anthony's Answering Service
Trial Balance
April 30, 19X9

Cash	_____	_____
Accounts receivable	_____	_____
Notes receivable	_____	_____
Prepaid insurance	_____	_____
Land	_____	_____
Accounts payable	_____	_____
Notes payable	_____	_____
Anthony, capital	_____	_____
Service revenue	_____	_____
Salary expense	_____	_____
Insurance expense	_____	_____
Total	_____	_____

VI. Beyond the Numbers

The following errors occurred in posting transactions from the journal to the ledger.

1. A payment of $170 for advertising was posted as a $170 debit to Advertising Expense and a $710 credit to Cash.
2. The receipt of $300 from a customer on account was posted as a $300 debit to Cash and a $300 credit to Fees Earned.
3. The purchase of Supplies on account for $140 was posted twice as a debit to Supplies and once as a credit to Accounts Payable.
4. The payment of $220 to a creditor on account was posted as a credit to Accounts Payable for $220 and a credit to Cash for $220.

For each of these errors, determine the following:
A. Is the trial balance out of balance?
B. If out of balance, what is the difference between the column totals?
C. Which column total is larger?
D. Which column total is correct?

Error	Out of balance?	Column Total difference	Larger column total	Correct column total
1.				
2.				
3.				
4.				

VII. Demonstration Problems

Demonstration Problem #1

The trial balance of Harry's Hiking Guides on May 1, 19X9 lists the entity's assets, liabilities, and owner's equity. The business was established by Harry Hancock.

| | Balance | |
Account Title	Debit	Credit
Cash	$ 8,000	
Equipment	24,000	
Accounts Payable		$ 5,000
Harry Hancock, Capital		27,000

During May, the business performed the following transactions:

1. In anticipation of expanding the business in the near future, Harry Hancock borrowed $75,000 from a local bank. A note payable in the name of the business was signed.
2. A small parcel of land was acquired for $50,000 cash. The land is expected to be used as the future location of the business.
3. Hiking trips were provided for clients. Cash totaling $6,000 was received for these trips.
4. Supplies costing $1,200 to be used in the business were purchased on account.
5. Hiking trips were provided for clients. Earned revenue on account totaled $3,500.
6. The following expenses were paid in cash:
   a. Salary expense, $4,000
   b. Rent expense, $1,400
   c. Advertising expense, $850
   d. Interest expense, $650
7. Harry Hancock withdrew $2,800 for personal use.
8. Paid $4,200 owed on account.
9. Received $2,100 cash on account for services previously rendered.

Required:

1. Using the T-account format, open the following ledger accounts for Harry's Hiking Guides with the balances as indicated.

   ASSETS
   Cash, $8,000
   Accounts receivable, no balance
   Supplies, no balance
   Equipment, $24,000
   Land, no balance

   LIABILITIES
   Accounts payable, $5,000
   Notes payable, no balance

OWNER'S EQUITY
Harry Hancock, capital, $27,000
Harry Hancock, withdrawals, no balance

REVENUE
Hiking revenue, no balance

EXPENSES
Salary expense, no balance
Rent expense, no balance
Interest expense, no balance
Advertising expense, no balance

2. Journalize the transactions using the format on page 39. Key each journal entry by its transaction letter.
3. Post to the T-accounts on the next two pages. Key all amounts by letter and compute a balance for each account.
4. Prepare the trial balance as of May 31, 19X9 using the format on page 41.

Requirements 1 and 3: (Open ledger accounts and post journal entries)

ASSETS

LIABILITIES

OWNER'S EQUITY

REVENUE

EXPENSES

Requirement 2 (Journal entries)

Date	Accounts and Explanation	PR	Debit	Credit

Requirement 4 (Trial balance)

Accounts	Debits	Credits
Cash		
Accounts Receivable		
Supplies		
Equipment		
Land		
Accounts Payable		
Notes Payable		
Harry Hancock, Capital		
Harry Hancock, Withdrawals		
Hiking revenue		
Salary expense		
Rent expense		
Interest expense		
Advertising expense		

Demonstration Problem #2

Using the information from the Trial Balance in Demonstration Problem # 1, prepare an Income Statement, Statement of Owner's Equity, and Balance Sheet.

Income Statement

Statement of Owner's Equity

Balance Sheet

SOLUTIONS

I. Matching

1. A	4. N	7. O	10. K	13. B
2. L	5. I	8. J	11. F	14. G
3. E	6. D	9. H	12. C	15. M

II. Multiple Choice

1. **D** The receipt of cash, an asset, for the performance of services causes an increase in owner's equity. This increase in owner's equity from providing services is called revenue. Cash is increased with a debit and revenue is increased with a credit.

2. **D** The recorded entry incorrectly increased expenses by $600. Accordingly, expenses are overstated. Since the entry should have debited Prepaid Insurance, but was not, assets are *understated.* Even though the entry is erroneous, it included both a debit and credit and the trial balance will balance.

3. **C** The $2,500 of debits to Accounts Receivable increased the balance, while the $1,700 of credits to Accounts Receivable decreased the balance. The net effect of the debits and the credits is $2,500 - $1,700 = $800, increase.

4. **C** The following equation is used to solve this problem:

    Beginning balance
    + increase   (new accounts)
    -   decrease   (payments)
    = ending balance

    Rearranged to solve for payments the equation is:
    Payments = beginning balance + new accounts - ending balance
    Payments = $3,000 + 1,750 - $2,850 = $1,900

5. **C** Of the combinations of accounts listed, only "Revenues and Expenses" are income statement accounts. All other responses include at least one balance sheet account.

6. **D** The posting reference provides a "trail" through the accounting records for future reference.

7. **A** A list of accounts and account numbers is called a chart of accounts.

8. **C** An entity may have as many revenue accounts as necessary. Each should be descriptive of the source of the revenue. Since the revenue earned from lending money is "interest," interest revenue is the appropriate account title.

9. **D** Withdrawals of cash from a business by the owner decreases the cash account balance and increases the balance in the withdrawals account. To decrease the cash balance it is necessary to credit the cash account; to increase the withdrawals account balance it is necessary to debit the withdrawals account.

10. D	The journal entry incorrectly credited (increased) the service revenue account balance. The correct entry should have been to credit (decrease) accounts receivable. As a result, assets (accounts receivable) are overstated and revenue (service revenue) is overstated.

III. Completion

1. A. 2	B. 3	C. 1	D. 4
(Source documents provide the information necessary to prepare journal entries. Journal entries are posted to the ledger. The trial balance is prepared from ledger balances.)

2. A. increase	B. decrease	C. increase	D. decrease	E. decrease	F. increase
   G. decrease	H. increase	I. increase	J. increase
(Debits increase accounts with a normal debit balance and decrease accounts with a normal credit balance. Assets and expenses have normal debit balances, while liabilities, owner's equity, and revenue have normal credit balances.)

3. A. debit	B. credit	C. debit	D. debit	E. credit	F. debit
   G. debit	H. credit	I. debit	J. debit
(Assets, expenses, and withdrawals have normal debit balances. Liabilities, owner's equity, and revenue have normal credit balances.)

IV. Daily Exercises

1. A. liability	B. asset	C. asset	D. asset	E. revenue	F. expense
2. A. credit	B. debit	C. debit	D. debit	E. credit	F. debit
3. None of the errors described will cause the trial balance to be out of balance. Errors (a) and (c) both included a debit and credit for the same amount, therefore the accounts contain equal values of debits and credits, so the trial balance will balance. Error (b) omitted the entire transaction, so the accounts will remain in balance. These errors are examples of one which will not be detected by the trial balance.

4.

Cash	1,150	
Accounts Receivable	850	
Supplies	180	
Furniture and Fixtures	4,600	
Accounts Payable		630
Notes Payable		1,500
Capital		2,200
Fees Earned		3,500
Insurance Expense	300	
Rent Expense	750	
Total	7,830	7,830

V. Exercises

1.

Date	Accounts	PR	Debit	Credit
7/1	Cash		5,000	
	John Collins, Capital			5,000
7/2	Equipment		2,000	
	Cash			600
	Notes Payable			1,400
7/3	Rent Expense		425	
	Cash			425
7/15	Cash		4,000	
	Service Revenue			4,000
7/17	John Collins, Withdrawals		1,100	
	Cash			1,100
7/19	Supplies		350	
	Accounts Payable			350
	Telephone Expense		169	
	Cash			169
7/21	Utility Expense		187	
	Utilities Payable (or Accounts Payable)			187
7/25	Salary Expense		1,750	
	Cash			1,750
7/28	Accounts Payable		350	
	Cash			350
7/31	Cash		4,000	
	Accounts Receivable		3,500	
	Service Revenue			7,500

2.

Grant's Dog Grooming Service
Trial Balance
May 31, 19X9

	Debit	Credit
Cash	$ 5,380	
Accounts receivable	2,075	
Grooming supplies	605	
Prepaid insurance	90	
Accounts payable		$ 1,250
Salaries payable		215
Grant, capital		3,625
Grooming revenue		7,545
Advertising expense	115	
Rental expense	640	
Food expense	975	
Salary expense	2,755	
Total	$12,635	$12,635

3.

Anthony's Answering Service
Trial Balance
April 30, 19X9

	Debit	Credit
Cash	$ 36,000	
Accounts Receivable	24,000	
Notes Receivable	4,000	
Prepaid Insurance	3,000	
Land	40,000	
Accounts Payable		$ 12,000
Notes Payable		2,000
Anthony, Capital		70,000
Service Revenue		30,000
Salary Expense	7,000	
Insurance Expense	0	
Total	$114,000	$114,000

VI. Beyond the Numbers

Error	Out of balance?	Column total difference	Larger column total	Correct column total
1.	yes	$540	credit	credit
2.	no			
3.	yes	$140	debit	credit
4.	yes	$440	credit	debit

VII. Demonstration Problems

Demonstration Problem #1 Solved and Explained

Requirement 1 (Open ledger accounts)

ASSETS

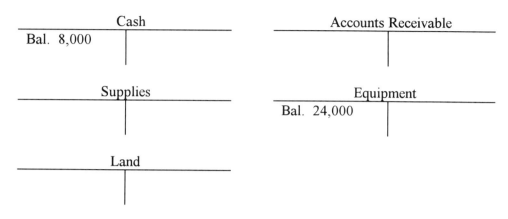

LIABILITIES

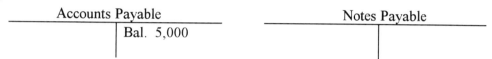

OWNER'S EQUITY

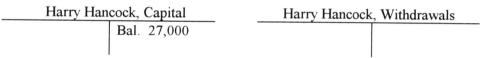

REVENUE

EXPENSES

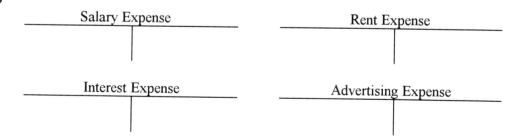

Requirement 2 (Journal entries)

Date	Accounts and Explanation		Debit	Credit
a.	Cash		75,000	
	Notes Payable			75,000
	Borrowed cash and signed note payable.			
b.	Land		50,000	
	Cash			50,000
	Purchased land for future office location.			
c.	Cash		6,000	
	Hiking Revenue			6,000
	Revenue earned and collected.			
d.	Supplies		1,200	
	Accounts Payable			1,200
	Purchased supplies on account.			
e.	Account Receivable		3,500	
	Hiking Revenue			3,500
	Performed services on account.			
f.	Salary Expense		4,000	
	Rent Expense		1,400	
	Advertising Expense		850	
	Interest Expense		650	
	Cash			6,900
	Paid cash expenses.			
g.	Harry Hancock, Withdrawals		2,800	
	Cash			2,800
	Owner withdrawal for personal use.			
h.	Accounts Payable		4,200	
	Cash			4,200
	Paid on account			
i.	Cash		2,100	
	Accounts Receivable.			2,100
	Received on account.			

Requirement 3 (Posting)

ASSETS

Cash			
Bal.	8,000		
(a)	75,000	(b)	50,000
(c)	6,000	(f)	6,900
(i)	2,100	(g)	2,800
		(h)	4,200
Bal.	27,200		

Accounts Receivable			
(e)	3,500	(i)	2,100
Bal.	1,400		

Supplies		
(d)	1,200	
Bal.	1,200	

Equipment		
Bal.	24,000	
Bal.	24,000	

Land		
(b)	50,000	
Bal.	50,000	

LIABILITIES

Accounts Payable			
		Bal.	5,000
(h)	4,200	(d)	1,200
		Bal.	2,000

Notes Payable			
		(a)	75,000
		Bal.	75,000

OWNER'S EQUITY

Harry Hancock, Capital			
		Bal.	27,000
		Bal.	27,000

Harry Hancock, Withdrawals		
(g)	2,800	
Bal.	2,800	

REVENUE

Hiking Revenue			
		(c)	6,000
		(e)	3,500
		Bal.	9,500

EXPENSES

Salary Expense		
(f)	4,000	
Bal.	4,000	

Rent Expense		
(f)	1,400	
Bal.	1,400	

Interest Expense		
(f)	650	
Bal.	650	

Advertising Expense		
(f)	850	
Bal.	850	

Requirement 4 (Trial Balance)

Accounts	Debits	Credits
Cash	$ 27,200	
Accounts Receivable	1,400	
Supplies	1,200	
Equipment	24,000	
Land	50,000	
Accounts Payable		$ 2,000
Notes Payable		75,000
Harry Hancock, Capital		27,000
Harry Hancock, Withdrawals	2,800	
Hiking revenue		9,500
Salary expense	4,000	
Rent expense	1,400	
Interest expense	650	
Advertising expense	850	
Total	$113,500	$113,500

Total debits = total credits. The accounts appear to be in balance. If the trial balance did not balance, we would look for an error in recording or posting.

Demonstration Problem #2 Solved

Harry's Hiking Guides
Income Statement
For the Month Ended May 31, 19X9

Revenues:		
Hiking Revenues		$9,500
Expenses:		
Salary Expense	$4,000	
Rent Expense	1,400	
Advertising Expense	850	
Interest Expense	650	
Total		6,900
Net Income		$2,600

Harry's Hiking Guides
Statement of Owner's Equity
For the Month Ended May 31, 19X9

Harry Hancock, Capital 5/1/X9		$27,000
Add: Net Income	2,600	
Less: Withdrawals	2,800	(200)
Harry Hancock, Capital 5/31/X9		$26,800

Harry's Hiking Guides
Balance Sheet
May 31, 19X9

ASSETS		LIABILITIES	
Cash	$ 27,200	Accounts Payable	$ 2,000
Accounts Receivable	1,400	Notes Payable	75,000
Supplies	1,200	Total Liabilities	77,000
Equipment	24,000		
Land	50,000	**OWNER'S EQUITY**	
		Harry Hancock, Capital	26,800
		Total Liabilities and	
Total Assets	$103,800	Owner's Equity	$103,800

Chapter 3—Measuring Business Income: The Adjusting Process

CHAPTER OVERVIEW

Chapter Three extends the discussion begun in Chapter Two concerning the recording of business transactions using debit and credit analysis. Therefore you should feel comfortable with the debit and credit rules when you begin. The learning objectives for this chapter are to

1. Distinguish accrual-basis accounting from cash-basis accounting.
2. Apply the revenue and matching principles.
3. Make adjusting entries at the end of the accounting period.
4. Prepare an adjusted trial balance.
5. Prepare the financial statements from the adjusted trial balance.

A1. Account for a prepaid expense recorded initially as an expense.
A2. Account for an unearned (deferred) revenue recorded initially as a revenue.

CHAPTER REVIEW

Objective 1 - Distinguish accrual-basis accounting from cash-basis accounting.

In **cash-basis accounting**, transactions are recorded only when cash is received or paid. In **accrual-basis accounting**, a business records revenues as they are earned and expenses as they are incurred, without regard to when cash changes hands. Revenues are considered earned when services have been performed or merchandise is sold because the provider has a legal right to receive payment. Expenses are considered incurred when merchandise or services have been used.

GAAP requires that businesses use the accrual basis so that financial statements will not be misleading. Financial statements would understate revenue if they did not include all revenues earned during the accounting period and would understate expenses if they did not include all expenses incurred during the accounting period.

Accountants prepare financial statements at specific intervals called accounting periods. The basic interval is a year, and nearly all businesses prepare annual financial statements. Usually, however, businesses need financial statements more frequently, at quarterly or monthly intervals. Statements prepared at intervals other than the one year interval are called **interim statements**.

Whether financial statements are prepared on an annual basis or on an interim basis, they are prepared at specific time intervals. The cutoff date is the last day of the time interval for which financial statements are prepared. All transactions that occur up to the cutoff date should be included in the accounts. Thus, if financial statements are prepared for January, all transactions occurring on or before January 31 should be recorded.

Objective 2 - Apply the revenue and matching principles.

The **revenue principle** guides the accountant on 1) when to record revenue and 2) the amount of revenue to record. Revenue is recorded when it is earned; that is, when a business has delivered a completed good or service. The amount of revenue to record is generally the cash value of the goods delivered or the services performed.

The **matching principle** guides the accountant on recording expenses. The objectives of the matching principle are 1) to identify the expenses that have been incurred in an accounting period; 2) to measure the expenses and 3) to match them against revenues earned during the same period. There is a natural association between revenues and some types of expenses. If a business pays its salespeople commissions based on amounts sold, there is a relationship between sales revenue and commission expense. Other expenses, such as rent, do not have a strong association with revenues. These types of expenses are generally associated with a period of time, such as a month or a year.

The **time-period concept** interacts with the revenue and the matching principles. It states that accounting information must be reported at regular intervals, and that income must be measured accurately each period.

Objective 3 - Make adjusting entries at the end of the accounting period.

Accountants use adjusting entries to obtain an accurate measure of the period's income, to bring the accounts up to date for the preparation of financial statements, and to properly record the effect of transactions which span more than one accounting period. End-of-period processing begins with the preparation of a trial balance, which is sometimes referred to as an unadjusted trial balance.

Adjusting entries fall into five categories: 1) **prepaid expenses**; 2) **depreciation**; 3) **accrued expenses**; 4) **accrued revenues**; and 5) **unearned revenues**. Prepaid expenses and unearned revenues are sometimes referred to collectively as **deferrals**, while accrued expenses and accrued revenues are called **accruals**.

1) **Prepaid expenses** are expenses that are paid in advance. They are assets because the future benefits are expected to extend beyond the present accounting period. If we pay advance rent of $3,000 ($1,000 per month for January, February, and March) on December 31, then on December 31 we will have Prepaid Rent of $3,000. None of the $3,000 payment is an expense during December because the payment benefits future periods. Rent expense will be recorded each month, as a portion of the $3,000 payment expires. Remember that the amount of a prepaid asset which has expired is an expense. Other examples of prepaid expenses are supplies, insurance, and sometimes, advertising. The adjusting entry for a prepaid expense always affects an asset account and an expense account.

2) **Depreciation** is recorded to account for the fact that plant assets decline in usefulness as time passes. Examples of plant assets include buildings, office equipment, and office furniture. One distinguishing feature of plant assets, compared with prepaid expenses, is that plant assets are usually useful for longer periods. Land is the only plant asset that does not depreciate.

The reduction in the usefulness of plant assets is recorded in a contra account called Accumulated Depreciation. **Contra accounts** always have companion accounts and have account balances opposite from the account balance of the companion accounts. For accumulated depreciation, the companion account is a plant asset account. The plant asset account has a debit balance, and the contra account,

Accumulated Depreciation, has a credit balance. The difference between these two amounts is called the asset's **book value**. The adjusting entry for depreciation always debits a depreciation expense and credits an Accumulated Depreciation account.

3) An **accrued expense** is an expense that a business has incurred but has not yet paid. Accrued expenses include salary expense for employees. If you have worked a summer job, then you know that there may be an interval of several days or even a week between the end of your pay period and the date that you receive your paycheck. If an accounting period ends during such an interval, then your employer's salary expense would be accrued for the salary that you have earned but have not yet been paid. Other examples of accrued expenses are interest and sales commissions.

4) **Accrued revenues** have been earned, but payment in cash has not been received nor has the client been billed. If Bob Bush's Appliance Repair completed $75 of repairs on a VCR on January 28, but did not receive payment until February 3, then accrued revenue of $75 would be recorded on January 31. The adjusting entry for accrued revenue always debits an asset (receivable) account and credits a revenue account.

5) **Unearned revenues** occur when cash is received from a customer before work is performed. Suppose that on March 15 you pay $80 for two tickets to a concert scheduled for April 7. The concert hall will not earn the $80 until April 7. Therefore, on March 15, the concert hall will debit Cash and credit Unearned Revenue. Unearned revenue is a liability account. In April, when the concert occurs, the concert hall earns the revenue and will debit Unearned Revenue and credit Revenue. The adjusting entry for unearned revenue always involves a liability (Unearned) account and a revenue account.

Note that each type of adjusting entry affects at least one income statement account and at least one balance sheet account. Also note that none of the adjusting entries has an effect on Cash. Adjusting entries are noncash transactions required by accrual accounting.

Objective 4 - Prepare an adjusted trial balance.

The general sequence for preparing an adjusted trial balance is:

1. Prepare an unadjusted trial balance.
2. Assemble the information for adjusting entries.
3. Journalize and post adjusting entries.
4. Compute the adjusted account balances.

Study Exhibit 3-10 in your text carefully to become familiar with the adjusted trial balance.

Objective 5 - Prepare the financial statements from the adjusted trial balance.

The **adjusted trial balance** provides the data needed to prepare the financial statements. The financial statements should always be prepared in the following order:

1. Income Statement
2. Statement of Owner's Equity
3. Balance Sheet

The reason for this order is quite simple. The income statement computes the amount of net income. Net income is needed for the statement of owner's equity. The statement of owner's equity computes the amount of ending capital. Ending capital is needed for the balance sheet. Exhibits 3-12, 3-13 and 3-14 in your text illustrate the flow of data from the income statement to the statement of owner's equity to the balance sheet.

The income statement starts with revenues for the period and subtracts total expenses for the period. A positive result is net income; a negative result is net loss.

The statement of owner's equity starts with the amount of capital at the beginning of the period, adds net income or subtracts net loss, and subtracts withdrawals. The result is the ending capital balance.

The balance sheet uses the asset and liability balances from the adjusted trial balance and the capital balance from the statement of owner's equity.

Note that none of the financial statements will balance back to the total debits and total credits on the adjusted trial balance. This is because the financial statements group accounts differently from the debit and credit totals listed on the adjusted trial balance. For example, the new balance for Capital on the balance sheet is a summary of the beginning Capital balance, the revenue and expense accounts used to obtain net income, and owner's withdrawals during the period.

Helpful Hints: What if the balance sheet does not balance?

1. Make sure that the balance sheet contains all asset and liability accounts with the correct balances. Check your math.
2. Be sure that you correctly transferred ending capital from the statement of owner's equity to the owner's equity section of the balance sheet.
3. Check to be sure that the statement of owner's equity is correct.
4. Check the income statement to be sure that all revenue and expense accounts have been recorded at the correct amounts. Check your math.

Objective A1 - Account for a prepaid expense recorded initially as an expense.

An alternative treatment for recording prepaid expenses into asset accounts (Prepaid Insurance, Supplies, Prepaid Rent, etc.) is to record them initially into an expense account (Insurance Expense, Supplies Expense, Rent Expense, etc.) If the accountant initially recorded the prepaid expense into an expense account, the adjusting entry will differ from that presented earlier. As an example, assume the company pays $1,800 for a one-year insurance policy on February 1. If the payment is recorded initially as an expense, the entry is

Feb. 1	Insurance Expense	1,800	
	Cash		1,800
	Purchased a one-year policy		

Assuming the accounts are adjusted on December 31, the adjusting entry is

Dec. 31	Prepaid Insurance	300	
	Insurance Expense		300
	To adjust for unexpired insurance		

After the adjusting entry is posted, the accounts would appear as follows:

Insurance Expense				Prepaid Expense		
2/1	1,800	300	12/31	12/31	300	
Balance	1,500					

The $1,500 balance in the Insurance Expense account will appear on the Income Statement, while the $300 balance in Prepaid Insurance will be listed in the asset section of the Balance Sheet.

Objective A2 - Account for an unearned (deferred) revenue recorded initially as a revenue.

An alternative treatment for recording unearned (deferred) revenue into a liability account (Unearned Fees) is to record it as revenue (Fees Earned) when received. If the accountant records the unearned revenue into a revenue account when received, the adjusting entry will differ from the previous discussion. As an example, assume a delivery service company receives $150,000 on December 30 for packages to be delivered on December 31 and January 2 and 3. As of the close of business on December 31, the company has earned $65,000 for packages delivered that day. If the $150,000 is recorded initially as revenue, the entry is

Dec. 30	Cash	150,000	
	Fees Earned		150,000
	Received $150,000		

Assuming the accounts are adjusted on December 31, the adjusting entry is

Dec. 31	Fees Earned	85,000	
	Unearned Fees		85,000
	To record fees received but not earned		

After the adjusting entry is posted, the accounts appear as follows:

	Fees Earned					Unearned Fees		
12/31	85,000	150,000	12/30				85,000	12/31
		65,000	Balance					

The $85,00 balance in Unearned Fees would be listed in the liability section of the Balance Sheet while the $65,000 balance in Fees Earned would appear on the Income Statement.

TEST YOURSELF

All the self-testing materials in this chapter focus on information and procedures that your instructor is likely to test in quizzes and examinations. Those questions followed by an * refer to information contained in the Appendix to the chapter.

I. Matching   *Match each numbered term with its lettered definition.*

_____ 1. contra asset
_____ 2. matching principle
_____ 3. prepaid expenses
_____ 4. unearned revenue
_____ 5. depreciation
_____ 6. plant asset
_____ 7. revenue principle
_____ 8. book value

_____ 9. deferrals
_____ 10. accruals
_____ 11. accumulated depreciation
_____ 12. valuation account
_____ 13. accrued expenses
_____ 14. liquidation
_____ 15. accrued revenues
_____ 16. cash-basis accounting

A. a category of miscellaneous assets that typically expire in the near future.
B. a liability created when a business collects cash from customers in advance of doing work for the customer
C. an asset account with a credit balance and a companion account
D. expense associated with spreading (allocating) the cost of a plant asset over its useful life
E. long lived assets, such as land, buildings, and equipment, that are used in the operations of the business
F. the basis for recording revenues that tells accountants when to record revenues and the amount of revenue to record
G. the basis for recording expenses that directs accountants to identify all expenses incurred during the period, to measure the expenses, and to match them against the revenues earned during that same period
H. a process of discontinuing operations and going out of business
I. revenues that have been earned but not recorded
J. an account used to determine the value of a related account
K. a collective term for accrued expenses and accrued revenues
L. expenses that have been incurred but not yet recorded
M. a balance sheet account credited when adjusting for depreciation
N. the difference between a plant asset account balance and its companion account balance
O. a collective term for prepaid expenses and unearned revenues
P. accounting that records transactions only when cash is received or paid

II. Multiple Choice   *Circle the best answer.*

1. An accountant who does not necessarily recognize the impact of a business event as it occurs is probably using:

   A. accrual-basis accounting
   B. cash-basis accounting

   C. income tax accounting
   D. actual-basis accounting

2. An example of accrual-basis accounting is:

   A. recording the purchase of land for cash
   B. recording utility expense when the bill is paid
   C. recording revenue when merchandise is sold on account
   D. recording salary expense when wages are paid

3. Which of the following is considered an adjusting entry category?

   A. accrued expenses   C. depreciation
   B. accrued revenues   D. all of the above

4. All of the following have normal credit balances except:

   A. Accumulated Depreciation   C. Unearned Rent
   B. Accounts Receivable   D. Wages Payable

5. The first financial statement prepared from the adjusted trial balance is the:

   A. income statement   C. statement of owner's equity
   B. balance sheet   D. order does not matter

6. Which of the following statements regarding the link between the financial statements is correct?

   A. Net income from the income statement goes to the balance sheet.
   B. Owner's equity from the balance sheet goes to the statement of owner's equity.
   C. Net income from the balance sheet goes to the income statement.
   D. Owner's equity from the statement of owner's equity goes to the balance sheet.

7. Bell Co. paid six months' rent on January 1 and appropriately debited Prepaid Rent for $7,200. On January 31, Bell should:

   A. credit Prepaid Rent for $6,000   C. debit Rent Expense for $6,000
   B. debit Rent Expense for $1,200   D. credit Cash for $7,200

8. A company has a beginning balance in Supplies $3,100. It purchases $3,200 of supplies during the period and uses $2,800 of supplies. If the accountant does not make an adjusting entry for supplies at the end of the period, then:

   A. assets will be understated by $2,500   C. expenses will be overstated by $2,800
   B. assets will be overstated by $2,800   D. expenses will be understated by $3,500

9. During September, a company received $6,000 cash for services rendered. It also performed $3,400 of services on account and received $2,700 cash for services to be performed in October. The amount of revenue to be included on the September income statement is:

   A. $6,000   C. $8,700
   B. $9,400   D. $12,100

10. A company correctly made an adjusting entry on December 31, 19X9 and credited Prepaid Insurance for $1,800. During 19X9 it paid $4,500 for insurance. The December 31, 19X9 balance in Prepaid Insurance was $3,000. What was the balance in the Prepaid Insurance account on January 1, 19X9?

A. $7,000
B. $ 300

C. $9,300
D. $4,800

11.* Bell Co. paid six months' rent on January and debited rent Expense for $7,200. On January 31, Bell should:

A. credit Prepaid Rent for $6,000
B. debit Rent Expense for $6,000

C. debit Prepaid Rent for $1,200
D. credit Rent Expense for $6,000

12.* On December 1, Fees Earned was credited for $12,000, representing six months of revenue for the period 12/1 to 6/1. On December 31, the company should:

A. credit Fees Earned for $10,000
B. debit Unearned Fees for $10,000

C. debit fees Earned for $10,000
D. credit Unearned fees for $2,000

III. Completion   *Complete each of the following statements.*

1. _____ basis accounting recognizes revenue when it is earned and expenses when they are incurred.
2. Adjusting entries categories include _____ , _____ , _____ , _____ , and _____ .
3. The end-of-period process of updating the accounts is called _____ .
4. Accumulated depreciation is an example of a(n) _____ account.
5. An amount that has been earned but not yet received in cash is a(n) _____ .
6. The revenue principle provides guidance to accountants as to _____ and _____ .
7. The objectives of the matching principle are: _____ , _____ and _____ .
8. Financial statements should be prepared in the following order: 1) _____ , 2) _____ , and 3) _____ .
9. The basic interval for financial statements is _____ , while statements prepared at other times and for shorter intervals of time are called _____ .
10. What is the difference between prepaid expense and unearned revenue? _____ _____ .

IV. Daily Exercises

1. Review the information provided in Multiple Choice question #9, but assume the bookkeeper was following cash-basis accounting. What amount would appear on the income statement as revenue?

2. List the following in correct sequence: trial balance, statement of owner's equity, record adjusting entries, income statement, adjusted trial balance, balance sheet, post the adjustments.

3. Record the following transaction in the space provided.

   Friday, 12/27   Paid the weekly wages, $4,000
   Tuesday, 12/31 Adjusted for two days accrued wages
   Friday, 1/3   Paid the weekly wages, $4,000

4. Classify each of the following as (a) prepaid expense, (b) accrued expense, (c) unearned revenues or (d) accrued revenue.

   _____ Fees earned but not recorded
   _____ A paid subscription series for five plays received by a community theater group
   _____ An airline ticket you just purchased for a flight at the end of the semester
   _____ The credit card charge the airline just recorded for your flight
   _____ Wages you earned last weekend, but won't receive until the end of the month
   _____ The check you just wrote for next semester's tuition

V. Exercises

1. Compute the missing amounts for each of the following independent Prepaid Insurance situations.

	1	2	3	4
Beginning balance	$1,500	C	$300	$7,600
Cash paid for premiums during the year	A	3,500	4,100	11,250
Total	B	D	4,400	18,850
Ending balance	2,200	700	2,000	F
Insurance expense	8,000	11,400	E	7,150

A._____   B._____   C._____   D._____   E._____   F._____

2. The accounting records of Ramino's Rental Service include the following unadjusted normal balances on September 30:

Accounts Receivable	$ 1,800
Supplies	610
Salary Payable	0
Unearned Revenue	900
Salary Expense	1,225
Service Revenue	5,100
Supplies Expense	0
Depreciation Expense	0
Accumulated Depreciation	1,100

The following information is available for the September 30 adjusting entries:

a. Supplies on hand, $440
b. Salaries owed to employees, $305
c. Service revenue earned but not billed, $180
d. Services performed which had been paid for in advance, $90
e. Depreciation, $110

Required:

1. Open the T-accounts.
2. Record the adjustments directly to the T-accounts. (Key each entry by letter.)
3. Compute the adjusted balance for each account.

Accounts Receivable	Supplies	Salary Payable

| Unearned Revenue | Service Revenue | Salary Expense |

| Supplies Expense | Depreciation Expense | Accumulated Depreciation |

3. The balance sheets for Jack's Studio had the following balances after adjusting entries:

	19X8	19X9
Supplies	$1,700	$1,075
Prepaid rent	2,400	800
Interest payable	1,100	200
Unearned revenue	3,150	4,100

Cash payments and receipts for 19X9 included

Payments for supplies	$2,500
Payments for rent	3,000
Payments of interest	1,400
Receipts from customers	81,000

How much supplies expense, rent expense, interest expense, and revenue were reported on the 19X9 income statement?

4. Treat Your Feet, a shoe repair shop, began the year with capital of $16,000. During the year, the owner invested $14,000 cash in his business and transferred to the business repair equipment valued at $17,500. During the year the business earned $74,000 and the owner withdrew $3,000 each month for his personal use. Prepare a statement of owner's equity for Treat Your Feet for the year ended December 31, 19X9.

Statement of Owner's Equity

VI. Beyond the Numbers

If a business is using cash-basis accounting, what is the amount listed on the Balance Sheet for Accounts Receivable, assuming clients have been billed $118,500 during the year and sent in payments totaling $93,000 by the end of the year?

VII. Demonstration Problems

Demonstration Problem #1

Point Videos, Inc. is in the business of renting videos. The trial balance for Point Videos, Inc. at December 31 of 19X9 and the data needed for year-end adjustments are as follows:

Trial Balance
December 31, 19X9

Cash	$19,415	
Accounts receivable	90	
Prepaid rent	1,200	
Supplies	400	
Rental tape library	24,000	
Accumulated depreciation—tape library		$12,000
Furniture	9,500	
Accumulated depreciation—furniture		3,800
Accounts payable		1,450
Salary payable		
Unearned tape rental revenue		1,300
Jayne Gold, capital		22,150
Jayne Gold, withdrawals	3,000	
Tape rental revenue		43,365
Salary expense	14,400	
Rent expense	6,600	
Utilities expense	2,800	
Depreciation expense—tape library		
Depreciation expense—furniture		
Advertising expense	2,660	
Supplies expense		
Total	$84,065	$84,065

Adjustment data:

    a. Depreciation for the year:
           - on the rental tape library, $6,000
           - on the furniture, $1,900
    b. Accrued salary expense at December 31, $120.
    c. Prepaid rent expired, $600.
    d. Unearned tape rental revenues which remain unearned as of December 31, $625.
    e. Supplies on hand at December 31, $230
    f. Accrued advertising expense at December 31, $115. (Credit Accounts Payable)

Required:

1. Prepare T-accounts for those accounts listed on the trial balance that are affected by the adjusting entries. Enter their December 31 unadjusted balances, then prepare and post the adjusting journal entries in the accounts. Key adjustment amounts by letter as shown in the text.
2. Using the form provided, enter the adjusting entries in the Adjustment columns, and prepare an adjusted trial balance, as shown in exhibit 3-10 of the text. Be sure that each account balance affected by an adjusting entry agrees with the adjusted T-account balances as calculated in Requirement 1.

Requirement 1 (T-accounts; adjusting journal entries; posting to ledger)

a.

Date	Accounts	PR	Debit	Credit
Dec. 31				

b.

Date	Accounts	PR	Debit	Credit
Dec. 31				

c.

Date	Accounts	PR	Debit	Credit
Dec. 31				

d.

Date	Accounts	PR	Debit	Credit
Dec. 31				

e.

Date	Accounts	PR	Debit	Credit
Dec. 31				

f.

Date	Accounts	PR	Debit	Credit
Dec. 31				

Requirement 2 (Adjusted trial balance)

Point Videos, Inc.
Preparation of Adjusted Trial Balance
For the Year Ended December 31, 19X9

Accounts	Trial Balance		Adjustments		Adjusted Trial Balance	
	Debit	Credit	Debit	Credit	Debit	Credit
Cash	$19,415					
Accounts receivable	90					
Prepaid rent	1,200					
Supplies	400					
Rental tape library	24,000					
Accumulated depreciation—tape library		$12,000				
Furniture	9,500					
Accumulated depreciation—furniture		3,800				
Accounts payable		1,450				
Salary payable						
Unearned tape rental revenue		1,300				
Jayne Gold, capital		22,150				
Jayne Gold, withdrawals	3,000					
Tape rental revenue		43,365				
Salary expense	14,400					
Rent expense	6,600					
Utilities expense	2,800					
Depreciation expense—tape library						
Depreciation expense—furniture						
Advertising expense	2,660					
Supplies expense						
	$84,065	$84,065				

Demonstration Problem #2

Refer to the adjusted trial balance in Demonstration Problem #1 and complete the following:

1. An income statement
2. A statement of owner's equity
3. A balance sheet

Income Statement

Statement of Owner's Equity

Balance Sheet

SOLUTIONS

I. Matching

1. C	5. D	9. O	13. L
2. G	6. E	10. K	14. H
3. A	7. F	11. M	15. I
4. B	8. N	12. J	16. P

II. Multiple Choice

1. **B** In cash-basis accounting the accountant does not record a transaction until cash is received or paid. In accrual-basis accounting, the accountant records a transaction when it occurs. Income tax accounting is appropriate for the preparation of income tax returns and actual-basis accounting has no meaning.

2. **C** Recording revenue when the merchandise is sold is the only event listed that does not involve the receipt or payment of cash. Accordingly, it would not be recorded using cash-basis accounting and is the only item that would be recorded under accrual-basis accounting.

3. **D** Adjusting entries assign revenues to the period in which they are earned and expenses to the period in which they are incurred. The five categories of adjusting entries are 1) prepaid expenses, 2) depreciation, 3) accrued expenses, 4) accrued revenues, and 5) unearned revenues

4. **B** Accounts Receivable is an asset account with a normal debit balance. The other items listed have normal credit balances.

5. **A** Since net income is required to prepare the statement of owner's equity, the income statement should be prepared first.

6. **D** The correct sequence is:
   1) Net income from the income statement goes to the statement of owner's equity.
   2) Owner's equity from the statement of owner's equity goes to the balance sheet.

7. **B** One month of rent will expire during January. Therefore, 1/6 X $7,200, or $1,200 will be expensed by the following journal entry:

Rent Expense	1,200	
Prepaid Rent		1,200

8. **B** The entry that should be made is:

Supplies Expense	2,800	
Supplies		2,800

   Failure to credit the Supplies account for $2,800 means that assets will be overstated by $2,800.

9. **B** With accrual accounting, total revenues in September will be $6,000 of revenues received in cash plus $3,400 of revenues that have been billed but not received.

10.   B   This problem requires you to work backward to find the solution.

Adjusted balance (given)	$3,000
Adjustment (given)	1,800
Unadjusted balance	$4,800

The unadjusted trial balance amount of $4,800 consists of the beginning balance and purchases made during the year. Since the purchases were $4,500 (given), the beginning balance must have been $300.

11.*   D   Because the entire prepayment was placed in an expense account, the correct adjusting entry is

Prepaid Rent	6,000	
Rent Expense		6,000

> Study Tip: When prepaid expenses are initially recorded into expense accounts, the adjusting entry will credit (i.e., reduce) the expense account and debit the asset account.

12.*   C   Because the $12,000 was placed into a revenue account on December 1, the following adjusting entry is required on December 31:

Fees Earned	10,000	
Unearned Fees		10,000

> Study Tip: When unearned revenue is initially recorded into a revenue account, the adjusting entry will debit (i.e., reduce) the revenue account and credit a liability (unearned) account.

III. Completion

1. Accrual
2. prepaid expenses, depreciation, accrued expenses, unearned revenue, accrued revenues (order not important)
3. adjusting the accounts
4. contra asset (A contra account has two distinguishing characteristics: (1) it always has a companion account, and (2) its normal balance is opposite that of the companion account. Accumulated depreciation's companion account is property, plant and equipment.)
5. accrued revenues
6. when to record revenue, the amount of revenue to record
7. to identify expenses which have been incurred, to measure the expenses, to match the expenses with revenues earned during the same time period
8. income statement, statement of owner's equity, balance sheet (order is important)
9. one year, interim statements
10. Prepaid expense is an asset of the business. Unearned revenue represents a liability for the business to perform services or deliver goods in the future. For every prepaid expense (asset) on the books of one business, there is a corresponding unearned revenue (liability) on the books of another business.

IV. Daily Exercises

1. $8,700 - representing all the cash received during September.
2. trial balance, prepare adjusting entries, post adjusting entries, adjusted trial balance, income statement, statement of owner's equity, balance sheet
3.

Dec. 27	Wages Expense	4,000	
	Cash		4,000
Dec. 31	Wages Expense	1,600	
	Wages Payable		1,600
	(2 days @ $800/day)		
Jan. 3	Wages Expense	2,400	
	Wages Payable	1,600	
	Cash		4,000

The Jan. 3 entry is rather unusual for issuing paychecks. However, note that $1,600 of the week's wages were already recorded (accrued) on Dec. 31, therefore only $2,400 of the weekly payroll remains an expense on Jan. 3.

4.
1. (d) - this is the definition of accrued revenues
2. (c) - unearned revenue because none of the plays have been presented
3. (a) - a prepaid expense to you because in theory, if you do not take the flight you can exchange the ticket or get a refund.
4. (c) - by accepting the charge, the airline has created an obligation to provide you with a future service.
5. (b) - to your employer and (d) to you
6. (c) - by accepting your check, your school is obligated to provide you with the courses you selected.

V. Exercises

1. Solutions are given in order worked. Note that D must be solved before C.

A.	$8,700	$1500 + A - $2,200	=	$8,000
B.	$10,200	$1,500 + A	=	B
		A	=	$8,700
		$1,500 + $8,700	=	B
D.	$12,100	D - $700	=	$11,400
C.	$8,600	C + $3,500	=	D
		D	=	$12,100
		C + $3,500	=	$12,100
E.	$2,400	$4,400 - $2,000	=	E
F.	$11,700	$18,850 - F	=	$7,150

2.

Accounts Receivable			Supplies			Salary Payable	
Bal. 1,800		Bal. 610				(b) 305
(c) 180			(a) 150			Bal. 305
Bal. 1,980		Bal. 440				

Unearned Revenue			Service Revenue			Salary Expense	
	Bal. 900		Bal. 5,100	Bal. 1,225	
(d) 90			(c) 180	(b) 305	
	Bal. 810		(d) 90	Bal. 1,530	
			Bal. 5,370		

Supplies Expense			Depreciation Expense			Accumulated Depreciation	
						Bal. 1,100
(a) 150		(e) 110				(e) 110
Bal. 150		Bal. 110				Bal. 1,210

3. Remember that Beginning balance + Additions - Reductions = Ending balance

For Supplies:

	Beginning balance	+	Supplies purchased for cash	-	Supplies expense	=	Ending balance
	$1,700	+	$2,500	-	?	=	$1,075

Supplies expense = $3,125

For Rent:

	Beginning balance	+	Rent paid	-	Rent expense	=	Ending balance
	$2,400	+	$3000	-	?	=	$800

Rent expense = $4,600

For Interest payable:

	Beginning balance	+	Interest expense	-	Cash paid for taxes	=	Ending balance
	$1,100	+	?	-	$1400	=	$200

Interest expense = $500

For unearned revenue:

	Beginning balance	+	Receipts from customers	-	Revenue earned	=	Ending balance
	$3,150	+	$81,000	-	?	=	$4,100

Revenue = $80,050

4.

Treat Your Feet
Statement of Owner's Equity
For the Year Ended December 31, 19X9

Capital, 1/1/19X9	$16,000	
Add: Cash invested	14,000	
Equipment		
transferred	17,500	
Net income	74,000	
	91,500	
Less: Withdrawals	36,000	
Capital, 12/31/19X9	$55,500	

VI. Beyond the Numbers

The answer is 0. Why? Because cash-basis accounting does not record revenue when a client is billed, only when the business receives payment. Therefore, while the business may send bills to clients, they are not recorded.

VII. Demonstration Problems

Demonstration Problem #1 Solved and Explained

Requirement 1 (T-accounts; adjusting entries; posting to ledger)

a.

Depreciation Expense—Tape Library	
(a) 6,000	
Bal. 6,000	

Accumulated Depreciation—Tape Library	
	Bal. 12,000
	(a) 6,000
	Bal. 18,000

Depreciation Expense—Furniture	
(a) 1,900	
Bal. 1,900	

Accumulated Depreciation—Furniture	
	Bal. 3,800
	(a) 1,900
	Bal. 5,700

Date	Accounts	PR	Debit	Credit
Dec. 31	Depreciation Expense—Tape Library		6,000	
	Accumulated Depreciation—Tape Library			6,000
	To record depreciation expense on tape library			
	Depreciation Expense—Furniture		1,900	
	Accumulated Depreciation—Furniture			1,900
	To record depreciation expense on furniture			

Explanation of Adjustment (a)

As a long-lived plant asset (such as building, furniture, machinery, equipment) becomes less useful, its cost is gradually transferred from the asset account to a depreciation expense account. The recording of depreciation expense for Point Videos, Inc., requires a debit of $7,900 ($6,000 on the rental tape library and $1,900 on furniture) to depreciation expense (expenses are increased with debits) and credits to the contra accounts of $6,000 to Accumulated Depreciation—Tape Library and $1,900 to Accumulated Depreciation —Furniture (assets are decreased with credits). Note that the original cost of the asset remains unchanged on the books of Point Videos, Inc. The reduction in book value of each asset is accomplished by increasing the asset's accumulated depreciation account.

Example: Change in book value of furniture.

Plant Assets	Before Adjustment	Change	After Adjustment
Furniture	$9,500	0	$9,500
Less accumulated depreciation	3,800	+1,900	5,700
Book value	$5,700	-$1,900	$3,800

b.

Salary Expense			Salary Payable	
Bal. 14,400				(b) 120
(b) 120				
Bal. 14,520				Bal. 120

Dec. 31	Salary Expense	120	
	Salary Payable		120
	To accrue salary expense		

Explanation of Adjustment (b)

Amounts owed employees for salary and wages unpaid as of the close of an accounting period must be accrued. The facts indicate that $120 must be accrued to record salary expense and the related liability. As a result, Salary Expense is debited $120 (expenses are increased by debits), and Salary Payable is credited $120 (liabilities are increased by credits).

c.

Rent Expense			Prepaid Rent	
Bal. 6,600			Bal. 1,200	(c) 600
(c) 600				
Bal. 7,200			Bal. 600	

Dec. 31	Rent Expense	600	
	Prepaid Rent		600
	To record rent expense		

Explanation of Adjustment (c)

Point Videos, Inc., paid two months' rent in advance early in December. This prepayment created an asset (Prepaid Rent) for Point Videos, Inc., in the form of a purchased future right to use the rental space. At the end of the year, the prepaid asset account must be adjusted for the amount of the prepayment that has expired. During December, one month's worth of the prepayment was used up. As a result, one month's prepaid rent of $600 is transferred to expense by crediting (assets are reduced by credits) the Prepaid Rent account and debiting (expenses are recorded as debits) the Rent Expense account. Note that one month's rent remains in the Prepaid Rent account.

d.

Tape Rental Revenue		Unearned Revenue	
Bal. 43,365			Bal. 1,300
(d) 675	(d) 675		
Bal. 44,040			Bal. 625

Dec. 31	Unearned Rent Revenue		675	
	Tape Rental Revenue			675
	To record revenue collected in advance.			

Explanation of Adjustment (d)

When cash is collected from customers before the agreed-upon product or service is provided, a liability is created. If $625 of the $1,300 of Unearned Rental Revenue remains unearned, then $675 has become earned revenue. The liability account Unearned Rental Revenue should be debited (a liability is reduced by a debit) and Tape Rental Revenue should be credited (a revenue is increased by a credit).

e.

Supplies Expense		Supplies	
(e) 170		Bal. 400	(e) 170
Bal. 170		Bal. 230	

Dec. 31	Supplies Expense		170	
	Supplies			170
	To record supplies expense.			

Explanation of Adjustment (e)

Supplies purchased for business use represent an asset until they are used. The Supplies account must be adjusted periodically to reflect supplies no longer on hand. Supplies of $230 remain on hand at December 31. Since $400 of supplies were on hand initially, it is clear that $170 of supplies have been used up ($400 - $230 = $170). Reduce the Supplies account by crediting it $170 (assets are decreased by credits) and record the $170 supplies expense by debiting Supplies Expense (expenses are recorded by debits).

f.

Advertising Expense			Accounts Payable	
Bal.	2,660		Bal.	1,450
(f)	115		(f)	115
Bal.	2,775		Bal.	1,565

Date	Accounts	PR	Debit	Credit
Dec. 31	Advertising Expense		115	
	Accounts Payable			115
	To record accrued advertising expense.			

Explanation of Adjustment (f)

The rationale for this entry is similar to that for the adjusting entry which accrued salary expense. Advertising Expense is increased by debiting the account (expenses are recorded by debits) and Accounts Payable is credited (liabilities are recorded by credits) to reflect the debt owed by Point Videos, Inc.

Requirement 2 (Adjusted trial balance)

Point Videos, Inc.
Preparation of Adjusted Trial Balance
For the Year Ended December 31, 19X9

Accounts	Trial Balance Debit	Trial Balance Credit	Adjustments Debit	Adjustments Credit	Adjusted Trial Balance Debit	Adjusted Trial Balance Credit
Cash	$19,415				$19,415	
Accounts receivable	90				90	
Prepaid rent	1,200			(c) 600	600	
Supplies	400			(e) 170	230	
Rental tape library	24,000				24,000	
Accumulated depreciation— tape library		$12,000		(a) 6,000		$18,000
Furniture	9,500				9,500	
Accumulated depreciation— furniture		3,800		(a) 1,900		5,700
Accounts payable		1,450		(f) 115		1,565
Salary payable				(b) 120		120
Unearned tape rental revenue		1,300	(d) 675			625
Jayne Gold, capital		22,150				22,150
Jayne Gold, withdrawals	3,000				3,000	
Tape rental revenue		43,365		(d) 675		44,040
Salary expense	14,400		(b) 120		14,520	
Rent expense	6,600		(c) 600		7,200	
Utilities expense	2,800				2,800	

Depreciation expense—tape library			(a) 6,000		6,000	
Depreciation expense—furniture			(a) 1,900		1,900	
Advertising expense	2,660		(f) 115		2,775	
Supplies expense			(e) 170		170	
	$84,065	$84,065	$9,580	$9,580	$92,200	$92,200

Demonstration Problem #2 Solved

Requirement 1

Point Videos, Inc.
Income Statement
For the Year Ended December 31, 19X9

Revenues:		
Tape rental revenue		$44,040
Expenses:		
Salary expense	14,520	
Rent expense	7,200	
Utilities expense	2,800	
Depreciation expense	7,900	
Advertising expense	2,775	
Supplies expense	170	
Total expenses		35,365
Net Income		$ 8,675

Requirement 2

Point Videos, Inc.
Statement of Owner's Equity
For the Year Ended December 31, 19X9

Owner's Equity 1/1/X9	$ 7,150
Add: Net Income	8,675
	15,825
Less: Withdrawals	3,000
Jayne Gold, Capital 12/1/X9	$12,825

Requirement 3

Point Videos, Inc.
Balance Sheet
December 31, 19X9

ASSETS

Cash		$19,415
Accounts Receivable		90
Prepaid Rent		600
Supplies		230
Tape Rental Library	24,000	
Less: Acc. Dep.—Library	18,000	6,000
Furniture	9,500	
Less: Acc. Dep.—Furniture	5,700	3,800
Total Assets		$30,135

LIABILITIES

Accounts Payable	$ 1,565
Salary Payable	120
Unearned Tape Rental Revenue	625
Total Liabilities	2,310

OWNER'S EQUITY

Jayne Gold, Capital	27,825
Total Liabilities and Owner's Equity	$30,135

Chapter 4—Completing the Accounting Cycle

CHAPTER OVERVIEW

Chapter Four introduces you to the final steps in the accounting cycle. Using the information you learned in the previous three chapters you are now ready to complete the accounting cycle, thereby preparing the financial records for the next accounting period. The learning objectives for this chapter are to

1. Prepare an accounting work sheet.
2. Use the work sheet to complete the accounting cycle.
3. Close the revenue, expense, and withdrawal accounts.
4. Correct typical accounting errors.
5. Classify assets and liabilities as current or long-term.
6. Use the current and debt ratios to evaluate a business.

CHAPTER REVIEW

OVERVIEW OF THE ACCOUNTING CYCLE

The **accounting cycle** is the process by which companies produce financial statements for a specific period.

The accounting cycle can be subdivided into two categories: work performed during the period and work performed at the end of the period.

Work performed during the period includes:
1. Starting with the ledger account balances at the beginning of the period.
2. Analyzing and journalizing transactions as they occur.
3. Posting entries to the ledger accounts.

Work performed at the end of the period includes:
1. Computing the unadjusted balance in each account at the end of the period.
2. Entering the unadjusted trial balance on the work sheet.
3. Using the adjusted trial balance or the full work sheet as a guide, a) prepare financial statements, b) record and post adjusting entries, c) record and post closing entries.
4. Preparing the post-closing trial balance.

Objective 1 - Prepare an accounting cycle.

A **work sheet** is an optional tool the accountant often uses to prepare financial statements. It is not part of a formal accounting system. Remember that in Chapter 3 you learned how to prepare an adjusted trial balance using the following steps:

1. Prepare the unadjusted trial balance.
2. Enter the adjustments.
3. Calculate the adjusted account balances.

The work sheet is completed using the following steps:

1. Extend the adjusted revenue and expense account balances to the Income Statement columns, which are located to the right of the Adjusted Trial Balance columns. Extend the adjusted asset, liability, and owner's equity account balances to the Balance Sheet columns, which are located to the right of the Income Statement columns.
2. Enter net income or net loss as a balancing amount on both the Income Statement and the Balance Sheet columns, and compute the adjusted column totals.

You should review Exhibits 4-2 through 4-6 in your text to be sure you understand the preparation of the adjusted trial balance.

Once the adjusted trial balance has been prepared (Steps 1-3), the adjusted asset, liability, and owner's equity account balances are transferred to the Balance Sheet columns, and the adjusted revenue and expense account balances are transferred to the Income Statement columns (Step 4). Note that each account will appear in either the Income Statement columns, or the Balance Sheet columns, but not both. Exhibit 4-5 in your text illustrates the process of transferring adjusted account balances to the Balance Sheet and Income Statement columns. At this point the debit and credit column totals are not necessarily equal in either the Income Statement or the Balance Sheet columns.

The final step in completing the work sheet is to obtain the net income or net loss amount and enter it as a balancing amount at the bottom of the Income Statement and Balance Sheet columns. If the transactions for the period result in net income, then the Income Statement column is debited and the Balance Sheet column is credited. If the result is a net loss, the Income Statement column is credited and the Balance Sheet column is debited.

Recall that net income increases owner's equity. On the work sheet, capital is recorded in the credit column of the balance sheet. Adding net income to the credit column of the balance sheet shows the effect of net income on owner's equity. Similar logic applies to a net loss, which appears on the work sheet in the debit column of the balance sheet, because a net loss decreases owner's equity.

Objective 2 - Use the work sheet to complete the accounting cycle.

Once the work sheet has been completed, financial statements must be prepared, adjusting entries must be recorded, and the accounts must be closed.

Exhibit 4-7 in your text illustrates financial statements prepared from a completed work sheet. (Remember that the work sheet is an optional tool, and that the financial statements can be prepared directly from the adjusted trial balance, as you learned in Chapter 3.)

Next, it is necessary to record the adjusting entries. Since the work sheet is not a journal or a ledger, the adjustments entered on the work sheet do not adjust the accounts. Adjusting journal entries must be prepared and posted to the accounts, as shown in Exhibit 4-8 of your text. Companies often do not record adjusting entries until after the work sheet is completed.

Objective 3 - Close the revenue, expense, and withdrawal accounts.

Closing the accounts refers to the process of preparing the accounts for the next accounting period. Closing involves journalizing and posting the **closing entries**. Closing the accounts sets the balances of revenues, expenses, and owner's withdrawals to zero. Remember that when the balance sheet is prepared, the owner's equity balance includes the summary effect of the revenue, expense, and owner's withdrawal accounts. These accounts are **temporary accounts**—they measure the effect on owner's equity for a single accounting period. This is in contrast to balance sheet accounts (except withdrawals) which are **permanent accounts**—they do not affect owner's equity.

The closing process uses a special holding account called **Income Summary**. The steps taken to close the accounts of an entity are:

1. For each account that appears in the Income Statement credit column of the work sheet, debit it for the amount of its balance (to zero it out). Credit Income Summary for the total amount of the debits.
2. For each account that appears in the Income Statement debit column of the work sheet, credit it for the amount of its balance. Debit Income Summary for the total amount of the credits.
3. If Income Summary has a credit balance, debit it for that amount (to zero it out) and credit Capital. If Income Summary has a debit balance, credit it for that amount and debit Capital. The amount of this third closing entry should agree with the net income (or loss) reported for the period.
4. For the Withdrawals account in the Balance Sheet column of the work sheet, credit it for the amount of its debit balance and debit Capital. Note that Withdrawal is neither a revenue nor an expense account, and thus is not closed to Income Summary.

Exhibit 4-9 in your text illustrates the closing process. Note that when the closing entries are posted, the balance in capital should be the same as the amount reported on the balance sheet.

The accounting cycle ends with the **post closing trial balance**. It contains the ending balances of the permanent, balance sheet accounts. Exhibit 4-10 in your text illustrates a post-closing trial balance.

Reversing entries are an optional step in the accounting cycle completed after the post-closing trial balance has been prepared. Reversing entries literally reverse a previous adjusting entry. Doing so allows the accountant to record a subsequent cash payment (for a previously accrued expense) or cash receipt (for a previously accrued revenue) in a routine manner.

Study Tip: If a business uses reversing entries, you can identify the adjusting entries which need to be reversed by tracing the effect of the adjustment to the balance sheet. If the adjustment increases total assets or total liabilities on the balance sheet, the adjusting entry should be reversed.

The complete **accounting cycle** can now be summarized as follows:

1. Analyze the transaction
2. Record and post the journal entry
3. Complete an unadjusted trial balance
4. Analyze the adjustments
5. Complete the adjusted trial balance
6. Complete the work sheet

7. Prepare the financial statements
8. Journalize and post the adjusting entries
9. Journalize and post the closing entries
10. Prepare a post-closing trial balance
11. Journalize and post the reversing entries

Objective 4 - Correcting typical accounting errors.

Typical accounting errors include 1) incorrect journal entries, 2) mistakes in posting, 3) transpositions, and 4) slides.

1. If a journal entry has been posted to an incorrect account, a correcting entry must be prepared. The correcting entry will contain a debit (or credit) to the correct account and a credit (or debit) to the incorrect account. The debit (or credit) to the incorrect amount will be offset by the credit (or debit) in the correcting entry.
2. If a debit is incorrectly posted as a credit, or vice versa, then total debits will not be equal to total credits. The amount of the error will be equal to one-half of the difference between total debits and total credits. When the amount of the error has been determined, you can go back to the journal to find the transaction and make the correction to the ledger.
3. A transposition occurs when the order of two digits is reversed. For example, $63 instead of $36. The amount of a transposition ($63 - $36, or $27) is always divisible by 9.
4. A slide occurs when one or more zeroes are added to or dropped from a number. For example, $500 instead of $50, or $50 instead of $500. The amount of the error ($500 - $50, or $450) is always divisible by 9.

Objective 5 - Classify assets and liabilities as current or long term.

Assets and liabilities are classified according to their liquidity. **Liquidity** is a measure of how quickly an item can be converted into cash. The balance sheet lists assets and liabilities in the order of their relative liquidity, with Cash, as the most liquid asset, listed first.

Current assets are those assets expected to be converted into cash, sold, or consumed within a year, or within the business normal operating cycle if longer than a year. Current assets include: 1) Cash, 2) Accounts Receivable, 3) Notes Receivable, 4) Inventory, and 5) Prepaid Expenses.

Long-term assets are all assets which are not current assets. Long-term assets include plant assets such as: 1) Land, 2) Buildings, and 3) Equipment.

Current liabilities are obligations due within one year or one accounting cycle if the accounting cycle is longer than one year. Current liabilities include: 1) Accounts Payable, 2) Notes Payable due within one year, 3) Salary Payable, 4) Unearned Revenue, and 5) Interest Payable.

Long-term liabilities are obligations due in future years. Long-term liabilities include: 1) Notes Payable due at least partly in more than one year, 2) Bonds Payable, and 3) Mortgages Payable.

(Helpful hint: Review Exhibits 4-11 and 4-12 in your text.)

Objective 6 - Use the current and debt ratios to evaluate a business.

Creditors like to be able to predict whether a borrower can repay a loan before the loan is made. Ratios of various items drawn from a company's financial statements can help creditors assess the likelihood that a loan can be repaid.

The **current ratio** measures the ability of a company to pay current liabilities (short-term debt) with current assets.

$$\text{Current ratio} = \frac{\text{Total current assets}}{\text{Total current liabilities}}$$

The **debt ratio** measures the relationship between total liabilities and total assets. The debt ratio is an indication of a company's ability to pay both current and long-term debt.

$$\text{Debt ratio} = \frac{\text{Total Liabilities}}{\text{Total Assets}}$$

TEST YOURSELF

All the self-testing materials in this chapter focus on information and procedures that your instructor is likely to test in quizzes and examinations.

I. Matching   *Match each numbered term with its lettered definition.*

_K_ 1. account format
_O I_ 2. closing the accounts
_B_ 3. current liability
_D_ 4. liquidity
_G_ 5. long-term asset
_J_ 6. report format
_H_ 7. debt ratio
_A_ 8. work sheet

_L_ 9. post-closing trial balance
_M O_ 10. accounting cycle
_I M_ 11. closing entries
_E_ 12. Income Summary
_C_ 13. long-term liability
_F_ 14. permanent accounts
_N_ 15. temporary accounts

A. a columnar document that is designed to help move data from the trial balance to the finished financial statements
B. a debt due to be paid within one year or one of the entity's operating cycles if the cycle is longer than a year
C. a liability other than a current liability
D. a measure of how quickly an item may be converted to cash
E. a temporary holding account into which revenues and expenses are transferred prior to their final transfer to the owner's equity account
F. accounts that are not closed at the end of the accounting period
G. an asset other than a current asset
H. ratio of total liabilities to total assets
I. entries that transfer the revenue, expense and owner withdrawal balances from these accounts to the owner's equity account
J. balance sheet format that lists the assets at the top, with the liabilities and owner's equity below
K. balance sheet format that lists the assets at the left, with the liabilities and owner's equity at the right
L. list of the ledger accounts and their balances at the end of the period after journalizing and posting the closing entries
M. process by which accountants produce an entity's financial statements for a specific period
N. revenue accounts, expense accounts, and withdrawals
O. step in the accounting cycle that prepares the accounts for recording the transactions of the next period

II. Multiple Choice   *Circle the best answer.*

1. Which of the following accounts will *not* appear on the post-closing trial balance?

    A. Accounts Receivable
    B. Rent Expense

    C. Capital
    D. Equipment

2. On a work sheet, which of the following is *not* extended from the adjusted trial balance to the balance sheet columns?

    A. liabilities
    B. capital

    C. assets
    D. revenues

3. What effect will adjusting entries usually have on the balance of the Accumulated Depreciation account?

    (A) increase   C. no effect
    B. decrease   D. cannot be determined

4. A company has a $7,000 net loss for 19X9. This amount is entered on the work sheet as:

    A. a debit on the income statement column   (C) a debit on the balance sheet column
    B. a credit on the balance sheet column   D. both A and B

5. Which of the following is *not* a temporary account?

    A. Salary Expense   C. Drawing
    B. Revenue   (D) Capital

6. Suppose a company has posted its closing entries to the Income Summary account. The account now has a debit balance. This means that the company had:

    (A) net income
    B. a net loss
    C. net income only if there were no owner withdrawals
    D. a net loss only if there were no owner withdrawals

7. Craine, Withdrawals has a balance of $1,800 before closing. What is the correct entry to close the Withdrawals account?

    (A) debit Capital and credit Withdrawals, $1,800
    B. debit Withdrawals and credit Income Summary, $1,800
    C. debit Withdrawals and credit Capital, $1,800
    D. debit Income Summary and credit Withdrawals, $1,800

8. Which of the following accounts would *not* be classified as a current assets?

    A. Accounts Receivable   C. Marketable Securities
    B. Cash   D. Equipment

9. The current ratio compares:

    A. current assets to long-term assets   C. current liabilities to long-term liabilities
    B. current assets to current liabilities   D. total liabilities to total assets

10. The Income Summary has debits of $88,000 and credits of $94,000. This means that the company had:

    A. $6,000 net income   C. $182,000 net income
    B. $6,000 net loss   D. $182,000 net loss

III. Completion   *Complete each of the following statements.*

1. The accounting cycle starts with _____.
2. Revenue and expense accounts are _____ accounts.
3. The optional summary device used for convenience in preparing financial statements is the _____.
4. The accounts that are never closed at the end of an accounting period are called _____ accounts.
5. Revenue and expense accounts are usually closed to the _____ account.
6. The Withdrawals account is closed to _____.
7. _____ refers to how quickly an asset can be converted into cash.
8. The accounting cycle ends with the _____.
9. _____ and _____ decrease owner's equity.
10. The debt ratio compares _____ to _____.
11. Optional entries completed after a post-closing trial balance are called _____.
12. The_____ is a measure of short-term liquidity.

IV. Daily Exercises

1. From the following list, present the current asset section of a balance sheet.

Accounts Payable	$ 5,000
Accounts Receivable	9,000
Cash	4,500
Inventory	11,000
Marketable Securities	8,500
Notes Payable (due in 60 days)	6,000
Notes Payable (due in 2 years)	18,000
Prepaid Insurance	1200
Salaries Payable	1,400
Supplies	350
Utilities Payable	280

2. Using the information in #1 above, calculate the current ratio.

3. On a work sheet, the asset and liability amounts appearing in the balance sheet columns are the same amounts listed on the financial statement; however, the amount for Capital on the work sheet is not the same figure listed on the financial statement. Why are the two amounts different?

4. Using the following balance sheet information, calculate the debt ratio.

Total current assets	$1.2 million
Total current liabilities	.8 million
Total property, plant, and equipment	4.4 million
Total long-term liabilities	2.1 million
Total investments and other assets	1.6 million
Total stockholders' equity	4.3 million

V. Exercises

1. The following transactions were recorded with an error in the original journal entry.

   A. Purchased equipment for $1,500 cash. Supplies was debited for $1,500; Cash was credited for $1,500
   B. Purchased equipment for $2,000 on account. Equipment was debited for $2,000; Cash was credited for $2,000.
   C. Received $800 cash for services to be rendered next month. Cash was debited for $800; Revenue was credited for $800.
   D. The owner withdrew $125 so he could pay his personal utilities bill. Utilities expense was debited for $125; Cash was credited for $125.

Prepare the correcting journal entry for each transaction.

A.

Date	Accounts and Explanation	PR	Debit	Credit

B.

Date	Accounts and Explanation	PR	Debit	Credit

C.

Date	Accounts and Explanation	PR	Debit	Credit

D.

Date	Accounts and Explanation	PR	Debit	Credit

2.

Elliot Company
Trial Balance
December 31, 19X9

Cash	$ 23,000	
Accounts receivable	6,000	
Prepaid advertising	3,600	
Supplies	4,200	
Notes payable		$15,400
Unearned revenue		3,400
Elliot, capital		12,200
Elliot, withdrawals	1,900	
Fees earned		18,000
Salary expense	5,600	
Rent expense	3,000	
Utilities expense	1,700	
	$49,000	$49,000

Additional information:
- a. Supplies at year end totaled $1,900.
- b. $1,700 of the Prepaid Advertising was expired at year end.
- c. Unearned revenues total $1,800 as of December 31.

Required:

1. Prepare the appropriate adjusting entries.
2. Prepare closing entries.

Requirement 1 (Adjusting entries)

GENERAL JOURNAL

Date	Accounts and Explanation	PR	Debit	Credit

Requirement 2 (Closing entries)

GENERAL JOURNAL

Date	Accounts and Explanation	PR	Debit	Credit

3. Using the information in Exercise 1 and 2, calculate the ending Capital balance.

Beginning Capital	$ _____
Plus: Net Income	_____
	_____
Less: Withdrawals	_____
Ending Capital	$ _____

4. Using the information in Exercise 1, 2, and 3, prepare a post-closing trial balance.

Elliot Company
Post-closing Trial Balance
December 31, 19X9

Cash	$_____	$_____
Accounts receivable	_____	_____
Prepaid advertising	_____	_____
Supplies	_____	_____
Notes payable	_____	_____
Unearned revenue	_____	_____
Elliot, Capital	_____	_____
	$_____	$_____

5. List the accounting cycle in the correct sequence.

VI. Beyond the Numbers

Given the following information, prepare a Statement of Owner's Equity. Also, journalize the last two closing entries and balance the accounts.

Income Summary			
12/31	82,000	12/31	96,000

Capital		
	Bal.	106,000
	5/5	9,000
	10/1	4,000

Withdrawals	
3/10	5,000
7/15	8,000
11/2	4,000

Statement of Owner's Equity

GENERAL JOURNAL

Date	Accounts and Explanation	PR	Debit	Credit

VII. Demonstration Problems

Demonstration Problem #1

1. Below are the trial balance columns of the work sheet of Pradesh Enterprises for the year ended November 30, 19X9. Using this trial balance, prepare the journal entries necessary to adjust the accounts of Pradesh Enterprises The additional data needed are provided below:

    a. Supplies on hand at November 30, 19X9, $895
    b. Depreciation expense, $1,820
    c. Accrued interest payable, $520
    d. Prepaid rent as of November 30, $4,300
    e. Unrecorded ticket orders charged on account by customers on November 30, 19X9, $2,775 (tickets were issued and used during November; debit Accounts Receivable)
    f. All but $12,500 of the unearned ticket revenue was earned at year end

Trial Balance

Accounts	Debit	Credit
Cash	$ 21,325	
Accounts receivable	1,555	
Prepaid rent	11,000	
Supplies	7,395	
Equipment	78,000	
Accumulated depreciation		$ 18,415
Accounts payable		4,925
Note payable		5,000
Interest payable		
Unearned ticket revenue		52,560
Sujan Pradesh, Capital		88,510
Sujan Pradesh, Withdrawals	13,000	
Admissions revenue		58,700
Salary expense	19,900	
Rent expense	37,000	
Interest expense	9,225	
Depreciation expense		
Advertising expense	29,710	
Supplies expense		
Total	$228,110	$ 228,110

2. Place each adjusting entry directly into the Adjustments columns of the work sheet and key each entry by letter. Complete the work sheet on page 95 using Exhibit 4-6 in your text as a guide.

3. Prepare the journal entries needed to close the accounts.

Requirement 1 (adjusting entries)

GENERAL JOURNAL

Date	Accounts and Explanation	PR	Debit	Credit

Requirement 2 (work sheet)

Pradesh Enterprises
Work sheet
For the Year Ended November 30, 19X9

Accounts	Trial Balance		Adjustments		Adjusted Trial Balance		Income Statement		Balance Sheet	
	Debit	Credit	Debit	Credit	Debit	Credit	Debit	Credit	Debit	Credit
Cash	$ 21,325									
Accounts receivable	1,555									
Prepaid rent	11,000									
Supplies	7,395									
Equipment	78,000									
Accumulated		$ 18,415								
Accounts payable		4,925								
Note payable		5,000								
Interest payable										
Unearned ticket revenue		52,560								
Sujan Pradesh, Capital		88,510								
Sujan Pradesh, Withdrawals	13,000									
Admissions revenue		58,700								
Salary expense	19,900									
Rent expense	37,000									
Interest expense	9,225									
Depreciation expense										
Advertising expense	29,710									
Supplies expense										
Total	$228,110	$228,110								

Completing the Accounting Cycle   95

Requirement 3 (closing entries)

GENERAL JOURNAL

Date	Accounts and Explanation	PR	Debit	Credit

Demonstration Problem #2

Refer to the completed work sheet in Demonstration Problem #1. Use the format on this page and pages 104 and 105 to:

1. Prepare the income statement for the year ended November 30, 19X9.
2. Prepare the statement of owner's equity for the year ended November 30, 19X9. Draw the arrow that links the income statement to the statement of owner's equity.
3. Prepare a classified balance sheet at November 30, 19X9 using the report format. All liabilities are current.
4. Using the balance sheet, calculate the current ratio and the debt ratio.
5. Prepare the post-closing trial balance. Confirm that your post-closing trial balance contains only permanent accounts.

Requirement 1 (Income Statement)

Pradesh Enterprises
Income Statement
For the Year Ended November 30, 19X9

Revenues:		
Expenses:		

Requirement 2 (Statement of Owner's Equity)

Pradesh Enterprises
Statement of Owner's Equity
For the Year November 30, 19X9

Sujan Pradesh, Capital 11/30/X8		
Add:		
Less:		
Sujan Pradesh, Capital 11/30/X9		

Requirement 3 (Balance Sheet)

Pradesh Enterprises
Balance Sheet
November 30, 19X9

Requirement 4 (current and debt ratios)

current ratio:

debt ratio:

Requirement 5 (post-closing trial balance)

Pradesh Enterprises
Trial Balance
November 30, 19X9

SOLUTIONS

I. Matching

1. K	4. D	7. H	10. M	13. C
2. O	5. G	8. A	11. I	14. F
3. B	6. J	9. L	12. E	15. N

II. Multiple Choice

1.   B   The post-closing trial balance contains the ending balances of the permanent accounts only. The temporary accounts (revenues, expenses and withdrawals) have been closed, have no balances and are not shown.

2.   D   Revenues are extended to the income statement columns. Assets, liabilities and capital are extended to the balance sheet columns.

3.   A   The adjusting entry for depreciation is
   Depreciation Expense   XX
       Accumulated Depreciation   XX
   The credit to accumulated depreciation increases the account balance.

4.   C   A net loss is entered as a credit on the income statement column of the work sheet and as a debit on the balance sheet column of the work sheet. Net income is entered as a debit on the income statement column of the income statement and as a credit on the balance sheet column of the work sheet.

5.   D   Revenue, expenses and withdrawals are temporary accounts. They are closed at the end of each accounting period.

6.   B   Closing has the effect of transferring all revenues to the credit side of Income Summary and all expenses to the debit side. If revenues are larger than expenses, income summary will have a credit balance which reflects net income. If expenses are greater than revenue, Income Summary will have a debit balance which reflects a net loss.

7.   A   The entry to close withdrawals is
   Capital   XX
       Withdrawals   XX
   Note that Withdrawals is closed directly to Capital and is not closed through Income Summary.

8.   D   Current assets are assets that are expected to be converted to cash, sold, or consumed during the next 12 months or within the business's normal operating cycle if longer than a year. Equipment would not fit this description while the other accounts listed do.

9.   B   The current ratio is current assets ÷ current liabilities.

10.   A   See the explanation for #6 above.

III. Completion

1. account balances at the beginning of the period (The accounting cycle is the process by which accountants produce the financial statements for a specific period of time. The cycle starts with the beginning account balances.)
2. temporary (Revenue, expenses and withdrawals are temporary accounts. They are closed at the end of each accounting period.)
3. work sheet (The work sheet is a columnar document that is designed to help move data from the trial balance to the finished financial statements.)
4. permanent (Permanent accounts, i.e., assets, liabilities and capital, are not used to measure income for a period and are not closed at the end of the period.)
5. Income Summary (Closing has the effect of transferring all revenues to the credit side of Income Summary and all expenses to the debit side. If revenues are larger than expenses, Income Summary will have a credit balance which reflects net income. If expenses are greater than revenue, Income Summary will have a debit balance which reflects a net loss.)
6. Capital (The entry to close withdrawals is always:

     Capital   XX
          Withdrawals   XX

    Note that Withdrawals is closed directly to Capital and is *not* closed through Income Summary.)
7. Liquidity (Balance Sheets list assets and liabilities in the order of their relative liquidity.)
8. post-closing trial balance
9. Net losses, withdrawals
10. total liabilities, total assets
11. reversing entries
12. current ratio (current assets ÷ current liabilities)

IV. Daily Exercises

1. From the following list, present the current asset section of a balance sheet.

Cash	$ 4,500
Marketable Securities	8,500
Accounts Receivable	9,000
Inventory	11,000
Prepaid Insurance	1200
Supplies	350
Total	$34,550

2. current ratio = current assets ÷ current liabilities

    current assets = $34,550 (from above)
         current liabilities =

Accounts Payable	5,000
Notes Payable	6,000
Salaries Payable	1,400
Utilities Payable	280
	12,680

current ratio = $34,550 ÷ $12,680 = 2.7 to 1 (rounded)

3. The Capital figure appearing on the work sheet has not been updated to reflect the effects of the income statement and drawing. Most account balances are updated when they are adjusted; however, capital becomes updated only when the accounts are closed. Remember, net income (from the income statement) is added to Capital on the Owner's Equity Statement. The ending balance amount from the Owner's Equity Statement is the updated amount listed on the Balance Sheet.

4. debt ratio = total liabilities ÷ total assets

total liabilities = $.8 million + 2.1 million = $2.9 million
total assets = $1.2 + 4.4 + 1.6 million = $7.2 million
debt ratio = $2.9 ÷ $7.2 million = .403 (rounded)

V. Exercises

1.

Date	Accounts and Explanation	PR	Debit	Credit
A.	Equipment		1,500	
	Supplies			1,500
B.	Cash		2,000	
	Accounts Payable			2,000
C.	Revenue		800	
	Unearned Revenue			800
D.	Withdrawals		125	
	Utilities Expense			125

2.

Requirement 1

Date	Accounts and Explanation	PR	Debit	Credit
A.	Supplies Expense		2,300	
	Supplies			2,300
	If ending supplies are $1,900, then $2,300 of supplies were used.			
B.	Advertising Expense		1,700	
	Prepaid advertising			1,700
	To record expired advertising.			
C.	Unearned Revenues		1,600	
	Fees Earned			1,600
	To adjust Unearned Revenues			

Requirement 2

Date	Accounts and Explanation	PR	Debit	Credit
	Fees Earned		19,600	
	Income Summary			19,600
	Income Summary		14,300	
	Salary Expense			5,600
	Rent Expense			3,000
	Utilities Expense			1,700
	Supplies Expense			2,300
	Advertising Expense			1,700
	Supplies Expense and Advertising Expense from Requirement 1 must be included.			
	Income Summary		5,300	
	Elliot, Capital			5,300
	Income Summary had a credit balance of $5,300 before this entry ($19,600 credit - $14,300 debit).			
	Elliot, Capital		1,900	
	Withdrawals			1,900

3.

Beginning Capital	$12,200
Plus: Net Income	5,300
	17,500
Less: Withdrawals	1,900
Ending Capital	$15,600

4.

Elliot Company
Post-closing Trial Balance
December 31, 19X9

Cash	$23,000	
Accounts receivable	6,000	
Prepaid advertising	1,900	
Supplies	1,900	
Notes payable		$15,400
Unearned revenue		1,800
Elliot, Capital		15,600
Totals	$32,800	$32,800

5.
1. Start with the balances in the ledger at the beginning of the period.
2. Analyze and journalize transactions as they occur.
3. Post entries to the ledger accounts.
4. Compute the unadjusted balance in each account at the end of the period.
5. Enter the trial balance on the work sheet, and complete the work sheet.
6. Prepare the financial statements.
7. Journalize and post the adjusting entries and the closing entries.
8. Prepare a post-closing trial balance.

VI. Beyond the Numbers

Income Summary			
12/31	82,000	12/31	96,000
12/31	14,000		
	-0-		

Capital				
12/31	17,000	Bal.	106,000
		5/5	9,000
		10/1	4,000
		12/31	14,000
		Bal.	116,000

Withdrawals			
3/10	5,000	12/31	17,000
7/15	8,000		
11/2	4,000		
	-0-		

Statement of Owner's Equity

Beginning Capital	$106,000
Add:	
Investment	13,000
Net Income	14,000
Less:	
Drawing	17,000
Ending Capital	$116,000

Date	Accounts and Explanation	PR	Debit	Credit
12/31	Income Summary		14,000	
	Capital			14,000
12/31	Capital		17,000	
	Withdrawals			17,000

VII. Demonstration Problems

Demonstration Problem #1 Solved and Explained

Requirement 1

(a) Nov. 30   Supplies Expense   6,500
                         Supplies   6,500
          To record supplies expense.

Calculation:

Supplies at the beginning of accounting period	$7,395
Supplies at the end of the accounting period	895
Supplies Expense (used up)	$6,500

A business must adjust its Supplies account to reflect supplies used up during each accounting period. Supplies are an asset to the business. When supplies are used in the business, the amount used up during the period must be transferred from the Supplies account to Supplies Expense. To decrease the asset, credit Supplies. To report the expense, debit Supplies Expense.

(b) Nov. 30   Depreciation Expense   1,820
                         Accumulated Depreciation - Equipment   1,820
          To record depreciation expense.

To reflect the decline in usefulness of long-lived assets, a portion of the asset's cost is systematically transferred from the asset to expense. Depreciation Expense is debited (expenses are recorded with debits) and the contra asset account Accumulated Depreciation - Equipment is credited (decreases in assets are recorded by credits).

(c) Nov. 30 Interest Expense   520
                         Interest Payable   520
          To record accrued interest expense.

Accrued interest is interest which is owed but is not required to be paid within the current accounting period. An adjusting entry must be made in order to update the interest account and properly match the expense to revenues in the period when the expense was incurred. Credit Interest Payable to reflect the increase in the liability owed, and debit Interest Expense to record the increase in expense.

(d) Nov. 30 Rent Expense   6,700
                         Prepaid Rent   6,700
          To record rent expense.

Prepaid rent must be reduced to adjust its balance for the amount of the asset total that has expired. Decrease the Prepaid Rent account (an asset) by crediting it, and increase Rent Expense by debiting the account.

Calculation:

Prepaid Rent at the beginning of accounting period $11,000
Prepaid Rent at the end of the accounting period   4,300
Rent Expense (used up) $ 6,700

(e) Nov. 30 Accounts Receivable   2,775
          Admissions Revenue   2,775
     To record admissions revenue.

Tickets sold on account in the last day or two of the month are occasionally not recorded for several days. To reflect this revenue in the proper accounting period, the adjusting entry must increase the Admissions Revenue account (by crediting it) and increase the Accounts Receivable (by debiting it). This is an example of accrued revenue.

(f) Nov. 30 Unearned Ticket Revenue   40,060
          Admissions Revenue   40,060
     To record admissions revenue.

Advance payment is a liability because the business owes the customer a service or product. The business records the liability in an unearned revenue account. This account must be adjusted at the close of each accounting period to reflect amounts earned during the period. Note that the liability Unearned Ticket Revenue is decreased by transferring $40,060 to the Admissions Revenue account. The unearned revenue, a liability, became revenue once the agreed-on service was performed.

Calculation:

Unearned ticket revenue at the beginning of the period $52,560
Unearned ticket revenue at the end of the period   12,500
Revenue Earned $40,060

Work Sheet:

If the adjusting entries are prepared correctly, completion of an accurate work sheet is relatively straightforward. The work sheet makes preparation of the financial statements fast and easy. The work sheet also provides a summary of all information needed to prepare the closing entries.

Errors made in the footing of individual columns of the work sheet are revealed and, of course, corrected prior to the formal preparation of the financial statements. As a result, the work sheet is a time saver. "Cross-footing" mistakes will occur less frequently if you use a ruler. Starting at the top of the work sheet and working from left to right, cross-foot and extend one column at a time. Working methodically, and slowly if necessary, saves time in the long run. You will become more efficient with practice.

Requirement 2

Pradesh Enterprises
Work Sheet
For the Year Ended November 30, 19X9

Accounts	Trial Balance Debit	Trial Balance Credit	Adjustments Debit	Adjustments Credit	Adjusted Trial Balance Debit	Adjusted Trial Balance Credit	Income Statement Debit	Income Statement Credit	Balance Sheet Debit	Balance Sheet Credit
Cash	$ 21,325				$ 21,325				$ 21,325	
Accounts receivable	1,555		(e) 2,775		4,330				4,330	
Prepaid rent	11,000			(d) 6,700	4,300				4,300	
Supplies	7,395			(a) 6,500	895				895	
Equipment	78,000				78,000				78,000	
Accumulated depreciation		$ 18,415		(b) 1,820		$ 20,235				$ 20,235
Accounts payable		4,925				4,925				4,925
Note payable		5,000				5,000				5,000
Interest payable				(c) 520		520				520
Unearned ticket revenue		52,560	(f) 40,060			12,500				12,500
Sujan Pradesh, capital		88,510				88,510				88,510
Sujan Pradesh, withdrawals	13,000				13,000				13,000	
Admissions revenue		58,700		(e) 2,775 (f) 40,060		101,535		101,535		
Salary expense	19,900				19,900		19,900			
Rent expense	37,000		(d) 6,700		43,700		43,700			
Interest expense	9,225		(c) 520		9,745		9,745			
Depreciation expense			(b) 1,820		1,820		1,820			
Advertising expense	29,710				29,710		29,710			
Supplies expense			(a) 6,500		6,500		6,500			
Total	$228,110	$228,110	55,610	55,610	$233,225	$233,225	111,375	101,535	121,850	131,690
Net loss								9,840	9,840	
							$111,375	$111,375	$131,690	$131,690

Requirement 3

GENERAL JOURNAL

Date	Accounts and Explanation	PR	Debit	Credit
Nov. 30	Admissions Revenue		101,535	
	Income Summary			101,535
	Income Summary		111,375	
	Salary Expense			19,900
	Rent Expense			43,700
	Interest Expense			9,745
	Depreciation Expense			1,820
	Advertising Expense			29,710
	Supplies Expense			6,500
	Sujan Pradesh, Capital		9,840	
	Income Summary			9,840
	NOTE: There was a net loss in this problem so			
	the capital account is debited, not credited.			
	Sujan Pradesh, Capital		13,000	
	Sujan Pradesh, Withdrawals			13,000

Closing entries zero out revenue, expense, and withdrawal accounts by transferring their amounts to the capital account. Revenues and expenses undergo the intermediate step of being transferred to a "holding" account called Income Summary.

The closing procedure can be broken down into four steps:
1. Close Revenues to Income Summary
2. Close Expenses to Income Summary
3. Close Income Summary to Capital
4. Close Withdrawals to Capital

Note how the above closing entries follow this sequence.

All information required for the first three adjusting entries can be taken directly from the Income Statement columns of the work sheet. Look at the Income Statement columns. Compare the income and expense figures with the first two closing entries, and compare the net loss figure with the third entry.

Demonstration Problem #2 Solved and Explained

Requirement 1

Pradesh Enterprises
Income Statement
For the Year Ended November 30, 19X9

Revenues:		
Admissions Revenue		$101,535
Expenses:		
Salary Expense	19,900	
Rent Expense	43,700	
Interest Expense	9,745	
Depreciation Expense	1,820	
Advertising Expense	29,710	
Supplies Expense	6,500	
Total Expenses		111,375
Net Income (Loss)		$ (9,840)

All the information for the Income Statement can be taken directly from the Income Statement columns of the work sheet.

Requirement 2 (Statement of Owner's Equity)

Pradesh Enterprises
Statement of Owner's Equity
For the Year Ended November 30, 19X9

Sujan Pradesh, Capital 11/30/X8		$88,510
Less: Net Loss	9,840	
Withdrawals	13,000	22,840
Sujan Pradesh, Capital 11/30/X9		$65,670

Beginning capital and withdrawals can be taken directly from the Balance Sheet columns of the work sheet. Net loss can be taken from the Income Statement. Ending capital is then calculated. The ending capital for this period will appear as the beginning capital on next year's work sheet and statement of owner's equity.

Requirement 3 (Balance Sheet)

Pradesh Enterprises
Balance Sheet
November 30, 19X9

ASSETS
Current Assets:

Cash	$21,325	
Accounts Receivable	4,330	
Prepaid Rent	4,300	
Supplies	895	
Total Current Assets		30,850

Plant Assets:

Equipment	78,000	
Less: Accumulated Depreciation	20,235	57,765
Total Assets		$88,615

LIABILITIES
Current Liabilities:

Accounts Payable	$4,925	
Notes Payable	5,000	
Interest Payable	520	
Unearned ticket revenue	12,500	
Total Liabilities		22,945

OWNER'S EQUITY

Sujan Pradesh, Capital	65,670
Total Liabilities and Owner's Equity	$88,615

Requirement 4

current ratio	=	current assets ÷ current liabilities
	=	$30,850 ÷ $22,945 = 1.34 : 1 (rounded)

debt ratio	=	total liabilities ÷ total assets
	=	$22,945 ÷ $88,615 = .26 (rounded)

Requirement 5

Pradesh Enterprises
Post-closing Trial Balance
November 30, 19X9

Accounts	Debit	Credit
Cash	$ 21,325	
Accounts receivable	4,330	
Prepaid rent	4,300	
Supplies	895	
Equipment	78,000	
Accumulated depreciation		$ 20,235
Accounts payable		4,925
Note payable		5,000
Interest payable		520
Unearned ticket revenue		12,500
Sujan Pradesh, capital		65,670
	$108,850	$108,850

A final check of the closing process is performed by preparing a post-closing trial balance. If any temporary account balances (Revenue, Expense, Income Summary, or Withdrawals) appear in the post-closing trial balance, a mistake has been made in closing the accounts. On a post-closing trial balance, the only accounts you should see are the balance sheet (permanent) accounts.

Chapter 5—Merchandising Operations and the Accounting Cycle

CHAPTER OVERVIEW

Throughout the previous four chapters you learned about the accounting cycle as it applies to a service business. In Chapter Five, the emphasis changes from a service business to a **merchandising business**—one which earns its revenue by selling products. Understanding this chapter will make subsequent chapters, particularly Chapters 6 and 9 easier to comprehend. The learning objectives for this chapter are to

1. Use sales and gross margin to evaluate a company.
2. Account for the purchase and sale of inventory.
3. Adjust and close the accounts of a merchandising business.
4. Prepare a merchandiser's financial statements.
5. Use the gross margin percentage and the inventory turnover ratios to evaluate a business.
6. Compute the cost of goods sold.

S1. Account for the purchase and sale of inventory.
S2. Compute cost of goods sold.
S3. Adjust and close the accounts of a merchandising business.
S4. Prepare a merchandiser's financial statements.

CHAPTER REVIEW

Objective 1 - Use sales and gross margin to evaluate a company.

When inventory is purchased, the merchandiser obtains an asset—inventory—which is held for resale to customers. When inventory is sold to customers, the amount of the sale is Sales Revenue, or simply Sales. However, once the inventory is sold to customers, it is no longer held by the merchandiser for sale, so it is no longer an asset. The cost of the inventory that has been sold to customers becomes Cost of Goods Sold, an expense. The difference between the amount of the sale and the cost of the inventory sold is called the **Gross Margin** or Gross Profit.

Gross Margin = Sales - Cost of Goods Sold

(Helpful hint: Review Exhibit 5-1 in your text.)

Accounting for a merchandising business is a bit more complex because the merchandiser must obtain inventory, pay for it, sell it to customers, collect from customers, and then obtain more inventory. This process is referred to as the **operating cycle**. (Review Exhibit 5-2 in your text.)

The two main accounting systems used for merchandise inventory are the **periodic system** and the **perpetual system**. The major difference between the two is the availability, within the accounting records, of an up-to-date (and therefore reasonably accurate) value for merchandise inventory on hand. When a perpetual system is used, this value is available, whereas the periodic system can only determine a value by an actual physical count (which is time consuming and expensive). With the increasing use of computers, more and more businesses have changed their systems from periodic to perpetual. For this reason, we use the perpetual system in our discussion of merchandise businesses (the periodic system is covered in the chapter supplement).

Objective 2 - Account for the purchase and sale of inventory.

Typically, the process of purchasing inventory and selling it to customers is a continuous process. A large business may have many different products it sells to customers, and may deal with many different suppliers.

When a merchandiser decides to purchase inventory, it sends a purchase order to its supplier. The supplier ships the merchandise and sends an invoice, or bill, to the merchandiser. After the inventory has been received and inspected, the merchandiser pays the supplier.

A **quantity discount** and a **purchase discount** (also called a cash discount) are two types of discounts a purchaser may be able to obtain. Both discounts are inducements from a seller to a buyer. A quantity discount offers a buyer the option of purchasing a larger number of units and, by doing so, obtaining a lower per unit cost. A purchase discount offers the buyer the option of paying an invoice promptly and, by doing so, obtaining a slight reduction in the total price paid. Quantity discounts are never recorded whereas purchase discounts are only recorded when earned. Review the following sequence of transactions and explanations:

Inventory	400	
Accounts Payable		400
Purchased inventory on account, term 1/15, n/30		
If paid within discount period (i.e., discount earned):		
Accounts Payable	400	
Cash		396
Inventory		4
If paid after discount period (i.e., discount not earned):		
Accounts Payable	400	
Cash		400

Frequently the buyer incurs the shipping cost on merchandise and, occasionally, goods need to be returned to the seller or an allowance requested by the buyer. Shipping costs incurred by the buyer are termed **freight-in** and can either be debited to the inventory account or debited to a unique account Freight-In. Either treatment reflects an added cost in acquiring goods for resale. Conversely, **returns and allowances** can be credited directly to the inventory account or credited to a special account Purchase Returns and Allowances. Either treatment is acceptable and both reflect a reduction in the cost of merchandise acquired.

When merchandise is sold and a perpetual inventory system is in use, two entries are required, as follows:

1) Cash (or Accounts Receivable)	XXX	
Sales		XXX
2) Cost of Goods Sold	XX	
Inventory		XX

Entry 1 records the sale at its selling price while Entry 2 transfers the cost of the sale from Inventory (an asset) to Cost of Goods Sold (an expense).

As mentioned earlier, sellers offer discounts to encourage prompt payment. On the seller's books, the entry to record a Sales Discount is

Cash	XX	
Sales Discount	X	
Accounts Receivable		XXX

When a return is accepted or an allowance is granted, the entry is:

Sales Return and Allowances	XX	
Accounts Receivable		XX

Sellers rarely debit either discounts or returns/allowances directly to the Sales account. Both Sales Discount and Sales Returns and Allowances are contra accounts to the Sales account. **Net Sales** is computed as follows:

> Sales Revenues (credit balance)
> - Sales Discounts (debit balance)
> - Sales Returns and Allowances (debit balance)
> = Net Sales (a calculation, not an account)

Objective 3 - Adjust and close the accounts of a merchandising business.

Adjusting entries for a merchandiser are like those for a service business. The general form of the **closing entries** for a merchandiser is basically the same as for a service business.

When a difference exists between the balance in the Inventory account and the result of a physical count of merchandise still on hand, the account needs to be adjusted so its balance agrees with the physical count. In most cases, this adjusting entry will be either

Cost of Goods Sold	XX	
Inventory		XX
When the Inventory account is overstated.		

Inventory	XX	
Cost of Goods Sold		XX
When the Inventory account is understated.		

The format for the **work sheet** is identical to the one introduced in Chapter 4, and the steps in completing the work sheet are the same. The closing process also remains unchanged, as follows:

1. Income Statement credit balances are transferred to the Income Summary account
2. Income Statement debit balances are transferred to the Income Summary account
3. The Income Summary account is closed to the Capital account (remember, the amount of this third closing entry must agree with net income or net loss)
4. The Withdrawals account is closed to the Capital account

Objective 4 - Prepare a merchandiser's financial statements.

The major difference between the financial statements of a merchandiser and those of a service business is the presence of Inventory on the merchandiser's balance sheet and Cost of Goods Sold on the merchandiser's income statement.

For many businesses, Inventory will be the largest current asset on the Balance Sheet. On the Income Statement, operating expenses are generally divided between Selling Expenses (those costs directly related to marketing the company's products) and General Expenses. Finally, non-operating revenues and expenses (called Other revenues and expenses) are listed separately. This allows the user to clearly distinguish between operating income and net income.

The Income Statement can be presented in either a **multiple-step format** or a **single-step format**. The multiple-step format clearly establishes significant relationships within the statement, whereas the single-step format groups together all revenues, then groups together all expenses and, in a single computation, deducts the expenses from the revenues (this is similar to the income statements illustrated in Chapters 1-4).

Objective 5 - Use the gross margin percentage and the inventory turnover ratios to evaluate a business.

A key measure of profitability for a merchandiser is the **gross margin percentage**.

$$\textbf{Gross margin percentage} \quad = \quad \frac{\textbf{Gross margin}}{\textbf{Net Sales Revenues}}$$

Inventory turnover measures the number of times a company sells its average level of inventory during a year.

$$\textbf{Inventory turnover} \quad = \quad \frac{\textbf{Cost of goods sold}}{\textbf{Average inventory}}$$

$$\textbf{Average inventory} \quad = \quad \frac{\textbf{Beginning inventory} + \textbf{Ending inventory}}{2}$$

(Helpful hint: Review Exhibits 5-10 and 5-11 in your text.)

The income statement reports revenues and expenses on an accrual basis (revenues earned and expenses incurred). The statement of cash flows includes three sections of cash flows—operating, investing, and financing activities. Cash flows from operating activities includes information about cash receipts from customers and cash payments to suppliers and employees. Exhibit 5-12 in your text compares an income statement with cash flows from operating activities.

Objective 6 - Compute cost of goods sold.

Gross Margin is the difference between Net Sales and Cost of Goods Sold, or

$$\text{Net Sales - Cost of Goods Sold = Gross Margin}$$

The perpetual inventory system described above maintains a Cost of Goods Sold account in the ledger; therefore, calculating gross margin is simple and quick. For control purposes, management may prefer to keep more detail regarding the purchase of inventory. When this occurs, these account balances need to be netted to arrive at the final cost, as follows:

Final cost = Cost of Goods Sold, where Cost of Goods Sold is

	Beginning Inventory
+	**Net Purchases**[*]
+	**Freight-In**
=	**Goods Available for Sale**
-	**Ending Inventory**
	Cost of Goods Sold

[*] **Net Purchases = Purchases - Purchase Discounts - Purchase Returns & Allowances**

(Helpful hint: Review Exhibit 5-13 in your text.)

Chapter 5 Supplement—Accounting for merchandise in a periodic inventory system.

Objective S1 - Account for the purchase and sale of inventory.

As mentioned earlier, some businesses use a **periodic inventory system** wherein the Inventory account is not updated each time merchandise is purchased or sold. Instead, when merchandise is acquired, a **Purchases account** is debited, as follows:

Purchases	XX	
Accounts Payable		XX

Amounts for freight, discounts and returns/allowances are also placed in separate accounts. Because all additions of merchandise are in the Purchase account, the Inventory account remains unchanged throughout the accounting period and is only updated at the end of the accounting cycle, usually when the closing entries are recorded. When sales occur in a periodic system, the revenue is recorded but a second entry is not recorded to update the inventory account.

Objective S2 - Compute cost of goods sold.

Whereas Cost of Goods Sold is an account balance in a perpetual inventory system, it becomes a computation in a periodic system, as follows:

$$
\begin{array}{l}
\text{Beginning Inventory} \\
+ \text{ Net Purchases*} \\
\underline{+ \text{ Freight-In}} \\
= \text{Merchandise Available for Sale} \\
\underline{- \text{ Ending Inventory}} \\
\text{Cost of Goods Sold}
\end{array}
$$

*Net Purchases = Purchases - Purchases Discounts - Purchase Returns and Allowances

(Helpful hint: Review Exhibit 5S-2 in your text.)

Objective S3 - Adjust and close the accounts of a business with merchandise inventory.

In a periodic system, the adjusting process is identical to that of a service business. However, the closing entries change slightly because the first two closing entries are used to update the Inventory account by removing the beginning inventory amount and replacing it with the ending inventory amount. The ease with which this transformation occurs is greatly facilitated by the work sheet, wherein the beginning inventory is extended from the trial balance to the Income Statement debit column and the ending inventory amount is placed on the work sheet in the Income Statement credit column (because it reduces Cost of Goods Sold) and the Balance Sheet debit column (because ending inventory is a current asset). By simply following the rules for closing entries using a work sheet, the change in the Inventory account occurs automatically after the first two closing entries have been recorded and posted (Study Exhibit 5S-3 carefully!).

Objective S4 - Prepare a merchandiser's financial statements.

The Statement of Owner's Equity for a merchandising business is similar to the Statement of Owner's Equity for a service business, while the only change in the Balance Sheet for a merchandising business is the addition of Inventory to the current asset section. However, there are significant changes in the Income Statement for a merchandising business. Now the Income Statement is prepared with four distinct sections, as follows:

1. Revenue from Sales
2. Cost of Goods Sold
3. Operating Expenses
4. Other revenue and expense

The Revenue from Sales section is the first presented and lists Sales and the contra revenue account balances. This section is summarized in the Net Sales calculation. Cost of Goods Sold uses the following formula:

$$
\begin{array}{l}
\text{Beginning Inventory} \\
\text{+ Net Purchases*} \\
\underline{\text{+ Freight-In}} \\
\text{= Merchandise Available for Sale} \\
\underline{\text{- Ending Inventory}} \\
\text{Cost of Goods Sold}
\end{array}
$$

*Net Purchases = Purchases - Purchases Discounts - Purchase Returns and Allowances

In order to present the Cost of Goods Sold information in an easily understood format, three-, and sometimes four-column paper is necessary. Once this section is completed, Gross margin (profit) is determined (gross margin = net sales - cost of goods sold). Thereafter, the Selling Expenses (those directly relating to marketing the company's products) are followed by the other operating expenses, called General Expenses. The sum of these two sections is Total Operating Expenses, which is subtracted from gross margin to arrive at Operating Income. Finally, any Other (meaning non-operating) Revenues or Expenses are listed to arrive at Net Income. Frequently much of this detail is omitted when the Income Statement is published, and the sections merely summarized for convenience.

(Helpful hint: Review Exhibit 5S-6 in your text.)

TEST YOURSELF

All the self-testing materials in this chapter focus on information and procedures that your instructor is likely to test in quizzes and examinations. Those questions followed by an *S* refer to information contained in the Appendix to the chapter.

I. Matching   *Match each numbered term with its lettered definition.*

_____ 1. Cost of Goods Sold

_____ 2. income from operations

_____ 3. multiple-step income statement

_____ 4. operating expenses

_____ 5. sales returns and allowances

_____ 6. single-step income statement

_____ 7. purchase returns & allowances

_____ 8. purchase discount

_____ 9. sales discount

_____ 10. gross profit

_____ 11. invoice

_____ 12. net sales

_____ 13S. net purchases

_____ 14. other revenue

_____ 15. other expense

_____ 16S. Purchases

_____ 17. sales revenue

_____ 18. quantity discount

A. a discount from supplier to merchandiser that lowers the price per item for volume purchases

B. a reduction in the amount receivable from a customer offered by the seller as an incentive for the customer to pay promptly

C. a reduction in the cost of inventory that is offered by a seller as an incentive for the customer to pay promptly

D. a seller's request for payment of a purchase

E. amount that a merchandiser earns from selling inventory

F. decreases in a buyer's debt that result from returning merchandise to the seller or receiving an allowance on the amount owed

G. decreases in the seller's revenue from a customer's return of merchandise or from granting to the customer an allowance from the amount the customer owes

H. excess of sales revenue over cost of goods sold

I. expense that is outside the main operations of a business

J. expenses, other than cost of goods sold, that are incurred in the entity's main line of business

K. format that contains only two sections, revenues and expenses

L. gross profit less operating expenses

M. income statement format that lists the figures within subsections and presents intermediate subtotals, such as gross profit and income from operations

N. purchases less purchase discounts and purchases returns & allowances

O. revenue that is outside the main operations of a business

P. sales revenue less sales discounts and sales returns & allowances

Q. merchandise acquired for resale using a periodic inventory system

R. an account in the perpetual system; a calculation in the periodic system

II. Multiple Choice *Circle the best answer.*

1. Which of the following companies would *not* be considered a merchandising entity?

   A. a clothing store
   B. a car dealership

   C. a restaurant
   D. a long-distance telephone company

2. A company will have a net loss if:

   A. cost of goods sold exceeds operating expenses
   B. operating expenses exceed gross profit

   C. sales exceed gross profit
   D. sales exceed operating expenses

3. Which of the following is classified as an operating expense?

   A. Cost of Goods Sold
   B. Rent Expense

   C. Sales Discount
   D. Interest Expense

4. A debit to Sales Returns and Allowances will:

   A. increase Inventory
   B. increase Net Purchases

   C. increase Net Sales
   D. decrease Net Sales

5. Which of the following does *not* have a credit balance?

   A. Purchase Discounts
   B. Purchase Returns and Allowances

   C. Freight-In
   D. Interest Revenue

6. A company purchases 50 stereo systems that sell for $300 each. There is a 20% quantity discount on the purchase. The journal entry would:

   A. debit Inventory $15,000
   B. credit Quantity Discount $3,000

   C. debit Inventory $12,000
   D. credit Cash $15,000

7. A company sells merchandise on June 1 for $1,200 with terms 1/15, n/30. If it receives payment for the merchandise on June 8, the entry to record the receipt would:

   A. credit Accounts Receivable $1,200
   B. credit Inventory $12

   C. credit Cash $1,200
   D. debit Inventory $1,188

8S. A company purchased merchandise for $3,200 on September 1 with terms 2/10, n/30. When it paid the account on September 12, the journal entry:

   A. debited Accounts Payable $3,136
   B. credited Purchase Discounts $64

   C. debited Purchases $3,200
   D. credited Cash $3,200

9. Which of the following accounts is *not* a contra account?

    A. Inventory
    B. Accumulated Depreciation

    C. Sales Returns and Allowances
    D. Sales Discounts

10S. In a merchandising company, the closing entries for the inventory account will:

    A. debit Inventory only for the amount of ending inventory
    B. debit Inventory only for the amount of beginning inventory
    C. debit Inventory for the amount of ending inventory and credit Inventory for the amount of beginning inventory
    D. debit Inventory for the amount of beginning inventory and credit Inventory for the amount of ending inventory

11. Gross Profit plus Cost of Goods Sold equals:

    A. Net Income
    B. Cost of Goods Available for Sale

    C. Net Sales
    D. Operating Income

12. To calculate the gross margin percentage,

    A. divide net sales by net income
    B. divide current assets by current liabilities

    C. divide total liabilities by total assets
    D. divide gross profit by net sales

III. Completion   *Complete each of the following statements.*

1. A merchandising entity earns its revenues by _____.
2. The largest single expense for most merchandisers is _____.
3. A seller's request for payment is called a(n) _____.
4S. A company debits the Purchases account when goods are acquired. It is using a _____ _____ inventory system.
5. The major difference between a merchandiser's balance sheet and a service entity's balance sheet is
_____.
6. The largest single current asset for most merchandisers is _____.
7. Sales minus Cost of Goods Sold is called _____.
8. A company credits the Inventory account when merchandise is sold. It is using a _____ _____ inventory system.
9. In a perpetual inventory system, Cost of Goods Sold is a(n) _____; in a periodic inventory system, Cost of Goods Sold is a(n) _____.
10. The four sections found on a multiple-step income statement for a merchandising business are
_____, _____, _____,
and _____.
11. The gross margin percentage is calculated as follows: _____
_____.
12. Inventory turnover is calculated by _____
_____.

IV. Daily Exercises

1. Record the following transactions in the space provided.

    5/4   Purchased merchandise from Golden, Inc., $1,400; term 2/10, n/60, FOB shipping point, freight of $65 added to the invoice.

    5/10   Returned $250 of merchandise to Golden, Inc.

    5/14   Sent a check to Golden, Inc. for the balance due.

Date	Accounts and Explanation	PR	Debit	Credit

2S. Record the transactions from #1 above, assuming a periodic inventory system.

Date	Accounts and Explanation	PR	Debit	Credit

3. Record the following transactions in the space provided.

3/11   Sold merchandise to J. Starrs, $900; term 2/10, n/30. The cost of the sale was $300.
3/16   Accepted a return of $150 from J. Starrs.
3/21   Received a check from J. Starrs for the amount due.

Date	Accounts and Explanation	PR	Debit	Credit

4S. Record the transaction from #3 above, assuming a periodic inventory system.

Date	Accounts and Explanation	PR	Debit	Credit

V. Exercises

1. The following information is available for Randy's Rejects for 19X9:

Beginning Inventory	$ 2,500
Ending Inventory	1,850
Operating Expenses	1,650
Cost of Goods Sold	15,975
Sales Discounts	255
Sales	21,500
Sales Returns and Allowances	165

Required:

1. What is net sales for 19X9?

2. What is Gross Profit for 19X9?

3. What is Net Income for 19X9?

4. What is the gross margin rate?

5. What is the inventory turnover rate?

2S. The following information is given for Julie's Junk for 19X9:

Beginning Inventory	$ 12,250
Gross Margin	7,500
Operating Expenses	3,100
Purchase Returns & Allowance	600
Purchase Discounts	550
Purchases	39,250
Sales Discounts	500
Sales	51,500
Sales Returns & Allowances	1,700

Required:

1. Compute net sales.

2. Compute net purchases.

3. Compute cost of goods sold.

4. Compute ending inventory.

5. Compute net income.

6. What is the inventory turnover rate?

3. Use the following information from Gina's Jeans for 19X9 to prepare an income statement through gross profit on sales:

Depreciation Expense	$ 500
Interest Expense	900
Interest Revenue	960
Inventory	1,300
Cost of Goods Sold	7,590
Rent Expense	400
Sales Discounts	125
Sales Returns & Allowances	85
Sales Revenues	10,150
Withdrawals	210

4. Using the information in #3 above, prepare the necessary closing entries.

Date	Accounts and Explanation	PR	Debit	Credit

VI. Beyond the Numbers

A business is offered the purchase discount term 1/15, n/60. At the same time, the business can borrow money from its bank at 10% interest. Assuming the business does not have sufficient cash on hand to take advantage of the discount, which would be less expensive—to lose the discount or to borrow the needed cash from the bank and take the discount? Support your answer.

_____

_____

_____

_____

_____

VII. Demonstration Problems

Demonstration Problem #1

On January 1, the Brooks Sisters had the following account balances:

Cash	$ 9,000	
Accounts receivable	16,000	
Inventory	21,000	
Other current assets	6,500	
Property, plant, and equipment (net)	85,000	
Account payable		$ 17,500
Long-term liabilities		48,000
Capital		72,000
Totals	$137,500	$137,500

During January, the following merchandise purchase and sales transactions occurred:

a. Sold merchandise on account to Jackson, $8,000; the cost of the merchandise was $3,200.
b. Purchased merchandise on account from Huston, $4,200, terms 1/10, n/30, FOB shipping point.
c. Received a freight bill for the Huston purchase, $130, terms n/7.
d. Sold merchandise on account to Perkins, $2,750; the cost of the merchandise was $925.
e. Paid the freight bill on the Huston purchase (#c above).
f. Received payment from Jackson (#a above) within the discount period.
g. Perkins returned $650 of merchandise; the cost of the merchandise was $210.
h. Paid Huston (#b above) within the discount period.
i. Sold merchandise on account to David, Inc., $3,600; the cost of the merchandise was $1,150.
j. Purchased merchandise on account from Tracy Co., $4,620, terms 3/20, n/60.
k. Received payment from Perkins (#d and #g above) within the discount period.
l. Returned $520 of merchandise to Tracy.
m. A $300 allowance was granted to David (#i above).
n. Paid Tracy (#j and #l above) within the discount period.
o. David, Inc. paid the balance due (#i and #m above) but did not earn a discount.
p. Sold merchandise on account to Somers Co., $5,025; the cost of the merchandise was $1,885.

Additional information:

1. The terms of all sales are 2/10, n/30, **FOB** destination.
2. Brooks Sisters records all purchase discounts, purchase returns and freight charges in the inventory account.

Required:

1. Place the opening balances into the T-accounts, identifying each.
2. Record the transactions (omit explanations).
3. Post the entries to the T-accounts, identifying each by letter.
4. Balance the accounts and prepare a trial balance.
5. Using the trial balance amounts, calculate the gross margin percentage.

Requirements 1, 3, and 4

Cash	Accounts receivable	Inventory

Other current assets	Property, plant, and equip.	Accounts payable

Long-term liabilities	Capital	Sales

Sales discount	Sales returns & allowance	Cost of goods sold

Requirement 2

Requirement 4

Accounts	Debit	Credit

Requirement 5

Demonstration Problem #2

Using the completed work sheet for Loc's Rocks on the following page:

1. Prepare a multiple-step income statement, statement of owner's equity, and balance sheet.
2. Journalize the adjusting and closing.
3. Prepare a postclosing trial balance.
4. Prepare a single-step income statement.
5. Calculate the gross margin percentage.
6. Calculate the inventory turnover ratio. The Beginning inventory was $36,000.

Loc's Rocks
Work Sheet
For the Year Ended December 31, 2000

Account	Trial Balance Debit	Trial Balance Credit	Adjustments Debit	Adjustments Credit	Income Statement Debit	Income Statement Credit	Balance Sheet Debit	Balance Sheet Credit
	$ 17,250						$ 17,250	
...able	19,100						19,100	
	42,000						42,000	
...plies	2,650			(a) 1,800			850	
'repaid advertising	8,000			(b) 3,500			4,500	
Equipment	91,400						91,400	
Accumulated depreciation		$ 39,100		(d) 7,800				$ 46,900
Accounts payable		22,675						22,675
Salary payable				(e) 810				810
Interest payable				(f) 225				225
Unearned sales revenue		1,420	(c) 900					520
Note payable, long-term		40,000						40,000
Loc Huynh, Capital		56,700						56,700
Loc Huynh, Withdrawals	20,000						20,000	
Sales revenue		297,460		(c) 900		$298,360		
Sales discounts	7,800				$ 7,800			
Sales returns and	6,210				6,210			
Cost of Goods Sold	148,310				148,310			
Salary expense	51,500		(e) 810		52,310			
Rent expense	18,000				18,000			
Depreciation expense			(d) 7,800		7,800			
Utilities expense	6,940				6,940			
Supplies expense			(a) 1,800		1,800			
Interest expense	3,775		(f) 225		4,000			
Advertising Expense	14,420		(b) 3,500		17,920			
Total	$457,355	$457,355	15,035	15,035	271,090	298,360	195,100	167,830
Net income					27,270			27,270
					$298,360	$298,360	$195,100	$195,100

Requirement 1 (Financial Statements)

Loc's Rocks
Income Statement
For the Year Ended December 31, 2000

Loc's Rocks
Statement of Owner's Equity
For the Year Ended December 31, 2000

Loc's Rocks
Balance Sheet
December 31, 2000

ASSETS		LIABILITIES	
		OWNER'S EQUITY	

Requirement 2 (adjusting and closing entries)

Accounts	Debit	Credit

Requirement 3 (Post-closing Trial Balance)

Loc's Rocks
Post-closing Trial Balance
December 31, 2000

Requirement 4 (Single-step Income Statement)

Loc's Rocks
Income Statement
For the Year Ended December 31, 2000

Requirement 5 (Gross margin)

_____

_____

_____

Requirement 6 (Inventory turnover ratio)

_____

_____

_____

SOLUTIONS

I. Matching

1. R	5. G	9. B	13S. N	17. E
2. L	6. K	10. H	14. O	18. A
3. M	7. F	11. D	15. I	
4. J	8. C	12. P	16S. Q	

II. Multiple Choice

1. **D** A merchandising entity earns its revenue by selling products. Of the entities listed, all sell products except the telephone company which sells a service .

2. **B** The basic income statement formula for a merchandising company is:

    Sales
    - Cost of goods sold
    = Gross margin
    - Operating expenses
    = Net income or (net loss)

    For a company to always have a net loss, operating expenses must be greater than gross margin.

3. **B** Cost of goods sold is the cost of inventory that the company sold to customers. Sales discounts is a contra-revenue account and interest expense is "other expense."

4. **D** Sales Returns and Allowances is contra to the Sales account. A credit to Sales Returns and Allowances increases its balance. Since it is contra to Sales this will decrease net sales.

5. **C** Freight-In is a cost of goods sold account, and has a normal debit balance. The other items listed all have normal credit balances.

6. **C** Quantity discounts are adjustments of the purchase price usually based on volume. Entries to record purchases are based on the net price of the merchandise after subtracting any available quantity discount.

7. **A** The terms 1/15, n/30 mean that a 1% discount is available if payment is received within fifteen days of the invoice date, otherwise the net amount of the invoice is due in 30 days. Since payment is received within the fifteen-day discount period, the journal entry to record the payment is:

Cash	1,188	
Inventory	12	
Accounts Receivable		1,200

8S.   D   The terms 2/10,n/30 mean that a 2% discount is available if payment is made within ten days of the invoice date, otherwise the net amount of the invoice is due in 30 days. Since payment was not made within the ten-day discount period the net amount is due. The journal entry to record the payment is:

    Accounts Payable   3,200
        Cash   3,200

9.   A   A contra account has two distinguishing characteristics: 1) it always has a companion account, and 2) its normal balance is opposite that of the companion account. Items B, C, and D are contra accounts. Only item A, Inventory, is not a contra account.

10S.   C   The purpose of the closing entry for inventory in a periodic system is two-fold: 1) remove the beginning inventory balance account and 2) enter the ending inventory balance into the account. Since inventory is a normal debit balance account, 1) is accomplished with a credit and 2) is accomplished with a debit.

11.   C   You are required to work backwards. Since Net Sales - Cost of Goods Sold = Gross Margin; therefore, Net Sales = Gross Margin + Cost of Goods Sold.

12.   D   The gross margin percentage divides gross profit by net sales.

III. Completion

1. selling products (This is in contrast to the entities studied through Chapter 4 that earned revenue by selling a service.)
2. Cost of Goods Sold (Cost of goods sold represents the entity's cost of the goods it sold to its customers.)
3. invoice (To the seller, the invoice results in a sale being recorded. To the purchaser, the same invoice results in a purchase being recorded.)
4. periodic (In a periodic system, Purchases is debited and Cash (or Accounts Payable) is credited.)
5. the Inventory account (The merchandiser earns revenue by selling a tangible product, inventory. The service entity earns its revenue by selling an intangible service.)
6. Inventory
7. Gross Margin or Gross Profit (The basic income statement formula for a merchandising company is:

        Sales
        - Cost of Goods Sold
        = Gross margin
        - Operating expenses
        = Net income (Net loss)

8. perpetual (Under the perpetual system, all merchandise is debited to the Inventory account when acquired and credited to the Inventory account when sold.)
9. account, calculation
10. 1) Revenue from Sales, 2) Cost of Goods Sold, 3) Operating Expenses, 4) Other Revenue and Expenses
11. gross margin divided by net sales
12. cost of goods sold divided by average inventory

IV. Daily Exercises

1.

5/4	Inventory	1,400	
	Freight-In (or Inventory)	65	
	Accounts Payable		1,465
5/10	Accounts Payable	250	
	Inventory		250
5/14	Accounts Payable	1,215	
	Purchase Discounts (or Inventory)		23
	Cash		1,192

Note: The cash discount applies only to the original purchase less the return. It does not apply to the freight charge.

2S.

5/4	Purchase	1,400	
	Freight-In	65	
	Accounts Payable		1,465
5/10	Accounts Payable	250	
	Purchase Returns/Allowance		250
5/14	Accounts Payable	1,215	
	Purchase Discounts		23
	Cash		1,192

Note: Under a periodic system, the Inventory account is not affected by any activity during the accounting period. Its beginning balance, representing beginning inventory, stays in the account until the end of the accounting period when it is removed and replaced by the accurate ending inventory figure (which becomes beginning inventory for the next accounting period.)

3.

3/11	Accounts Receivable	900	
	Sales		900
	Cost of Goods Sold	300	
	Inventory		300
3/16	Sales Returns and Allowances	150	
	Accounts Receivable		150
	Inventory	50	
	Cost of Goods Sold		50

3/21	Cash	735	
	Sales Discount	15	
	Accounts Receivable		750

With a perpetual inventory system, sales and sales returns/allowances require double entries—one to record the sale (or return) and a second entry to update the inventory account. The sale is recorded at selling price, while the inventory entry is recorded at cost. Because the cost of the product was one-third the selling price (see 3/11 entry), the return is recorded using the same proportion.

4S.

| 3/11 | Accounts Receivable | 900 | |
| | Sales | | 900 |

| 3/16 | Sales Returns and Allowances | 150 | |
| | Accounts Receivable | | 150 |

3/21	Cash	735	
	Sales Discounts	15	
	Accounts Receivable		750

V. Exercises

1.

Requirement 1

Sales - Sales Returns & Allowances - Sales Discount = Net Sales
$21,500 - $165 - $255 = $21,080

Requirement 2

Net Sales - Cost of Goods Sold = Gross Profit (or Gross Margin)
$21,080 - $15,975 = $5,105

Requirement 3

Gross Margin - Operating Expenses = Net Income
$5,105 - $1,650 = $3,455

Requirement 4

Gross Margin ÷ Net Sales
$5,105 ÷ $21,080 = 24.2%

Requirement 5

Cost of Goods Sold ÷ Average Inventory
Average Inventory = ($2,500 + $1,850) ÷ 2 = $2,175
$15,975 ÷ $2,175 = 7.3 times

2S.

Requirement 1

Sales - Sales Discounts - Sales Returns & Allowances = Net Sales
$51,500 - $500 - $1,700 = $49,300

Requirement 2

Purchases - Purchase Discounts - Purchase Returns & Allowances = Net Purchases
$39,250 - $550 - $600 = $38,100

Requirement 3

Net Sales - Cost of Goods Sold = Gross Profit
Cost of Goods Sold = $49,300 - $7,500 = $41,800

Requirement 4

Beginning Inventory + Net Purchase - Ending Inventory = Cost of Goods Sold
Therefore, Ending Inventory = Beginning Inventory + Net Purchase - Cost of Goods Sold
Ending Inventory = $12,250 + $38,100 - $41,800 = $8,550

Requirement 5

Gross Profit - Operating Expenses = Net Income
$7,500 - $3,100 = $4,400

Requirement 6

Inventory turnover rate = Cost of Goods Sold ÷ Average Inventory
Average Inventory = ($12,250 + $8,550) ÷ 2 = $10,400
Inventory Turnover Rate = $41,800 ÷ $10,400 = 4 times

3.

Revenues from Sales			
Sales		$10,150	
Less: Sales Discount	125		
Sales Returns/Allowance	85	210	
Net Sales			9,940
Less: Cost of Goods Sold			7,590
Gross Profit			$2,450

4.

Date	Accounts and Explanation	PR	Debit	Credit
	Sales Revenue		10,150	
	Interest Revenue		960	
	Income Summary			11,110
	Income Summary		9,600	
	Cost of Goods Sold			7,590
	Interest Expense			900
	Sales Discounts			125
	Rent Expense			400
	Depreciation Expense			500
	Sales Returns & Allowances			85
	Income Summary		1,510	
	Capital			1,510
	Capital		210	
	Withdrawals			210

VI. Beyond the Numbers

It would be less expensive to let the discount lapse compared with borrowing money from the bank at 10% interest. The term 1/15, n/60 means you pay 1% for extending the payment period an additional 45 days. This computes to about 8% interest or about 2% less than your bank is charging. As an example, assume you receive an invoice for $10,000, with terms 1/15, n/60. If you pay within the discount period, you will save $100 (1% × $10,000).

To borrow $10,000 for 45 days at 10% would cost $125 ($10,000 × 10% × 45/360) in interest. Therefore, it is not cost beneficial to borrow the funds.

VII. Demonstration Problems

Demonstration Problem #1 Solved and Explained

Requirements 1, 3, and 4

Cash			
Bal.	9,000	130	(c)
(f)	7,840	4,158	(h)
(k)	2,058	3,977	(n)
(o)	3,300		
Bal.	13,933		

Accounts receivable			
Bal. 16,000		8,000	(f)
(a)	8,000	650	(g)
(d)	2,750	2,100	(k)
(i)	3,600	300	(m)
(p)	5,025	3,300	(o)
Bal. 21,025			

Inventory			
Bal. 21,000		3,200	(a)
(b)	4,200	925	(d)
(c)	130	42	(h)
(g)	210	1,150	(i)
(j)	4,620	520	(l)
		123	(n)
		1,885	(p)
Bal. 22,315			

Other current assets		Property, plant, and equip.		Accounts payable	
Bal. 6,500		Bal. 85,000		(e) 130	17,500 Bal.
				(h) 4,200	4,200 (b)
				(l) 520	130 (c)
				(n) 4,100	4,620 (j)
					17,500 Bal.

Long-term liabilities		Capital		Sales	
	48,000 Bal.		72,000 Bal.		8,000 (a)
					2,750 (d)
					3,600 (i)
					5,025 (p)
					19,375 Bal.

Sales discount		Sales returns & allowance		Cost of goods sold	
(f) 160		(g) 650		(a) 3,200	210 (g)
(k) 42		(m) 300		(d) 925	
Bal. 202		Bal. 950		(i) 1,150	
				(p) 1,885	
				Bal. 6,950	

Requirement 2

a.	Accounts Receivable (Jackson)		8,000	
	Sales			8,000
	Cost of Goods Sold		3,200	
	Inventory			3,200
b.	Inventory		4,200	
	Accounts Payable (Huston)			4,200
c.	Inventory		130	
	Accounts Payable			130
d.	Accounts Receivable (Perkins)		2,750	
	Sales			2,750
	Cost of Goods Sold		925	
	Inventory			925
e.	Accounts Payable		130	
	Cash			130

f.	Cash		7,840	
	Sales Discount		160	
	Accounts Receivable (Jackson)			8,000
g.	Sales Returns & Allowance		650	
	Accounts Receivable (Perkins)			650
	Inventory		210	
	Cost of Goods Sold			210
h.	Accounts Payable (Huston)		4,200	
	Inventory			42
	Cash			4,158
i.	Accounts Receivable (David, Inc.)		3,600	
	Sales			3,600
	Cost of Goods Sold		1,150	
	Inventory			1,150
j.	Inventory		4,620	
	Accounts Payable (Tracy Co.)			4,620
k.	Cash		2,058	
	Sales Discount		42	
	Accounts Receivable (Perkins)			2,100
l.	Accounts Payable (Tracy)		520	
	Inventory			520
m.	Sales Returns & Allowance		300	
	Accounts Receivable (David)			300
n.	Accounts Payable (Tracy)		4,100	
	Inventory			123
	Cash			3,977
o.	Cash		3,300	
	Accounts Receivable (David)			3,300
p.	Accounts Receivable (Somers Co.)		5,025	
	Sales			5,025
	Cost of Goods Sold		1,885	
	Inventory			1,885

Requirement 4

Cash	$ 13,933	
Accounts receivable	21,025	
Inventory	22,315	
Other current assets	6,500	
Property, plants, and equipment (net)	85,000	
Account payable		$ 17,500
Long-term liabilities		48,000
Capital		72,000
Sales		19,375
Sales discount	202	
Sales returns & allowance	950	
Cost of goods sold	6,950	
Totals	$156,875	$156,875

Requirement 5

Gross margin percentage = Gross margin ÷ Net sales
Net Sales = $19,375 - $202 - $950 = $18,223

Gross margin = Net sales - Cost of goods sold
$\qquad$ = $18,223 - $6,950
$\qquad$ = $11,273

Gross margin percentage = $11,273 ÷ $18,223 = 61.9% (rounded)

Points to remember:

1. When a company uses a perpetual inventory system and records a sale, two transactions are required. One transaction records the sales (at the selling price) while the second transfers the cost of the sale from the Inventory account to the Cost of Goods Sold account.
2. Because of #1 above, a sales return also requires two entries. However, a sales allowance (transaction (m) in the problem) only requires one entry because no merchandise is being returned.
3. In a perpetual system, the company can record all purchase discounts, purchase returns, and freight charges in the Inventory account (as this problem required) or establish separate accounts for these items. If the latter policy is followed, the balance in the Cost of Goods Sold account would need to be adjusted for the discounts, returns, and freight charges to reflect the total cost.

Demonstration Problem #2 Solved and Explained

Requirement 1

Loc's Rocks
Income Statement
For the Year Ended December 31, 2000

Sales revenue		$298,360	
Less: Sales discounts	7,800		
Sales returns & allowances	6,210	14,010	
Net Sales			$284,350
Cost of goods sold			148,310
Gross margin			136,040
Operating expenses:			
Salary Expense		52,310	
Rent Expense		18,000	
Depreciation Expense		7,800	
Utilities Expense		6,940	
Supplies Expense		1,800	
Advertising Expense		17,920	104,770
Income from operations			31,270
Other expenses:			
Interest Expense			4,000
Net income			$ 27,270

Loc's Rocks
Statement of Owner's Equity
For the Year Ended December 31, 2000

Loc Huynh, Capital 1/1/2000	$56,700
Add: Net Income	27,720
	83,970
Less: Withdrawals	20,000
Loc Huynh, Capital 12/31/2000	$63,970

Loc's Rocks

Balance Sheet

December 31, 2000

ASSETS			LIABILITIES		
Current:			Current:		
Cash	$17,250		Accounts payable	$22,675	
Accounts receivable	19,100		Salary payable	810	
Inventory	42,000		Interest payable	225	
Supplies	850		Unearned sales revenue	520	
Prepaid advertising	4,500		Total liabilities		$ 24,230
Total current assets		$ 83,700	Long term:		
			Notes payable		40,000
Plant:			Total liabilities		64,230
Equipment	91,400				
Less: Accumulated			OWNER'S EQUITY		
Depreciation	46,900	44,500	Loc Huynh, Capital		63,970
			Total liabilities and owner's		
Total assets		$128,200	equity		$128,200

Requirement 2 (adjusting and closing entries)

	ADJUSTING ENTRIES		Debit	Credit
(a)	Supplies Expense		1,800	
	Supplies			1,800
(b)	Advertising Expense		3,500	
	Prepaid Advertising			3,500
(c)	Unearned Sales Revenue		900	
	Sales Revenue			900
(d)	Depreciation Expense		7,800	
	Accumulated Depreciation			7,800
(e)	Salary Expense		810	
	Salary Payable			810
(f)	Interest Expense		225	
	Interest Payable			225
	CLOSING ENTRIES			
12/31	Sales Revenue		298,360	
	Income Summary			298,360
	Close revenue to Income Summary.			

12/31	Income Summary		271,090	
	Sales Discounts			7,800
	Sales Returns and Allowances			6,210
	Cost of Goods Sold			148,310
	Salary Expense			52,310
	Rent Expense			18,000
	Depreciation Expense			7,800
	Utilities Expense			6,940
	Supplies Expense			1,800
	Interest Expense			4,000
	Advertising Expense			17,920
	Close all expenses to Income Summary.			
12/31	Income Summary (298,360 - 271,090)		27,270	
	Loc Huynh, Capital			27,270
	Close Income Summary to capital.			
12/31	Loc Huynh, Capital		20,000	
	Loc Huynh, Withdrawals			20,000
	Close withdrawals to capital.			

Requirement 3

Loc's Rocks
Post-closing Trial Balance
December 31, 2000

Cash	$ 17,250	
Accounts receivable	19,100	
Inventory	42,000	
Supplies	850	
Prepaid advertising	4,500	
Equipment	91,400	
Accumulated depreciation		$ 46,900
Accounts payable		22,675
Salary payable		810
Interest payable		225
Unearned sales revenue		520
Note payable, long-term		40,000
Loc Huynh, capital		63,970
	$175,100	$175,100

Requirement 4 (Single-step Income Statement)

Loc's Rocks
Income Statement
For the Year Ended December 31, 2000

Net Sales		$284,350
Less:		
Cost of goods sold	148,310	
Operating expenses	104,770	
Interest expense	4,000	257,080
Net income		$ 27,270

Requirement 5 (Gross margin)

Gross Margin Percentage = Gross Margin ÷ Net Sales
Gross Margin = 136,040 ÷ 284,350 = 47.8%

Requirement 6 (Inventory turnover ratio)

Inventory turnover ratio	=	Cost of goods sold ÷ Average inventory
	=	$148,310 ÷ [($42,000 + $36,000) ÷ 2]
	=	$148,310 ÷ $39,000
	=	3.8 times

Chapter 6—Accounting Information Systems: Special Journal, Control Accounts, and Subsidiary Ledgers

CHAPTER OVERVIEW

Chapters 1 through 5 covered the accounting cycle for both service businesses (Chapters 1-4) and merchandising businesses (Chapter 5). Throughout those chapters frequent reference was made to the use of computers at various steps in the accounting cycle. We now turn our attention to an accounting information system and a more in-depth discussion of computers in accounting. In addition, we introduce special journals and subsidiary ledgers. The learning objectives for this chapter are to

1. Describe the features of an effective accounting information system.
2. Understand how computerized and manual accounting systems are used.
3. Understand how spreadsheets are used in accounting.
4. Use the sales journal, the cash receipts journal, and the accounts receivable subsidiary ledger.
5. Use the purchases journal, the cash disbursements journal, and the accounts payable subsidiary ledger.

CHAPTER REVIEW

Objective 1 - Describe the features of an effective accounting information system.

An **accounting information system** is the combination of people, procedures, and business records that a company maintains to manage financial data. Because each business has specific needs, businesses develop an accounting information system to meet their individual needs.

An effective information system provides **control, compatibility, flexibility**, and a **favorable cost/benefit relationship. Internal controls** are methods and procedures that a business uses to safeguard assets, authorize transactions, and ensure accuracy of the accounting records. **Compatibility** means that the information system works smoothly with the business's other operations. A system is **flexible** if it can be easily adapted to changes in the way a business operates. A **favorable cost/benefit relationship** is one in which the benefits of the system are greater than the cost of the system.

Computers process data with accuracy and speed. The basic components of a computer system are 1) **hardware**, 2) **software**, and 3) **personnel. Hardware** is the electronic equipment which makes up the system—the computers, disk drives, monitors, printers, and so on. Modern systems can share information through the use of **networks. Software** is the set of instructions that directs the computer to perform specific tasks. Some software packages operate independently from other activities while others, particularly in larger companies, are integrated into the company's overall database. **Personnel** are key to the success of all information systems, along with security measures to insure the confidentiality of the information contained within the system.

Objective 2 - Understand how computerized and manual accounting systems are used.

Inputs, processing, and **outputs** are the three stages of **information processing. Inputs** represent the business source documents—the things which represent transactions and therefore need to be entered into the system. **Processing** means getting the information from the source document into the accounting system. Manually, this means journalizing and posting. A computerized system does the same thing but considerably faster and much less formally. **Outputs** are the reports used for decision making, including the financial statements.

Both systems require the accountant to classify transactions. In a computerized system, you select the proper processing environment from a **menu**, which is a list of options organized by function. Once an option has been selected, transactions are recorded. Information is processed in one of two ways: 1) **on-line processing** or 2) **batch processing**. On-line processing posts information continuously while batch processing allows transactions to be checked before being posted automatically.

Accounting reports, the outputs, are displayed or printed automatically in a computerized system by simply selecting the appropriate options from a menu.

Review Exhibit 6-6 in your text carefully so you understand the differences between manual and computerized systems.

Objective 3 - Understand how spreadsheets are used in accounting.

Spreadsheets are computer programs which allow for masses of data to be entered, updated, corrected, deleted, etc. electronically. A spreadsheet looks like the manual work sheet introduced in Chapter 4. The **columns** are identified with letters while the **rows** are identified with numbers. The intersection of any particular row and column is called a cell. The **cell** is the place where information is stored. The information in the cell can be words, numbers or a formula. (See Exhibit 6-7 for an example of a simple spreadsheet.) The use of formulas allow for amounts to be changed with results changing automatically.

Objective 4 - Use the sales journal, the cash receipts journal, and the accounts receivable subsidiary ledger.

Special journals are used by businesses to increase the efficiency of the accounting system. This is accomplished when specific types of transactions (for instance, those involving debits to the Cash account) are removed from the general journal and recorded together in a special journal (for instance, a Cash Receipts Journal) which has been designed for only that type of transaction. Four commonly used special journals are the **Sales Journal**, the **Cash Receipts Journal**, the **Purchases Journal** and the **Cash Disbursements Journal**. The general journal is not a special journal because it can accommodate any type of transactions.

The **sales journal** is used to record all credit sales. If the company uses a perpetual inventory system the sales journal will also record the cost of the sale. As credit sales are recorded, the business keeps track of each credit customer by posting the transaction to the customer's account which is contained in the **subsidiary ledger**. A subsidiary ledger contains the day-to-day detail of a general ledger account. In this discussion therefore, the customers ledger will contain all of the current balances for each customer while the Accounts Receivable account in the general ledger contains a balance representing the total amount owed by customers. To maintain agreement between the two, credit sales are posted periodically to both the Sales and Accounts Receivable accounts in the General Ledger. Because Accounts Receivable has a subsidiary ledger attached to it, it is called a **control account**. Study Exhibit 6-10 in your text to understand the posting process when a sales journal is used.

A **cash receipts journal** is the second type of special journal. It contains all transactions which include a debit to cash, regardless of the corresponding credit(s). In other words, all receipts of cash are now recorded together. The posting process for the cash receipts journal is similar to that of the sales journal. Receipts from customers are posted to their individual accounts, thereby maintaining current account balances. Posting to general ledger accounts occurs periodically, thereby maintaining the debit/credit equality of the general ledger and agreement between the control account and the customers subsidiary ledger. Review Exhibit 6-11 in your text carefully.

Objective 5 - Use the purchases journal, the cash disbursements journal, and the accounts payable subsidiary ledger.

The **purchases journal** is the third type of special journal. It is used to record all credit purchases. In other words, anytime the business acquires anything on account, that transaction will be recorded in the purchases journal. Because businesses deal with a large number of vendors it is important to maintain current accounts payable balances for each. This is accomplished by setting up and maintaining an **accounts payable subsidiary ledger**. The posting procedure for it is identical to the one discussed above for customers. Study Exhibit 6-12 carefully.

The fourth type of special journal is the **cash disbursements journal**. This journal contains all transactions which include a credit to the cash account (i.e., a cash payment). The posting procedures for the cash disbursements journal is identical to the posting procedure for the cash receipts journal. Study Exhibit 6-13 carefully in your text.

TEST YOURSELF

All the self-testing materials in this chapter focus on information and procedures that your instructor is likely to test in quizzes and examinations.

I. Matching *Match each numbered term with its lettered definition.*

_____ 1. subsidiary ledger
_____ 2. cash disbursements journal
_____ 3. control account
_____ 4. spreadsheet
_____ 5. cash receipts journal
_____ 6. on-line processing
_____ 7. sales journal
_____ 8. accounting information system
_____ 9. batch processing

_____ 10. cell
_____ 11. formula
_____ 12. hardware
_____ 13. menu
_____ 14. purchases journal
_____ 15. software
_____ 16. general journal
_____ 17. general ledger

A. an account whose balance equals the sum of the balances in a group of related accounts in a subsidiary ledger
B. book of accounts that provides supporting details on individual balances, the total of which appears in a general ledger account
C. a computer program which organizes information into columns and rows
D. the intersection of a particular column and row on a spreadsheet
E. computerized accounting for transaction data on a continuous basis
F. computerized accounting for similar transactions in a group
G. a mean of expressing relationships among various cells in a spreadsheet
H. equipment that makes up a computer system
I. set of programs, or instructions, that cause the computer to perform the work desired
J. a list of options in a computer program
K. special journal used to account for all purchases of inventory, supplies, and other assets on account
L. special journal used to account for cash payments made by check
M. special journal used to account for cash collections
N. special journal used to account for credit sales
O. the combination of personnel, records, and procedures that a business uses to meet its need for financial data
P. the journal used to report all transactions that do not fit one of the special journals
Q. ledger of accounts that are reported in the financial statements

II. Multiple Choice *Circle the best answer.*

1. The activity sequence of the basic information processing model is:

   A. organize data, process data, and collect data
   B. collect data, organize and process data, and communicate information
   C. process data, organize data, and collect data
   D. organize data, collect data, and communicate information

2. Internal controls are designed to:

   A. only protect assets
   B. only achieve maximum revenue
   C. only ensure accurate accounting records
   D. protect assets and ensure accurate accounting records

3. Electronic linkages allowing different computers to share information are called:

   A. spreadsheets   C. networks
   B. software   D. databases

4. One way of protecting data security is by using:

   A. software   C. spreadsheets
   B. passwords   D. menus

5. A firm's payment to a supplier for merchandise inventory purchased on account is recorded in the:

   A. cash receipts journal   C. cash disbursements journal
   B. purchases journal   D. sales journal

6. Amounts owed by customers for credit sales are found in the:

   A. accounts receivable journal   C. sales journal
   B. accounts receivable subsidiary ledger   D. general ledger

7. Which of the following transactions is *not* recorded in the cash receipts journal?

   A. adjusting prepaid rent   C. receipt of customer payments
   B. borrowing money from the bank   D. sale of equipment for cash

8. A debit posted to Accounts Payable in the general ledger would come from the:

   A. cash disbursements journal   C. purchases journal
   B. sales journal   D. cash receipts journal

9. When using a formula on an electronic spreadsheet, the symbol for multiply is:

   A. x   C. /
   B. @   D. *

10. Which of the following is a control account?

   A. Prepaid Rent   C. Capital
   B. Salary Payable   D. Accounts Receivable

III. Completion   *Complete each of the following statements.*

1. The procedures that a business uses to protect its assets are called _____.
2. When special journals are used, cash sales are recorded in the _____.
3. A general ledger account with a subsidiary ledger attached to it is called a _____.
4. When goods are returned, the buyer issues a _____ while the seller acknowledges the return by issuing a _____.
5. _____ are software programs organized by columns and rows.
6. An effective accounting information system should include four features: _____, _____, _____, and _____.
7. The three components that form a computerized accounting system are: _____, _____, and _____.
8. The intersection of a row and column in a spreadsheet is called a _____.
9. The three stages of data processing are _____, _____, and _____.
10. In a computerized system, posting occurs continuously with _____.

IV. Daily Exercises

1. Indicate in which journal each of the following transactions would be recorded. Use *S* for the Sales Journal, *P* for the Purchases Journal, *CR* for the Cash Receipts Journal, *CD* for the Cash Disbursements Journal, and *J* for the General Journal.
    - _____ A. Purchases of merchandise on account
    - _____ B. Purchases of merchandise for cash
    - _____ C. Sale of merchandise on account
    - _____ D. Sale of merchandise for cash
    - _____ E. Merchandise returned for credit on account
    - _____ F. Merchandise returned by customer for cash
    - _____ G. Payment of salaries
    - _____ H. Receipt of cash payment on account
    - _____ I. Sales discount taken by a customer
    - _____ J. Purchase discounts taken
    - _____ K. Owner's withdrawal of cash
    - _____ L. Depreciation expense

2. Record the following transactions in the space provided.

    a. Sold merchandise on account to Duncan Miller, $2,100, terms 2/10, n/30. The cost of the inventory was $1,025.
    b. Duncan Miller returned $600 from the sale. The cost of the returned goods was $280.
    c. Received payment from Duncan Miller for the amount due. Miller paid within the discount period.

Date	Accounts and Explanation	PR	Debit	Credit

3. Review the transactions in #2 above, specifically (b). In the space below, construct a special journal for Sales Returns and Allowance.

V. Exercises

1. Enter the following transactions in the purchases journal or the cash disbursements journal of Annie's Auto Supply Shop below. (You may omit posting references and check numbers.)

7/2	Purchased mufflers on account from Acme, $3,000, terms 1/10, n/30
7/3	Purchased bumpers for cash, $425
7/5	Annie withdrew $1,200 for personal use
7/6	Purchased miscellaneous replacement parts on account from Steve's Wholesalers, $1,650, terms 2/15, n/60
7/7	Paid telephone bill, $181
7/8	Purchased office equipment on account from Office Supply, Inc., $265, terms n/30
7/10	Paid for the July 2 purchase
7/13	Paid $2,000 to the bank on a loan
7/20	Purchased batteries from Acme on account, $892, terms 1/10, n/30
7/27	Paid Steve's Wholesalers the balance due

Purchases Journal

Date	Account Credited	Terms	CREDITS Accounts Payable	Purchases	DEBITS Other Accounts Title	Amount

Cash Disbursements Journal

Date	Account Debited	DEBITS Other Accounts	Accounts Payable	CREDITS Purchase Discounts	Cash

2. After Bernadette Green had completed all posting for the month of April, the sum of the balances in the Accounts Payable subsidiary ledger did not agree with the balance in the Accounts Payable control account in the general ledger. Assume the control account balance is correct. Locate and correct the errors in the subsidiary ledger accounts and determine the correct balance for each subsidiary account.

Name: Ellen Smith
Address: 321 Golf Club

Date	Item	Post Ref.	Debit	Credit	Balance
4/1	Balance	√			1,225
4/3		P		650	1,875
4/19		CD	1,225		650
4/22		J	75		725

Name: Lee Brelie
Address: 229 Bishop

Date	Item	Post Ref.	Debit	Credit	Balance
4/1	Balance	√			2,450
4/20		P		950	3,400
4/26		CD	2,450		950

Name: Helen Kalkstein
Address: 2402 University Ave.

Date	Item	Post Ref.	Debit	Credit	Balance
4/1	Balance	√			890
4/6		CD	890		-
4/22		P		1,025	1,025
4/26		J	275		800

3. Refer to the correct solution for Exercise 2 above and construct the Accounts Payable control account as it would appear for the month of April assuming Bernadette Green has only Smith, Brelie, and Kalkstein in her Accounts Payable ledger.

Accounts Payable

Date	Accounts	PR	Debit	Credit	Balance

4. Analyze each of the following and indicate when the error will come to the attention of the accountant.

a. When adding the columns in the cash disbursements journal, the cash credit column was totaled at $16,439. The actual total was $16,339.

_____
_____
_____

b. The receipt of a $800 check from a customer in payment of the account was recorded and posted as $80.

_____
_____
_____

c. When posting from the Cash Receipts journal, a check for $410 from Allen company was correctly recorded but posted to Alan Company in the subsidiary ledger.

_____
_____
_____

d. A credit sale of $980 to Sanders, Inc. was correctly recorded in the sales journal but was not posted to their account in the subsidiary ledger.

_____
_____
_____

VI. Beyond the Numbers

In this chapter you were introduced to control accounts and subsidiary ledgers, specifically Accounts Receivable which controls the customers ledger and Accounts Payable which controls the creditors ledger. What other general ledger accounts might be suitable for subsidiary ledgers and how might the subsidiary ledger be organized?

General Ledger account	Subsidiary ledger organized by
_____	_____
_____	_____
_____	_____
_____	_____
_____	_____

VII. Demonstration Problems

Demonstration Problem #1

A spreadsheet for Loc's Rocks follows. All column subtotals and totals are identified with the letters *m* through *z*. For each cell, present the formula so that the correct figure will automatically be printed as the spreadsheet is completed.

Loc's Rocks
Work Sheet
For the Year Ended December 31, 19X9

	A	B	C	D	E	F	G	H	I
1		Trial Balance		Adjustments		Income Statement		Balance Sheet	
2	Accounts	Debit	Credit	Debit	Credit	Debit	Credit	Debit	Credit
3	Cash	17,250						17,250	
4	Accts rec.	19,100						19,100	
5	Inventory	42,000						42,000	
6	Supplies	2,650			1,800			850	
7	Prepaid exp.	8,000			3,500			4,500	
8	Equipment	91,400						91,400	
9	Acc. dep.		39,100		7,800				46,900
10	Accts pay.		22,675						22,675
11	Salary pay.				810				810
12	Interest pay.				225				225
13	Unearned rev.		1,420	900					520
14	Note pay.		40,000						40,000
15	Loc, capital.		56,700						56,700
16	Loc, drawings	20,000						20,000	
17	Sales revenue		297,460		900		298,360		
18	Sales discounts	7,800				7,800			
19	Ret. & allow.	6,210				6,210			
20	Cst of gds sld	148,310				148,310			
21	Salary expense	51,500		810		52,310			
22	Rent expense	18,000				18,000			
23	Dep. exp.			7,800		7,800			
24	Util. expense	6,940				6,940			
25	Supp. expense			1,800		1,800			
26	Int. expense	3,775		225		4,000			
27	Adv. exp.	14,420		3,500		17,920			
28	Total	*m*	*n*	*o*	*p*	*q*	*t*	*v*	*x*
29						*r*			*y*
30						*s*	*u*	*w*	*z*

m. _____	t. _____
n. _____	u. _____
o. _____	v. _____
p. _____	w. _____
q. _____	x. _____
r. _____	y. _____
s. _____	z. _____

Demonstration Problem #2

During April, Konfection Corporation had these transactions:

4/2   Issued invoice No. 1079 to record credit sale to Gardner, Inc., $800. All credit sales are made on the company's standard terms of 1/10, n/30. Cost of the sale was $275.

4/5   Collected cash of $390 from Le, Inc. in full payment of their account receivable.

4/6   Collected note receivable, $10,000 plus interest of $600.

4/8   Issued invoice No. 1080 for sale on account to Molina, Inc., $1,200. Cost of the sale was $550.

4/14   Received $792 cash from Gardner, Inc., in settlement of their account receivable, net of discount, from the sale arising on April 2.

4/18   Sold inventory on account to Saecho, Inc., issuing invoice No. 1081 for $2,000. Cost of the sale was $975.

4/25   Received $3,005 from Langston, Inc., in full settlement of its account receivable. (The discount period has expired.)

4/28   Issued invoice No. 1082 to Langston Inc. for sale of $950. Cost of the sale was $390.

4/29   Sold goods on credit to Saecho, Inc., issuing invoice No. 1083 for $630. Cost of the sale was $280.

4/30   Issued credit in the amount of $1,325 for inventory that Saecho, Inc. returned because it had spoiled during shipment. The goods were discarded.

Selected accounts from the general ledger of Konfection Corporation show the following balances at April 1:

Acct. No.	Account Title	Balance		Acct. No.	Account Title	Balance
12	Cash	$5,662		400	Sales Revenues	-
20	Accounts Receivable	10,110		410	Sales Discounts	-
25	Inventory	23,685		420	Sales Returns and Allowances	-
30	Supplies	872		501	Cost of Goods Sold	-
40	Note Receivable	10,000		601	Interest Revenue	-

Konfection accounts receivable subsidiary ledger includes the following accounts and balances at April 1:

Account Title	Balance
Langston, Inc.	$ 3,005
Gardner, Inc.	1,080
Saecho, Inc.	4,725
Molina, Inc.	910
Le, Inc.	390
	$10,110

Required:

1. Open the general ledger and the accounts receivable subsidiary ledger accounts given, and insert their balances at April 1. Place a check mark (√) in the posting reference column for each April 1 balance.
2. Record the transactions on page 9 of a sales journal, page 18 of a cash receipts journal, and page 2 of a general journal as appropriate. Note: Record sales returns and allowances in the general journal.
3. Post to the general ledger and the accounts receivable subsidiary ledger. Use complete posting references, including the account number as given above. The sales journal and cash received from customers should be posted daily to the accounts receivable subsidiary ledger, as should any sales returns and allowances from the general journal. Other journals should be posted at the end of the month.
4. Prove the accuracy of posting by showing that the total of the balances in the subsidiary ledger equals the general ledger balance in Accounts Receivable.

Requirements 1 and 3 (open ledgers; post to ledgers)

Accounts Receivable Subsidiary Ledger   General Ledger

Langston, Inc.

Date	Ref.	Debit	Credit	Balance

Cash   12

Date	Ref.	Debit	Credit	Balance

Gardner, Inc.

Date	Ref.	Debit	Credit	Balance

Accounts Receivable 20

Date	Ref.	Debit	Credit	Balance

Saecho, Inc.

Date	Ref.	Debit	Credit	Balance

Inventory   25

Date	Ref.	Debit	Credit	Balance

Molina, Inc.

Date	Ref.	Debit	Credit	Balance

Supplies   30

Date	Ref.	Debit	Credit	Balance

Le, Inc.				
Date	Ref.	Debit	Credit	Balance

Notes Receivable				40
Date	Ref.	Debit	Credit	Balance

Sales Revenue				400
Date	Ref.	Debit	Credit	Balance

Sales Discount				410
Date	Ref.	Debit	Credit	Balance

Sales Returns and Allowances				420
Date	Ref.	Debit	Credit	Balance

Cost of Goods Sold				501
Date	Ref.	Debit	Credit	Balance

Interest Revenue				601
Date	Ref.	Debit	Credit	Balance

Requirement 2

SALES JOURNAL

Date	Account Debited	Invoice No.	Post Ref.	Debit A/R Credit Sales	Debit CGS Credit Inventory

CASH RECEIPTS JOURNAL

	DEBIT		CREDIT			
					Other Accounts	
Date	Cash	Sales Discount	Accounts Receivable	Account Title	Post Ref.	Amount

GENERAL JOURNAL

Date	Accounts and Explanation	PR	Debit	Credit

Requirement 4

Schedule of Accounts Receivable

Customer	Balance

SOLUTIONS

I. Matching

1. B	4. C	7. N	10. D	13. J	16. P
2. L	5. M	8. O	11. G	14. K	17. Q
3. A	6. E	9. F	12. H	15. I	

II. Multiple Choice

1. B Data are first collected, then organized and processed, and finally communicated.

2. D Internal controls are the methods and procedures used to authorize transactions, safeguard assets, and ensure the accuracy of accounting.

3. C Networks are the linkages which permit information sharing.

4. B Access to computer information can be protected by assigning passwords to potential users.

5. C All cash payments are recorded in the cash disbursements journal.

6. B Amounts owed to the business by its customers for merchandise purchased on account are accounts receivable of the business. Details of customers accounts receivable are maintained in the Accounts Receivable Subsidiary Ledger.

7. A The cash receipts journal is used to record all cash received by the business. Of the items listed, only "adjusting prepaid rent" does not involve the receipt of cash.

8. A The normal posting sources for Accounts Payable in the general ledger are the cash disbursements journal for cash payments that reduce the Accounts Payable balance and the purchases journal for inventory purchases which increase the Accounts Payable balance. The entry from the cash disbursements journal would be a debit to Accounts Payable. (Note: a debit or credit memo entry from the general journal might also be posted to Accounts Payable.)

9. D The symbol for multiply is *.

10. D A control account is a general ledger account with a balance equal to the sum of the balances of a group of related accounts in a subsidiary ledger. Of the accounts listed, only accounts receivable has a related subsidiary ledger.

III. Completion

1. internal controls (Internal controls are the methods and procedures used to authorize transactions, safeguard assets, and ensure the accuracy of accounting records.)
2. Cash Receipts Journal
3. Control account
4. debit memo, credit memo
5. spreadsheets
6. control, compatibility, flexibility, favorable cost/benefit relationship (order not important)

7. hardware, software, personnel (order not important)
8. cell
9. inputs, processing, outputs (order important)
10. on-line processing

IV. Daily Exercises

1. A. P   B. CD   C. S   D. CR   E. J   F. CD
    G. CD   H. CR   I. CR   J. CD   K. CD   L. J

2.

(a)	Accounts Receivable - Miller		2,100	
	Sales			2,100
	Cost of Goods Sold		1,025	
	Inventory			1,025
(b)	Sales Returns and Allowances		600	
	Accounts Receivable - Miller			600
	Inventory		280	
	Cost of Goods Sold			280
(c)	Cash		1,470	
	Sales Discounts		30	
	Accounts Receivable - Miller			1,500

3.

Date	Customer	Ref.	Debit Sales Returns and Allowances Credit A/R	Debit Inventory Credit CGS

V. Exercises

1.

Purchases Journal

Date	Account Credited	Terms	CREDITS Accounts Payable	DEBITS Purchases	DEBITS Other Accounts Title	DEBITS Other Accounts Amount
7/2	Acme	1/10,n/30	3,000	3,000		
7/6	Steve's Wholesalers	2/15,n/60	950	950		
7/18	Office Supply Co.		265		Equipment	265
7/20	Acme	1/10,n/30	892	892		

Cash Disbursements Journal

Date	Account Debited	DEBITS Other Accounts	DEBITS Accounts Payable	CREDITS Purchase Discounts	CREDITS Cash
7/3	Purchases	425			425
7/5	Withdrawals	1,200			1,200
7/7	Telephone exp.	181			181
7/10	Acme		3,000	30	2,970
7/13	Note Payable	2,000			2,000
7/27	Steve's Wholesalers		950		950

Note: 7/10 discount = 1% x $3,000 = $30

2.

Name: Ellen Smith					
Address: 321 Golf Club					
Date	Item	Post Ref.	Debit	Credit	Balance
4/1	Balance	√			1,225
4/3		P		650	1,875
4/19		CD	1,225		650
4/22		J	75		~~725~~ 575

Name: Lee Brelie					
Address: 229 Bishop					
Date	Item	Post Ref.	Debit	Credit	Balance
4/1	Balance	√			2,450
4/20		P		950	3,400
4/26		CD	2,450		950

Name: Helen Kalkstein
Address: 2402 University Ave.

Date	Item	Post Ref.	Debit	Credit	Balance	
4/1	Balance	√			890	
4/6		CD	890		-	
4/22		P		1,025	1,025	
4/26		J	275		800	750

3.

Accounts Payable

Date	Accounts	PR	Debit	Credit	Balance
4/1	Balance	√			4,565
4/22		J	75		4,490
4/26		J	275		4,215
4/30		P		2,625	6,840
4/30		CD	4,565		2,275

4.

a. Before posting column totals from a special journal, the debit/credit equality of the totals should be verified. When this is done, the credit column totals will be $100 more than the debit column totals.

b. Since the transaction was recorded as $80, the trial balance will balance and there will be agreement between the control account and the subsidiary ledger. However, our records indicate the customer still owes us $720 ($800 less the $80 receipt). No doubt the error will be brought to our attention when we re-bill the customer for an amount they have already paid.

c. As in b) above, the trial balance will balance and the control/subsidiary will agree. However Allen Company will be re-billed even though they paid the account. When this happens the error will be detected.

d. This error should come to our attention when we attempt to reconcile the control account with the total of the individual balances in our receivables subsidiary. The control account balance will be correct while the total of the subsidiary will be understated $980.

VI. Beyond the Numbers

There are a number of different accounts you could have listed as potential control accounts. The list that follows contains only some of the possibilities.

General Ledger account	Subsidiary ledger organized by
Merchandise Inventory	different types of inventory items
Prepaid Insurance	individual policies
Office Furniture	specific type—chairs, desks, etc.
Notes Payable	individual payees
Salary Expense	individual employee's wages

You set up a subsidiary ledger when the amount of activity is large enough to warrant the additional detail. Doing so keeps the general ledger "cleaner" while still providing the detail (in the subsidiary ledger) when needed.

VII. Demonstration Problems

Demonstration Problem #1 Solved

m. @sum(B3..B27) {add cell b3 through b27}

n. @sum(C9..C17)
o. @sum(D13..D27)
p. @sum(E6..E17)
q. @sum(F18..F27)
r. =(G28-F28) {sales - total expenses}
s. =(F28+F29)

t. =G17 {assign this cell the same value as cell G17}
u. =G28
v. @sum(H3..H16)
w. =H28
x. =@sum(I9..I15)
y. =(H28-I28)
z. =(I28+I29)

Demonstration Problem #2 Solved and Explained

Requirements 1 and 3

Accounts Receivable Subsidiary Ledger

General Ledger

Langston, Inc.

Date	Ref.	Debit	Credit	Balance
4/1	√			3,005
4/25	CR 18		3,005	0
4/28	S. 9	950		950

Cash   12

Date	Ref.	Debit	Credit	Balance
4/1	√			5,662
4/30	CR 18	14,787		20,449

Gardner, Inc.

Date	Ref.	Debit	Credit	Balance
4/1	√			1,080
4/2	S 9	800		1,880
4/14	CR 18		800	1,080

Accounts Receivable

Date	Ref.	Debit	Credit	Balance
4/1	√			10,110
4/30	GJ 2		1,325	8,785
4/30	S 9	5,580		14,365
4/30	CR 18		4,195	10,170

Saecho, Inc.

Date	Ref.	Debit	Credit	Balance
4/1	√			4,725
4/18	S 9	2,000		6,725
4/29	S 9	630		7,355
4/30	GJ 2		1,325	6,030

Inventory   25

Date	Ref.	Debit	Credit	Balance
4/1	√			23,685
4/30	S 9		2,470	21,215

Molina, Inc.

Date	Ref.	Debit	Credit	Balance
4/1	√			910
4/8	S 9	1,200		2,110

Le, Inc.

Date	Ref.	Debit	Credit	Balance
4/1	√			390
4/5	CR 18		390	0

Supplies 30

Date	Ref.	Debit	Credit	Balance
4/1	√			872

Notes Receivable 40

Date	Ref.	Debit	Credit	Balance
4/1	√			10,000
4/6	CR 18		10,000	0

Sales Revenue 400

Date	Ref.	Debit	Credit	Balance
4/1	√			0
4/30	S 9		5,580	5,580

Sales Discount 410

Date	Ref.	Debit	Credit	Balance
4/1	√			0
4/30	CR 18	8		8

Sales Returns and Allowances 420

Date	Ref.	Debit	Credit	Balance
4/1	√			0
4/30	GJ 2	1,325		1,325

Cost of Goods Sold 501

Date	Ref.	Debit	Credit	Balance
4/1	√			0
4/30	S 9	2,470		2,470

Interest Revenue 601

Date	Ref.	Debit	Credit	Balance
4/1	√			0
4/6	CR 18		600	600

Requirement 2

SALES JOURNAL

Date	Account Debited	Invoice No.	Post Ref.	Debit A/R Credit Sales	Debit CGS Credit Inventory
4/2	Gardner, Inc.	1079	√	800	275
4/8	Molina, Inc.	1080	√	1,200	550
4/18	Saecho, Inc.	1081	√	2,000	975
4/28	Langston, Inc.	1082	√	950	390
4/29	Saecho, Inc.	1083	√	630	280
				5,580	2,470
				(20) (400)	(501) (25)

CASH RECEIPTS JOURNAL

	DEBIT			CREDIT		
					Other Accounts	
Date	Cash	Sales Discount	Accounts Receivable	Account Title	Post Ref.	Amount
4/5	390		390	Le, Inc.	√	
4/6	10,600			Note Rec.	40	10,000
				Interest Rev.	601	600
4/14	792	8	800	Gardner, Inc.	√	
4/25	3,005		3,005	Langston, Inc.	√	
	14,787	8	4,195			10,600
	(12)	(410)	(20)			(√)
	14,795				14,795	

GENERAL JOURNAL

Date	Accounts and Explanation	PR	Debit	Credit
4/30	Sales Returns and Allowances	420	1,325	
	Accounts Receivable—Saecho, Inc.	20/√		1,325
	To record return of merchandise from Saecho, Inc. for goods spoiled during shipment. The goods were discarded.			

Requirement 4

Schedule of Accounts Receivable

Customer	Balance
Langston, Inc.	$ 950
Gardner, Inc.	1,080
Saecho, Inc.	6,030
Molina, Inc.	2,110
	$10,170

Note: The $10,170 total of the accounts receivable subsidiary ledger agrees with the accounts receivable controlling account.

<u>Explanations</u>

As you have probably noticed in your studies to date, there are a large number of similar transactions that occur in each problem set. This is true in the real world for most businesses as well. By using specialized journals, it is possible to save a significant amount of time in both the recording and posting of like transactions. The most common special journals are:

Special Journal	Used to Record
Cash receipts journal	all collections of cash
Cash disbursements journal	all disbursements of cash
Sales journal	merchandise sales on account
Purchases journal	all purchases on account

Actually using these specialized journals is a relatively straightforward task requiring little more than careful entry and systematic posting of the data into the appropriate subsidiary ledger account.

Chapter 7—Internal Control, Managing Cash, and Making Ethical Judgments

CHAPTER OVERVIEW

In Chapter 6, you learned about an accounting information system. This chapter follows that discussion by introducing you to internal control and the processes a business follows to control the organization's assets. As cash is the most liquid asset, this chapter applies internal control concepts to cash. However, internal control applies to all assets—topics covered in the next three chapters. The learning objectives for this chapter are to

1. Define internal control.
2. Identify the characteristics of an effective system of internal control.
3. Prepare a bank reconciliation and related journal entries.
4. Apply internal controls to cash receipts.
5. Apply internal controls to cash disbursements, including petty cash transactions.
6. Use a budget to manage cash.
7. Make ethical judgments in business.

CHAPTER REVIEW

Objective 1 - Define internal control.

Internal control is a system of methods and procedures designed to safeguard assets, ensure reliable accounting records, promote efficiency, and encourage adherence to company policies. A Federal law, the **Foreign Corrupt Practice Act**, passed in 1977, requires companies under SEC jurisdiction to maintain a system of internal control.

Objective 2 - Identify the characteristics of an effective system of internal control.

An effective system of internal control has four characteristics:
1. **Competent, reliable, and ethical personnel**. Paying competitive salaries, training people thoroughly, and providing adequate supervision help to promote competence.
2. **Assignment of responsibilities**. All duties to be performed must be identified, and responsibility for the performance of those duties must be assigned to appropriate people.
3. **Proper authorization**. An organization generally has a written set of rules that outlines approved procedures. Proper authorization must be obtained for deviations from standard policies.
4. **Separation of duties**. Separation of duties is designed to limit the possibility of fraud or theft in the handling of assets. The company must have:
   a) separation of operations from accounting
   b) separation of the custody of assets
   c) separation of the authorization of transactions from the custody of related assets
   d) separation of duties within the accounting function

Auditors evaluate the system of internal control to estimate the reliability of the accounting systems. Auditors also help to spot areas where improvements in internal control can be made. **Internal auditors** are employees of the company. **External auditors** are employed by public accounting firms and are hired by a business to audit its books.

Business documents and records are designed according to each company's needs. Source documents and records include sales invoices, purchase orders, and special journals. Good internal control requires documents to be prenumbered. A gap in the numbered sequence will call attention to a missing document.

Additional controls include electronic sensors (for inventory), fireproof vaults (for cash), point-of-sale terminals (also for cash), fidelity bonds (for employee theft), and electronic data processing auditors (for computer systems).

The limitations of an internal control system are determined by the opportunities available for collusion and the resources that management devotes to the system. Collusion between two or more people working together to defraud the firm may go undetected by the system of internal control. Internal control must be designed and judged in light of the costs and the benefits.

Using a bank account promotes internal control over cash. For accounting purposes, cash includes currency, coins, checks, money orders, and bank accounts. Banks safeguard cash and provide detailed records of transactions. Cash is the most common means of exchange, and it is also the most tempting asset for theft.

Documents used to control bank accounts include signature cards, deposit tickets, checks, and bank statements. Banks usually send monthly statements to depositors. The bank statement shows the beginning balance in the account, all transactions recorded during the month, and the ending balance. The bank also returns canceled checks with the statement.

Electronic Fund Transfer (EFT) is a system that relies on electronic impulses to account for cash transactions. EFT systems reduce the cost of processing cash transactions by reducing the documentary evidence of transactions. This lack of documentation poses a challenge to managers and auditors to enforce the internal control system.

Bank reconciliations are necessary because there are usually differences between the time that transactions are recorded on a business's books and the time that those transactions are recorded by the bank. For example, if you mail a check to a supplier on the last day of the month, you will record it on that day. However, the check will not clear your bank until the supplier has received it and deposited it in his bank, several days later.

Objective 3 - Prepare a bank reconciliation and related journal entries.

The general format for a bank reconciliation is:

BANK		BOOKS	
	Balance, last day of month		Balance, last day of month (trial balance of general ledger)
+	Deposits in transit		
-	Outstanding checks	+	Bank collections
±	Correction of bank errors	+	Interest paid on deposits
		-	Service charge
		±	Correction of book errors
	Adjusted bank balance	=	Adjusted book balance

Adjustments to the bank balance never require preparation of journal entries. Adjustments to the bank balance include the following items:

1. Deposits in transit have been recorded by the company, but not by the bank. There is often a time lag of a day or two until the deposit is sent to the bank and posted by the bank.
2. Outstanding checks are checks issued by the company and recorded on its books, but the checks have not yet been paid by the bank. There is a time lag of several days until the checks are cashed or deposited by the payee and sent to the business's bank to be paid.
3. Corrections of bank errors are the responsibility of the bank. The bank should be notified, and the corrections should appear on the next statement.

Adjustments to the books always require preparation of journal entries. Adjustments to the book balance include the following items:

1. The bank collects money on behalf of depositors. Examples are a lock-box system where customers pay directly to the bank account. A bank may also collect on a note receivable for the depositor. The bank will notify the depositor of these collections on the bank statement. The journal entry for the collection of a note receivable and the related interest is:

Cash	XXX	
Note Receivable		XX
Interest Revenue (if applicable)		X

2. Interest Revenue is sometimes paid on the checking account. The journal entry to record the interest is:

Cash	XX	
Interest Revenue		XX

3. Service charges are the bank's fees for processing transactions. The journal entry for a service charge is:

Miscellaneous Expense	X	
Cash		X

4. Nonsufficient funds (NSF) checks are customer checks that have been returned by the customer's bank because the customer's account did not have sufficient funds in the account to cover the amount of the check. Checks may also be returned if the maker's account has closed, the date is stale, the signature is not authorized, the check has been altered, or the check form is improper. The amount of returned checks is subtracted from the book balance and the following journal entry is made:

Accounts Receivable	XX	
Cash		XX

5. The cost of printing checks is handled like a service charge. The journal entry is:

Miscellaneous Expense	XX	
Cash		XX

6. Errors on the books must be handled on a case by case basis. If checks are recorded on the books for the wrong amount, then an entry must be prepared to correct the original entry.

Study Exhibit 7-5 carefully. Be sure you understand the components of a bank reconciliation and the journal entries needed to correct the Cash account balance.

When reported on the balance sheet, most companies list "Cash and equivalents"—this includes cash and other items similar enough to be included with cash (such as petty cash, short-term time deposits, and certificates of deposit).

Objective 4 - Apply internal controls to cash receipts.

The objective of internal control over cash receipts is to ensure that all cash is deposited in the bank and recorded correctly in the company's accounting records.

A cash register is a good device for management control over cash received in a store. Positioning the machine so that customers see the amounts rung up discourages cashiers from overcharging customers and pocketing the excess over actual prices. Issuing receipts requires cashiers to record the sale. Comparing actual receipts to control tapes maintained by the machine discourages theft.

For payments received from customers by mail, separation of duties among different people promotes good internal control. The mail room clerk should open all mail and record incoming payments. The mail room should deliver checks to the cashier for deposit, and send remittance advices to the accounting department for posting. Comparison of mail room totals, cashier totals, and accounting totals should be made daily.

Where large numbers of cash transactions occur, there is often a small difference between actual cash received and cash recorded. An account entitled **Cash Short and Over** is used to account for such differences. The account is debited for cash shortages and credited for cash overages. An example of the journal entry to record an overage is:

Cash	20,014	
Cash Short and Over		14
Sales		20,000

A debit balance in Cash Short and Over appears on the income statement as a miscellaneous expense; a credit balance in Cash Short and Over appears as Other Revenue. A large debit or credit balance in the account (representing shortage or overage) should be investigated promptly. (Helpful hint: Review Exhibit 7-7 in your text.)

Objective 5 - Apply internal controls to cash disbursements, including petty cash transactions.

Payment by check is a good control over cash disbursements. However, before a check can be issued, additional control procedures have occurred. For instance, companies require approved purchase orders before goods and/or services can be acquired, receiving reports verifying that goods received conform to the purchase order, an invoice which agrees with both the purchase order and receiving report, and, finally, an authorized check in payment of the invoice. Additionally, many companies require two signatures before a check can be sent.

(See Exhibit 7-10 in your text.)

Businesses keep a **petty cash** account to have cash on hand for minor expenses which do not warrant preparing a check. Such expenses include taxi fares, local delivery costs, and small amounts of office supplies.

Suppose a petty cash fund of $200 is established. The cash is placed under the control of a custodian and the following entry is made:

Petty Cash	200	
Cash		200

This type of entry is also used to increase the amount in the fund, say from $200 to $300:

Petty Cash	100	
Cash		100

Note that once the fund is established, no entry is made to the Petty Cash account except to change the total amount in the fund.

Petty cash is disbursed using petty cash tickets, which document the disbursements. Cash on hand plus the total of the petty cash tickets should always equal the fund balance. This is referred to as an **imprest fund**. If the fund comes up short, debit Cash Short and Over. If the opposite occurs, credit Cash Short and Over.

A petty cash fund must be periodically replenished, particularly on the balance sheet date. A check is drawn for the amount of the replenishment. An entry is made as follows:

Various accounts listed on petty cash tickets	XX	
Cash		XX

Note that the expenses on the petty cash tickets are recorded in the journal when the fund is replenished.

Objective 6 - Use a budget to manage cash.

A **budget** is a quantitative expression of a plan that helps managers coordinate the organization. Cash budgeting, therefore, is a way to manage cash. This is accomplished by developing a plan for future cash receipts and disbursements. The cash budget starts with the amount of cash on hand at the beginning of the period. To this is added the budgeted cash receipts. Sources of cash receipts will include revenue transactions, the sale of assets, proceeds from borrowing money, and customers paying their accounts. Budgeted cash disbursements will include expenditures for operating activities, acquisition of assets, and payments of debt. Once these budgeted receipts and disbursements have been determined, they can be compared with the expected receipts and disbursements. If the results of the expected cash activity exceed the budgeted activity, the managers will have the opportunity to invest the excess and generate additional revenue (the interest earned on the invested cash.) If the budgeted activity exceeds the expected activity, the company will need to arrange financing in order to maintain the desired amount of cash. Exhibit 7-12 illustrates a typical format for a cash budget.

Objective 7 - Make ethical judgments in business.

Most businesses have codes of ethics to which their employees are expected to conform. In addition, the accounting profession has the AICPA Code of Professional Conduct and the Standards of Ethical Conduct for Management Accountants. In many situations, the ethical course of action is clear. However, when this is not the case, the following steps may prove helpful:

1. Determine the facts
2. Identify the ethical issues
3. Specify the alternatives
4. Identify the people involved
5. Assess the possible consequences
6. Make the decision

Review the decision guidelines at the end of Chapter 7.

TEST YOURSELF

All the self-testing materials in this chapter focus on information and procedures that your instructor is likely to test in quizzes and examinations.

I. Matching *Match each numbered term with its lettered definition.*

_____ 1. external auditors
_____ 2. Foreign Corrupt Practices Act
_____ 3. bank statement
_____ 4. budget
_____ 5. electronic fund transfer
_____ 6. nonsufficient funds check
_____ 7. outstanding check
_____ 8. service charge

_____ 9. cash budget
_____ 10. bank collection
_____ 11. bank reconciliation
_____ 12. check
_____ 13. deposit in transit
_____ 14. imprest system
_____ 15. internal control
_____ 16. petty cash
_____ 17. voucher

A. a deposit recorded by the company but not by its bank
B. a check for which the payer's bank account has insufficient money to pay the check
C. a check issued by a company and recorded on its books but not yet paid by its bank
D. a document authorizing a cash disbursement
E. a document for a particular bank account that shows its beginning and ending balances and lists the month's transactions that affect the account
F. a document that instructs the bank to pay a designated person or business a specified amount of money
G. a fund containing a small amount of cash that is used to pay minor expenditures
H. a quantitative expression of a plan to help managers coordinate the entity's activities
I. a plan for cash receipts and disbursements during a future period
J. a system that accounts for cash transactions by electronic impulses rather than paper documents
K. a method of accounting for petty cash by which the balance in the Petty Cash account is compared to the sum of cash on hand plus petty cash disbursement tickets
L. bank's fee for processing a depositor's transactions
M. collection of money by the bank on behalf of a depositor
N. employed by public accounting firms; hired to audit a client's books
O. requires certain companies to maintain a system of internal controls
P. process of explaining the reasons for the difference between a depositor's records and the bank's records of the depositor's bank account
Q. the organizational plan and all related measures adopted by an entity to safeguard assets, ensure accurate and reliable accounting records, promote operational efficiency, and encourage adherence to company policies

II. Multiple Choice   *Circle the best answer.*

1. Bob McIvor handles cash receipts and has the authority to write off accounts receivable. This violates separation of:

    A. custody of assets from accounting
    B. operations from accounting
    C. duties within the accounting function
    D. authorization of transactions from custody of related assets

2. Felipe Toledo keeps both the cash receipts journal and the cash disbursements journal. This violates separation of:

    A. custody of assets from accounting
    B. operations from accounting

    C. duties within the accounting function
    D. authorization of transactions from custody of related assets

3. Which of the following items does *not* require a journal entry?

    A. interest paid on checking account
    B. deposits in transit

    C. collection by bank of note receivable
    D. bank service charge

4. The journal entry to record an NSF check returned by the bank is:

    A. debit Cash, credit Accounts Receivable
    B. debit Accounts Payable, credit Cash

    C. debit Accounts Receivable, credit Cash
    D. debit Miscellaneous Expense, credit Cash

5. Which of the following is *not* an internal control procedure for cash receipts?

    A. comparing actual cash to cash register tape totals
    B. pricing merchandise at uneven amounts
    C. paying bills by check
    D. enabling customers to see amounts entered on cash receipts

6. A debit balance in Cash Short and Over is reported on the income statement as:

    A. Other Revenue
    B. Cost of Goods Sold

    C. General Expenses
    D. Miscellaneous Expenses

7. Which of the following documents is prepared first?

    A. purchase requisition
    B. receiving report

    C. purchase order
    D. check

8. Which of the following documents is prepared last?

    A. purchase requisition
    B. receiving report

    C. purchase order
    D. check

9. Which of the following would not be included in a cash budget?

A. depreciation
B. withdrawals by owners
C. interest received
D. payments for expenses

10. Which of the following is *not* an internal control for cash?

A. fidelity bonds
B. point-of-sale terminal
C. electronic sensors
D. fireproof vault

III. Completion   *Complete each of the following statements.*

1. _____ is a measure of making small cash disbursements quickly.
2. Under the Foreign Corrupt Practices Act, _____ is (are) responsible for maintaining adequate internal controls.
3. _____ auditors are regular employees of a business; _____ auditors are independent of the business.
4. In a good internal control system, the following functions are separated:
   a)_____
   b)_____
   c)_____
   d)_____
5. _____ is usually the first asset listed on the balance sheet.
6. In preparing a cash budget, the first amount listed is _____.
7. When preparing the bank reconciliation, outstanding checks are _____ from the _____.
8. What account(s) is (are) debited when Petty Cash is replenished? _____
9. _____ insure a company against theft by an employee.
10. _____ is a temporary account used to reconcile discrepancies which result from cash transactions.

IV. Daily Exercises

1. Indicate how each of the following items is treated in a bank reconciliation. Use *AB* for additions to the bank balance; *AF* for additions to the firm's balance; *DB* for deductions from the bank balance; and *DF* for deductions from the firm's balance.
   _____ A. A deposit for $143 was not recorded in the books
   _____ B. A check for $34 was entered in the books as $43
   _____ C. Bank collection of a note receivable
   _____ D. Bank service charges
   _____ E. A deposit was credited by the bank to the firm's account in error
   _____ F. Deposits in transit
   _____ G. Interest earned on checking account
   _____ H. Outstanding checks
   _____ I. NSF checks

2. Examine your answers in Daily Exercise #1 and indicate which reconciling items will require a journal entry.

3. A small law firm maintains a $150 imprest petty cash fund. At the end of the month, there were receipts for expenditures totaling $128 and $21 in coins and currency. In the space below, record the entry to replenish the fund.

4. There are only three circumstances where the account Petty Cash is used in a journal entry. What are they?

IV. Exercises

1. Lee's bank statement gave an ending balance of $518.00. Reconciling items include: deposit in transit, $225.00; service charge, $9.00; outstanding checks, $189.00; and interest earned on her checking account, $1.50. What is the adjusted bank balance after the bank reconciliation is prepared?

2. Using the information in Exercise 1 above, what was the unadjusted ending balance in Lee's checking account?

3. During the month of November, Hillmuth Photo Co., had the following transactions in its Petty Cash fund.

   11/1   Established Petty Cash fund, $300
   11/6   Paid postage, $29
   11/8   Paid freight charges, $43
   11/11   Purchased office supplies, $31
   11/22   Paid miscellaneous expenses, $28
   11/30   Replenished the Petty Cash fund ($167 was in the fund)

   Prepare the journal entries required by each of the above transactions.

Date	Accounts and Explanation	PR	Debit	Credit

4. From the following information, present a Cash Budget for the year ended June 30, 19X9.

Proceeds from note receivable	$150,000
Purchases for inventory	110,000
Receipts from customers	285,000
Withdrawal by owner	55,000
Proceeds from sale of equipment	21,500
Payments for interest and taxes	108,000
Cash required for operating expenses	92,250
Debt payments	81,700

The cash balance as of July 1, 19X8, is $95,500. The budgeted cash balance for June 30, 19X9, is $100,000.

Cash Budget
For the Year Ended June 30, 19X9

VI. Beyond the Numbers

At the Fat Lady Sings Opera House, you notice that there is a box office at the entrance where the cashier receives cash from customers and, with a press of a button, a machine ejects serially numbered tickets. To enter the opera house, a customer must present his or her ticket to the door attendant. The attendant tears the ticket in half and returns the stub to the customer. The other half of the ticket is dropped into a locked box.

1. What internal controls are present in this scenario?
2. What should management do to make these controls more effective?
3. How can these controls be rendered ineffective?

VII. Demonstration problems

Demonstration Problem #1

The following petty cash transactions occurred in March:

3/1	Management decided to establish a petty cash fund. A check for $200 was written and cashed with the proceeds given to Becky Matsubara, who was designated custodian of the fund.
3/1	The owner of the business immediately took $25 for lunch money.
3/4	$12.95 was disbursed to reimburse an employee for an air-express package paid for with personal funds.
3/6	COD freight charges on Supplies were paid, $22.00.
3/9	$29 was spent on postage stamps while the postage meter was being repaired.
3/11	The owner "borrowed" another $35 from the fund.
3/12	COD freight charges on merchandise were paid, $31.
3/13	Because the fund was running low, Ms. Matsubara requested a check to replenish it for the disbursements made. As there was $44.45 on hand, Ms. Matsubara requested a check for $155.55. However, her supervisor authorized a check for $355.55 so sufficient funds would be on hand and only require monthly replenishment.
3/16	The monthly charge for the office newspaper was paid, $18.
3/19	COD charges on merchandise were paid, $47.
3/20	The owner took $55 from the fund.
3/22	Ms. Matsubara took $12 from the fund to purchase coffee and supplies for the office coffee room.
3/25	The owner's spouse arrived by taxi. The fare of $19 plus a $3 tip was paid from the petty cash fund.

3/26	$35 was paid from the fund to have the front windows washed.
3/28	A coworker did not have lunch money. Ms. Matsubara gave the coworker $15 from the fund and took a post-dated check for that amount.
3/31	The company decided to replenish the fund on the last working day each month. There was $93.00 left in the fund.

Required:

1. Record the appropriate transactions in the General Journal.
2. Post any entries to the Petty Cash account.

Requirement 1(General Journal entries)

Date	Accounts and Explanation	PR	Debit	Credit

Requirement 2 (Post entries to Petty Cash Fund)

Petty Cash Fund

Demonstration Problem #2

Selected columns of the cash receipts journal and the check register of Martin Co. appear as follows on January 31, 19X9:

Cash Receipts Journal (Posting reference is CR)		Check Register (Posting reference is CD)	
Date	Cash Debit	Check No.	Cash Credit
Jan. 3	$ 242	669	$ 232
7	701	670	2,114
12	408	671	445
14	900	672	756
24	2,715	673	905
31	382	674	105
		675	781
		676	828
Total	$5,348	Total	$6,166

The cash account of Martin Co. shows the following information on January 31, 19X9:

Cash

Date	Item	PR	Debit	Credit	Balance
Jan. 1	Balance				$ 5,682
31		CR 1	5,348		11,030
31		CD 2		6,166	4,864

Martin Co. received the following bank statement on January 31, 19X9.

Bank Statement for Martin Co.

Beginning balance		$ 5,682
Deposits and other credits:		
Jan. 4	242	
8	701	
11	1,830	BC
13	408	
15	900	
25	2,715	
31	16	INT
	6,812	

Checks and other debits:

Jan. 3	$ 725	
7	223	
11	2,114	
12	445	
15	756	
20	175	NSF
24	905	
30	781	
31	14	SC
	6,138	
Ending balance:	$6,356	

Legend:

BC = Bank Collection   NSF = Nonsufficient Funds Check

SC = Service Charge   INT = Interest Earned

Additional data for the bank reconciliation:

1. The $1,830 bank collection on Jan. 11 includes $130 interest revenue. The balance was attributable to the collection of a note receivable.
2. The correct amount of Check Number 669 is $223, a payment on account. The Martin Co. bookkeeper mistakenly recorded the check in the check register as $232.
3. The NSF check was received from Rick's Restaurant.
4. The bank statement includes a $725 deduction for a check drawn by Morton Co. The bank has been notified of its error.
5. The service charge consists of two charges: $4 for the monthly account charge and $10 for the NSF check.

Required:

1. Prepare the bank reconciliation of Martin Co. on January 31, 19X9.
2. Record the entries based on the bank reconciliation. Include explanations.

Requirement 1 (Bank reconciliation)

Martin Co.
Bank Reconciliation
January 31, 19X9

Requirement 2 (Entries based on bank reconciliation)

Date	Accounts and Explanation	PR	Debit	Credit

SOLUTIONS

I. Matching

1. N	4. H	7. C	10. M	13. A	16. G
2. O	5. J	8. L	11. P	14. K	17. D
3. E	6. B	9. I	12. F	15. Q	

II. Multiple Choice

1.   D   Handling cash receipts and having authority to write off accounts receivable puts the person in a position to illegitimately write off an account on which payment has been received. This is a violation of separation of the authorization of transactions from custody of related assets.

2.   C   Independent performance of various phases of accounting helps to minimize errors and the opportunities for fraud. The cash receipts journal and the cash disbursements journal are two duties within the accounting function that should be separated.

3.   B   Deposits in transit are cash receipts that have been recorded in the cash receipts journal of the business but have not yet been recorded by the bank. The other items listed are items that will be reflected in the banks records, but have not yet been recorded on the books of the business.

4.   C   An NSF check represents a previously recorded cash receipt that has no substance and, accordingly, must be reversed; reduce cash (credit) and reestablish the receivable (debit).

5.   C   Paying bills by check is an internal control procedure for cash disbursements, not cash receipts. The other items listed are internal control procedures for cash receipts.

6.   D   A debit balance means a cash shortage exists. It is reported as a miscellaneous expense.

7.   A   The purchasing process starts when the sales department identifies need for merchandise and prepares a purchase requisition. The purchase order, receiving report, and voucher follow in that order.

8.   D   The check is prepared last.

9.   A   Depreciation is a non-cash item and would not be included in a cash budget.

10.   C   Electronic sensors attempt to control inventory, not cash.

III. Completion

1. Petty Cash fund
2. management (Companies under SEC jurisdiction are required to maintain an appropriate system of internal control. This requirement is a responsibility of the management of the company.)
3. Internal; external (Internal auditors report directly to the company's president or audit committee of the board of directors. External auditors audit the entity as a whole and usually report to the stockholders.)
4. custody of assets from accounting, authorization of transactions from custody of related assets, operations from accounting, duties within the accounting function

5. Cash (Assets are listed in order of relative liquidity; cash is listed first because it is the most liquid.)
6. beginning cash balance
7. deducted, balance per bank
8. Various expense accounts (Note that the Petty Cash account is debited or credited only when the amount of the fund is changed.)
9. fidelity bonds
10. Cash Short and Over

IV. Daily Exercises

1. A) AF   B) AF   C) AF   D) DF   E) DB   F) AB   G) AF   H) DB
   I) DF
2. Items A, B, C, D, G, and I will all require a journal entry.
3. Miscellaneous Expense   128
   Cash Short and Over   1
       Cash   129
4. The Petty Cash account is part of a journal entry when
   a. the fund is established
   b. the size of the fund is increased
   c. the size of the fund is decreased

V. Exercises

1.

Balance per bank statement	$518
Add:	
Deposit in transit	225
	743
Deduct:	
Outstanding checks	189
Adjusted bank balance	554

2. This requires you to work backwards. Start by setting up what is known and then solve for the unknown balance. Remember that the adjusted balance in the checkbook will equal the adjusted bank balance on the bank reconciliation.

Balance per checkbook	?
Add:	
Interest earned	1.50
	?
Deduct:	
Service charge	9.00
Adjusted bank balance	554

Book balance + 1.50 - 9.00 = 554
Book balance = 561.50

3.

Date	Accounts and Explanation	PR	Debit	Credit
11/1	Petty Cash		300	
	Cash			300
11/30	Miscellaneous Expense		28	
	Postage Expense		29	
	Freight Expense		43	
	Supplies		31	
	Cash Short and Over		2	
	Cash			133

Note that you make an entry to record the various expenses only when the Petty Cash fund is replenished.

4.

Cash Budget
For the Year Ended June 30, 19X9

Cash balance, 7/1/X8		$ 95,500
Estimated cash receipts		
Receipts from customers	$285,000	
Proceeds from sale of equipment	21,500	
Proceeds from note receivable	150,000	456,500
Estimated cash disbursements		
Purchases of inventory	110,000	
Withdrawals by owner	55,000	
Payments for interest and taxes	108,000	
Operating expenses	92,250	
Payments for debt	81,700	446,950
Cash available (needed) before new financing		105,050
Budgeted cash balance, 6/30/X9		100,000
Cash available for additional investments		$ 5,050

VI. Beyond the Numbers

1. Notice that there is separation of duties—one person issues the ticket and collects the money, and the other person oversees the admission to the opera house. Thus, a ticket is necessary to gain entrance.

The tickets are serially numbered. Management can determine the amount of cash that should be in the drawer by multiplying the price of each ticket by the number of tickets issued.

2. To make the controls effective, management should 1) record the serial number of the first and last ticket sold on each cashier's shift, 2) maintain control over the unsold tickets, and 3) count the cash at the beginning and end of each shift.

3. The controls are ineffective if there is collusion by the cashier and the door attendant. The door attendant may choose to keep the entire ticket instead of tearing it in half. The ticket is then given to the cashier to be sold again. The cashier can then pocket the cash received for the "used" tickets. Remember, internal controls are ineffective if everyone colludes.

VII. Demonstration Problems

Demonstration Problem #1

Requirement 1

Only three entries were required in this problem! Remember, the purpose of a petty cash fund is to make small disbursements while avoiding the time and cost of writing checks. Therefore, entries are only recorded when a fund is established, when the fund balance is changed, and when the fund is replenished.

3/1	Petty Cash Fund	200.00	
	Cash		200.00
3/13	Drawing	60.00	
	Postage	41.95	
	Supplies	22.00	
	Freight-in (or Inventory)	31.00	
	Cash Short and Over	1.50	
	Petty Cash Fund	200.00	
	Cash		355.55

Amounts taken by the owner are charged to the Drawing account. Freight charges on merchandise are debited to Freight-In (or Inventory). Freight charges on assets are debited to the asset account, not to Freight-In. Freight-In is a cost of goods sold account and the Supplies are for use, not for resale. Finally, the receipts plus remaining cash did not reconcile to the beginning balance so Cash Short and Over was debited for the difference.

3/31	Freight-In (or Inventory)	47	
	Drawing	77	
	Accounts Receivable	15	
	Miscellaneous Expense	65	
	Cash Short and Over	3	
	Cash		207

The newspaper, coffee money, and window washing were all charged to Miscellaneous Expense, although they could be debited to separate accounts. The post-dated check is charged to Accounts Receivable because it represents an amount the employee owes the business. Allowing an employee to "borrow" from the petty cash fund violates effective internal control procedures and should be stopped immediately. If permitted to continue, the petty cash fund will contain nothing but a stack of post-dated checks!

Requirement 2

Petty Cash Fund		
3/1	200	
3/13	200	
Bal.	400	

Assuming the company is correct in its estimates that a $400 balance is sufficient for the petty cash fund, the general ledger account, Petty Cash Fund, will remain as presented above, with the $400 balance undisturbed.

Demonstration Problem #2

Requirement 1

Martin Co.
Bank Reconciliation
January 31, 19X9

BANK:		
Balance 1/31		6,356
Add:		
Deposit in transit of 1/31		382
Correction of bank error		725
		7,463
Less:		
Outstanding checks		
Check # 674	105	
Check # 676	828	933
Adjusted bank balance 1/31		6,530
BOOKS:		
Balance 1/31		4,864
Add:		
Bank collection of note receivable, including interest of $130		1,830
Interest earned on bank balance		16
Error - Check #669		9
		6,719
Less:		
Service charge		14
NSF check		175
Adjusted bank balance 1/31		6,530

Explanation: bank reconciliation

1. A bank reconciliation prepared on a timely basis provides good internal control over a company's cash accounts. Comparing the cash balance in the general ledger with the cash balance maintained by the bank makes errors easy to detect.

2. The month-end balance shown in the general ledger rarely agrees with the month-end balance shown on the bank statement. The difference generally occurs for one of two reasons:

    1. Timing differences: These occur because of the time lag that occurs when one recordkeeper records a transaction before the other. Typical timing differences include:

        - Deposits in transit (the bank has yet to record)
        - Outstanding checks (the bank has yet to record)
        - Bank service charges (the company has yet to record)
        - Notes collected by the bank (the company has yet to record)
        - Interest earned on account (the company has yet to record)
        - NSF checks (the company has yet to record)

    2. Errors: An error must result in an adjustment by the recordkeeping party that made the error. If the error is made by the company, a general journal entry is made. The correcting entry will include an increase or decrease to the Cash account. Note that if the bank has made the error, the proper procedure is to notify the bank promptly. Since the company's records are accurate, no journal entry is needed.

Requirement 2

Date	Accounts and Explanation	PR	Debit	Credit
a.	Cash		1,830	
	Note Receivable			1,700
	Interest Revenue			130
	Note Receivable collected by the bank.			
b.	Cash		16	
	Interest Revenue			16
	Interest earned on bank balance.			
c.	Miscellaneous Expense		4	
	Cash			4
	Bank service charge.			
d.	Accounts Receivable - Rick's Restaurant		185	
	Cash			185
	NSF check returned by bank plus service charge.			
e.	Cash		9	
	Accounts Payable			9
	To correct error in recording Check #115			

<u>Explanations: Journal Entries</u>

Entries (a) and (b) are necessary to record the increase in the cash account attributable to 1) the collection of interest and principal on the note receivable, and 2) interest earned on the account paid by the depository bank. These are timing differences which occur because of the time lag between the recording of an item on the bank's books and the books of the company. The bank has already recorded these items in its records (as evidenced by the bank statement), and the company must do so when it learns of the transaction(s).

Entries (c) and (d), which are similar to entries (a) and (b) reduce cash on the company's books. These timing differences have already been recorded by the bank. Entry (c) reduces cash for checking account (or other) service charges for the monthly period and brings the account up to date. The entry for the NSF check is necessary to establish an account receivable for Rick's Restaurant. They had paid the company with a check that was deposited in the cash account. Because the check was returned unpaid for nonsufficient funds, the company must pursue collection of the debt and record on its books that $185 is still owed.

Entry (e) represents the correction of an error. Check #669 was recorded in the cash disbursements journal as a reduction to Cash of $233 instead of $223.

Note: No entry is required for the bank error. Once notified, the bank needs to correct their books.

Chapter 8—Accounts and Notes Receivable

CHAPTER OVERVIEW

In Chapter 7 you learned about the importance of internal control, with the specific application of internal control procedures to cash and other highly liquid current assets. Chapter 8 extends the discussion to include other current assets, specifically receivables—both accounts and notes. Subsequent chapters will cover merchandise inventory (Chapter 9) and fixed assets (Chapter 10). The learning objectives for this chapter are to

1. Design internal controls for receivables.
2. Use the allowance method of accounting for uncollectibles. Estimate uncollectibles by the percentage of sales and the aging approaches.
3. Use the direct write-off method of accounting for uncollectibles.
4. Account for notes receivable.
5. Report receivables on the balance sheet.
6. Use the acid-test ratio and days' sales in receivables to evaluate a company's position.
7. Report cash flows from receivables transactions on the statement of cash flows.

CHAPTER REVIEW

Receivables arise when goods or services are sold on credit. The basic types of receivables are **accounts receivable** and **notes receivable**.

Accounts receivable are amounts that customers owe a business for purchases made on credit. They should be collectible according to a firm's normal terms of sale, such as net 30 days. Accounts receivable are sometimes called **trade receivables**, and are current assets.

Notes receivable occur when customers sign formal agreements to pay for their purchases. These agreements are called **promissory notes**, and usually extend for periods of 60 days or longer. The portion of notes receivable scheduled to be collected within a year is a current asset; the remaining amount is a long-term asset.

Other receivables includes miscellaneous items such as loans to employees.

(Helpful hint: Review Exhibit 8-1 in your text for the correct statement placement of these receivables.)

Objective 1 - Design internal controls for receivables.

The main issues in controlling and managing the collection of receivables are:

1. extending credit only to creditworthy customers
2. separating cash-handling, credit, and accounting duties
3. pursuing collection from customers to maximize cash flow

The main issues in accounting for receivables are:

1. measuring and reporting receivables at the net realizable value (the amount we expect to collect)
2. measuring and reporting the expense associated with uncollectible accounts

It is imperative that cash-handling and cash accounting duties be separated; otherwise, too many opportunities exist for employees to steal cash from the company. This is true in both the receivables department and the credit department.

Extending credit to customers involves the risk that some customers will not pay their obligations. Uncollectible Account Expense (also called Doubtful Account Expense or Bad Debt Expense) occurs when a business is unable to collect from some credit customers. This expense is a cost of doing business, and should be measured, recorded, and reported. Two methods used by accountants are the **allowance method** and the **direct write-off method**.

The **allowance method** is the preferred way to account for Uncollectible Account Expense (it is better for matching the expense with revenue earned). This method estimates and records collection losses before specific uncollectible accounts are identified.

Allowance for Uncollectible Accounts is a contra account to Accounts Receivable. Remember, contra accounts are subtracted from a related account. Examples from earlier chapters are Accumulated Depreciation (which is subtracted from a related plant asset) and Sales Discounts (which is subtracted from Sales Revenue). On the balance sheet, Accounts Receivable would appear as follows:

Accounts Receivable	XXX
- Allowance for Uncollectible Accounts	(XX)
= Net Accounts Receivable	XXX

Objective 2 - Use the allowance method to estimate uncollectible receivables. Estimate uncollectibles by the percentage of sales and the aging approaches.

Using the allowance method requires an estimate of uncollectible accounts.

The **percentage of sales method** estimates uncollectible accounts as a percentage of sales, using past experience to set the percentage. The amount of the journal entry is equal to credit sales times the bad debt percentage, and is recorded as:

Uncollectible Account Expense	XX	
Allowance for Uncollectible Accounts		XX

Aging the accounts involves grouping accounts receivable according to the length of time they have been outstanding. Accounts are usually grouped into 30-day increments, such as 1-30, 31-60, 61-90, and over 90 days. Different percentages of the total receivables in each group are estimated to be uncollectible. The amount for each group is equal to the total receivables in that group times the estimated uncollectible percentage for that group.

The amount of the journal entry will be what is needed to bring the Allowance account to the estimated amount calculated using the aging method. Therefore, if the existing balance in the Allowance for

Uncollectible Accounts is a credit, the amount of the journal entry will be less than the estimate. If the existing balance in the Allowance for Uncollectible Accounts is a debit, the amount of the journal entry will be greater than the estimate.

The expense is recorded as:

Uncollectible Account Expense	XX	
Allowance Uncollectible Accounts		XX

> **Study Tip**: When using an estimate based on sales, adjust *for* the estimate; when using an estimate based on accounts receivable, adjust *to* the estimate.

(Review Exhibit 8-2 in your text.)

When using the allowance method, specific accounts receivable are written off when the credit department determines that the receivable is not collectible. Specific accounts are written off with this journal entry:

Allowance for Uncollectible Accounts	XX	
Accounts Receivable		XX

Note that this entry does not affect expense because the estimated expense has already been recorded.

Objective 3 - Use the direct write-off method of accounting for uncollectibles.

Using the **direct write-off method**, the company writes off an account receivable directly to an expense account. In other words, the allowance account is not used.

The journal entry for a direct write-off is:

Uncollectible Account Expense	XX	
Accounts Receivable		XX

The direct write-off method is easy to use. Its major drawback is that the bad debt expense is not matched with the revenues to which it pertains because the expense is usually recorded long after the corresponding revenue is recorded.

In the retail industry, credit card usage has become universal. Credit cards enable merchants to reduce the risk of uncollectible accounts and to eliminate accounts receivable subsidiary ledgers.

When a customer presents a credit card as payment for a purchase, a sales slip is prepared. The merchant keeps one copy, the customer keeps one copy, and one copy is forwarded to the credit card company. The credit card company charges the merchant a fee for processing the charge sale. This fee is usually a percentage of sales, and ranges up to 5%. The merchant records:

Accounts Receivable - Credit Card Co.	XX	
Sales Revenue		XX

When the credit card company receives the charge slips, it processes them, bills its cardholders, and reimburses the merchant. The merchant records this entry:

Cash	XX	
Credit Card Discount Expense	XX	
Accounts Receivable - Credit Card Co.		XX

Bankcard sales (VISA, MasterCard) are treated differently from the credit card sales treated above. When a customer uses a bankcard, the transaction is immediately recorded at both the bank and the merchant. Therefore, the transaction is similar to a cash sale because the business receives its cash at the point of sale.

Credit balances in particular customers' accounts (usually the result of overpayments or returns following payments) represent obligations to the business and should be reported on the balance sheet as liabilities (rather than "netted" against the debit balances in Accounts Receivable).

Objective 4 - Account for notes receivable.

Notes receivable are more formal than accounts receivable. Usually, the maker (debtor) will sign a promissory note and must pay the principal amount plus interest to the payee (creditor) on the maturity date. The maturity value is the sum of the principal amount plus the interest.

Review Exhibit 8-5 in your text to be certain you are familiar with the following terms:

Promissory note	Interest period (note period or note term)
Maker	Maturity date (due date)
Payee	Maturity value
Principal amount	Interest rate
Interest	

The formula for computing interest is :

Principal × Interest Rate × Time = Interest Amount

Study the examples in the text. It is important to be able to compute interest based on years, months, and days.

Generally notes arise from three events, as follows:

1)
Notes Receivable	XX	
Sales		XX

Sold goods and received a promissory note.

2)
Notes Receivable	XX	
Accounts Receivable		XX

Receipt of a note from a customer is payment of the account.

3)　　　Notes Receivable　　　　　　　XX
　　　　　　Cash　　　　　　　　　　　　　　　XX
　　　Loaned money and received a promissory note.

Interest revenue is earned as time passes, and not just when cash is collected. If the interest period of the note extends beyond the current accounting period, then part of the interest revenue is earned in the current accounting period and part is earned in the next accounting period.

Interest must be accrued (you were introduced to accrued revenue in Chapter 3) for the amount which has been earned in the current period but not yet collected. The entry to record accrued interest is:

　　　Interest Receivable　　　　　　　XX
　　　　　　Interest Revenue　　　　　　　　XX

On the maturity date, the payee will record collection of the note with this entry:

　　　Cash　　　　　　　　　　　　　　XX
　　　　　　Notes Receivable　　　　　　　　XX
　　　　　　Interest Receivable　　　　　　　XX
　　　　　　Interest Revenue　　　　　　　　XX

This entry records: 1) the amount of cash received; 2) the collection of the note; 3) the collection of the interest receivable from the prior accounting period; and 4) the collection of the remaining interest revenue earned in the current accounting period.

A note receivable is a negotiable instrument. Frequently, a business will sell a note receivable to a bank to raise cash. Selling a note receivable before its maturity date is called **discounting a note receivable**. The seller receives less than the maturity value (that is, gives up some of the interest revenue) in exchange for receiving cash. The discounted value, called the proceeds, is the amount the seller (business) receives from the purchaser (bank).

　　　Proceeds are computed as:
　　　　　　Principal amount of the note
　　　　　　+ Interest (Principal × Rate × Time) (entire length of note)
　　　　　　= Maturity Value
　　　　　　- Discount (Maturity value × Discount Rate × Time) (time bank holds note)
　　　　　　= Proceeds

The business records the following entry when selling a note receivable:

　　　Cash　　　　　　　　　　　　XX (Proceeds)
　　　　　　Notes Receivable　　　　　　　　XX (Face Value of Note)
　　　　　　Interest Revenue　　　　　　　　XX (difference if Proceeds > Face Value)

Sometimes the proceeds are less than the principal amount. In this situation, the entry is:

Cash	XX	
Interest Expense	XX	
Notes Receivable		XX

Review Exhibit 8-6 in your text.

A **contingent liability** is a potential liability—one that may or may not occur. If the maker of the note fails to pay the maturity value to the new payee (bank), the seller (business) must pay the new payee (bank). Thus, the liability is potential. Contingent liabilities are not reported on the balance sheet, but are reported in the footnotes to the financial statements. Notes receivable which have been discounted represent contingent liabilities.

If the maker of the note does not pay at maturity, the maker has **dishonored** (defaulted on) the note. The note agreement is no longer negotiable, but the payee (creditor) still has a claim against the maker (debtor). The payee usually transfers the claim from Notes Receivable to Accounts Receivable and records the interest revenue earned:

Accounts Receivable	XX	
Notes Receivable		XX
Interest Revenue		XX

If the business has sold the note, the contingent liability becomes an actual liability when the note is dishonored. The business is obligated to pay the note purchaser (the bank) the maturity value of the note. The business records the dishonored note:

Accounts Receivable	XX	
Cash		XX

Objective 5 - Report receivables on the balance sheet.

Firms report the value of accounts receivable on the balance sheet in various ways:

1. As a net value:

Accounts Receivable (less Allowance of $XX for Uncollectibles)	$XXX

2. With footnotes:

Current Receivables (note X)	$XXX

3. With detail in the body of the balance sheet:

Accounts Receivable	$XXX	
Less: Allowance for Uncollectibles Accounts	XX	$XXX

Objective 6 - Use the acid-test ratio and the days' sales in receivables to evaluate a company's position.

The **acid-test (quick) ratio** measures the ability of a business to pay all of its current liabilities if they become due immediately.

$$\text{Acid-test Ratio} = \frac{\text{Cash} + \text{Short-term investment} + \text{Net current receivables}}{\text{Current Liabilities}}$$

Study Tip: Remember that inventory, supplies, and prepaid expenses are not used to compute the acid-test ratio.

Days' sales in receivables (also called the collection period) measures the average days an account receivable is outstanding.

$$\text{One day's sales} = \frac{\text{Net Sales}}{365}$$

$$\text{Days' sales in average accounts receivable} = \frac{\text{Average Net Accounts Receivable}}{\text{One day's sales}}$$

$$\text{Average Net Accounts Receivable} = \frac{\text{Beginning Receivables} + \text{Ending Receivables}}{2}$$

Objective 7 - Report cash flows from receivables transactions on the statement of cash flows.

The cash flows statement organizes cash receipts and payments into three categories: operating activities, investing activities, and financing activities (the first two sections are illustrated in Exhibit 8-8 in your text). The receipt of cash from customers and the receipt of cash interest are both classified as operating activities because they relate to the business operations. Lending money (for which a promissory note is received) and collecting a note receivable are classified as investing activities on the cash flows statement.

TEST YOURSELF

All the self-testing materials in this chapter focus on information and procedures that your instructor is likely to test in quizzes and examinations.

I. Matching   *Match each numbered term with its lettered definition.*

_____ 1. aging of accounts receivable
_____ 2. Allowance for Uncollectible Accounts
_____ 3. contingent liability
_____ 4. direct write-off method
_____ 5. discounting a notes receivable
_____ 6. interest
_____ 7. maturity date
_____ 8. payee
_____ 9. promissory note
_____ 10. Uncollectible Account Expense

_____ 11. allowance method
_____ 12. creditor
_____ 13. debtor
_____ 14. dishonor a note
_____ 15. interest period
_____ 16. maker of a note
_____ 17. maturity value
_____ 18. principal amount
_____ 19. receivable
_____ 20. interest rate

A. a potential liability
B. the party to a credit transaction who obtains a receivable
C. the party to a credit transaction who makes a purchase and credits a payable
D. failure of the maker of a note to pay at maturity
E. a method of accounting for bad debts in which the company records uncollectible account expense and credits the customer's account receivable when the credit department decides that a customer's account receivable is uncollectible
F. selling a note receivable before its maturity
G. revenue to the payee for loaning out the principal, and expense to the maker for borrowing the principal
H. the person who signs a note and promises to pay the amount required by the note agreement
I. the date on which the final payment of a note is due
J. the person who receives promised future payment on a note
K. the amount loaned out or borrowed
L. a written promise to pay a specified amount of money on a particular future date
M. a monetary claim against a business or an individual which is acquired by selling goods and services on credit or by lending money
N. a way to estimate bad debts by analyzing individual accounts receivable according to the length of time they have been due
O. a contra asset account related to accounts receivable
P. a method of recording collection losses based on estimates made prior to determining that specific accounts are uncollectible
Q. the percentage rate multiplied by the principal amount to compute the amount of interest on a note
R. the time during which interest is computed
S. the sum of the principal and interest due at the maturity of a note
T. cost of extending credit that arises from the failure to collect from credit customers

II. Multiple Choice   *Circle the best answer.*

1. Using the allowance method, writing off a specific account receivable will:

   A. increase net income
   B. decrease net income

   C. not affect net income
   D. affect net income in an undetermined manner

2. Uncollectible Account Expense is:

   A. a component of Cost of Goods Sold
   B. an operating expense

   C. a reduction to Sales
   D. an Other Expense

3. Which of the following will occur if Uncollectible Account Expense is not recorded at the end of the year?

   A. Expenses will be overstated.
   B. Net Income will be understated.

   C. Liabilities will be understated.
   D. Assets will be overstated.

4. Net Accounts Receivable is equal to:

   A. Accounts Receivable - Allowance for Uncollectible Accounts
   B. Accounts Receivable + Allowance for Uncollectible Accounts
   C. Accounts Receivable - Uncollectible Account Expense
   D. Accounts Receivable + Uncollectible Account Expense

5. Accounts Receivable has a debit balance of $22,500 and the Allowance for Uncollectible Account has a credit balance of $1,500. A specific account of $200 is written off. What is the amount of net receivables after the write-off?

   A. $22,300
   B. $21,300

   C. $21,000
   D. $20,800

6. Allowance for Uncollectible Accounts is:

   A. an expense account
   B. a contra liability account

   C. a contra asset account
   D. a liability account

7. A 120-day note receivable reported on the balance sheet is classified as a:

   A. current asset
   B. long-term asset

   C. current liability
   D. long-term liability

8. Interest is equal to:

   A. Principal × Rate
   B. Principal ÷ Rate ÷ Time

   C. Principal × Rate ÷ Time
   D. Principal × Rate × Time

9. When a company discounts a note receivable, how much cash is typically received?

   A. more than the maturity value
   B. the maturity value
   C. less than the maturity value
   D. the principal amount

10. Which of the following does not describe a business's cost of extending credit to customers who do *not* pay?

   A. Bad Debt Expense
   B. Uncollectible Account Expense
   C. Account Receivable Expense
   D. Doubtful Account Expense

III. Completion   *Complete each of the following statements.*

1. The direct write-off method of accounting for bad debt violates the _____ principle.
2. Cash receipts from customers are listed in the _____ activities section of the statement cash flows.
3. The method of estimating bad debts that focuses on the balance sheet is the _____ method.
4. The method of estimating bad debts that focuses on the income statement is the _____ method.
5. A _____ liability will become an actual liability and require payment only if certain events occur in the future.
6. The collection of a note receivable is listed in the _____ activities section of the cash flows statement.
7. The _____ measures the ability of a business to pay all its current liabilities if they become due immediately.
8. To calculate the average days an account receivable is outstanding, average net accounts receivable is divided by _____.
9. On a promissory note, the person signing the note is called the _____ and the person (a business) to whom the promise of payment is being made is called the _____.
10. The discount period refers to the length of time _____.

IV. Daily Exercises

1. Marty's Art Mart uses the Allowance method to account for bad debt. Indicate whether the effect that each of the following transactions will have on gross Accounts Receivable, the Allowance for Bad Debt, net Accounts Receivable, and Bad Debt Expense. Use + for increases and - for decreases, and 0 for no effect.

	Gross Accounts Receivable	Allowance for Bad Debt	Net Accounts Receivable	Bad Debt Expense
An account receivable is written off	_____	_____	_____	_____
An account receivable is reinstated	_____	_____	_____	_____
A customer pays his account receivable	_____	_____	_____	_____
1.5% of $900,000 in sales is estimated to be uncollectible	_____	_____	_____	_____
3% of $80,000 in accounts receivable is estimated to be uncollectible (the balance in the allowance account is a credit of $200)	_____	_____	_____	_____

2. Compute the missing amounts. Use the 360-day year.

	Principal	Interest rate	Duration	Interest	Maturity Value
A.	$ 3,000	12%	3 months	_____	_____
B.	$10,000	9%	90 days	_____	_____
C.	_____	6%	30 days	_____	$9,045
D.	$ 4,000	_____	6 months	$320	_____

3. From the following list, present the current asset section of the balance sheet:

Accounts Receivable (short-term)	$ 84,400
Accounts Receivable (long-term)	110,000
Allowance for Uncollectible Accounts	5,270
Cash	165,090
Inventory	277,420
Marketable Securities	61,200
Notes Receivable (60-days)	18,000
Notes Receivable (2-year)	32,000
Prepaid Expense	17,973

4. From the items in Daily Exercise #3, list those that would be used in calculating the acid-test ratio.

5. Upshaw Co. uses an allowance method in accounting for bad debts. Three months ago, it wrote off a $1,550 receivable from customer Jones. In today's mail, Upshaw receives a check from Jones for the entire amount along with a note apologizing for the delay in paying the delinquent invoice. Record the entry for the $1,550 check from Jones.

6. Review the circumstances in #5 above, but assume Upshaw Co. uses the direct write-off method for bad debts. Record the entry for the $1,550 payment.

V. Exercises

1. Santa Fe Market has a $210,000 balance in Accounts Receivable on December 31, 19X9. The Allowance for Uncollectible Accounts has a $700 credit balance. Credit sales totaled $650,000 for the year.

   a. If Santa Fe Market uses the percentage of sales method and estimates that 1.5% of sales may be uncollectible, what is the Uncollectible Account Expense for 19X9?

   b. What is the ending balance in the Allowance for Uncollectible Accounts after adjustments?

   c. Would your answer be different if the Allowance for Uncollectible Accounts had a $700 debit balance?

2. Assume the same account balances in Exercise #1 for Santa Fe Market:

   a. If Santa Fe Market uses the aging of Accounts Receivable method and has determined that $11,000 of Accounts Receivable is uncollectible, what is the Uncollectible Account Expense for 19X9?

   b. What is the ending balance in the Allowance for Uncollectible Accounts after adjustments?

c. Would your answers be different if the Allowance for Uncollectible Accounts had a $700 debit balance?

3. A $18,000, 90-day, 9% note is discounted at the bank at 12%, 30 days before maturity. What is the appropriate journal entry?

4. A $6,000, 120-day, 6% note is discounted at the bank at 9%, 90 days before maturity. What is the appropriate journal entry?

VI. Beyond the Numbers

Review the information given in Exercises 3 and 4 above, but assume the interest rate and discount rate in each was reversed.

Therefore, in Exercise 3, the note carried a 12% interest rate while the bank was offering a 9% discount and in Exercise 4 the note carried a 9% interest rate while the bank was offering a 6% discount rate. In each case, at what point during the term of each note should the business discount the note? Support your answer.

VII. Demonstration Problems

Demonstration Problem #1

Henderson, Inc. manufactures machine parts. The company's year end trial balance for 19X9 reported the following:

	Debit	Credit
Accounts Receivable	3,125,200	
Allowance for Uncollectible Accounts		62,050

Assume that net credit sales for 19X9 amounted to $39,750,000 and Allowance for Uncollectible Accounts has not yet been adjusted for 19X9.

Required:

1. At the end of 19X9, the following accounts receivable were deemed uncollectible:

Shen Inc.	$ 4,125
Brown Corporation	9,360
Gonzalez Products	7,140
APL Co.	10,010
Total	$31,635

   Prepare the 19X9 journal entry necessary to write off the above accounts.

2. Assume that the company uses the percentage of sales method to estimate Uncollectible Account Expense. After analyzing industry averages and prior years' activity, management has determined that Uncollectible Account Expense for 19X9 should be 0.5% of net credit sales. Prepare the journal entry to record and adjust Uncollectible Account Expense.

3. Show the balance sheet presentation for Accounts Receivable after the adjustment in #2 has been posted.

4. Assume that the company uses the aging of accounts receivable method. The aging schedule prepared by the company's credit manager indicated that an Allowance of $205,000 for uncollectible accounts is appropriate. Prepare the appropriate journal entry.

5. Show the balance sheet presentation for Accounts Receivable after the adjustment in #4 has been posted.

6. Calculate the days' sales in receivables assuming the adjustment in #4 above and beginning net receivables were $2,742,107.

Requirement 1 (Write-off of uncollectible accounts)

Date	Accounts and Explanation	PR	Debit	Credit

Requirement 2 (Adjustment to record Uncollectible Account Expense using the percentage of sales method)

Date	Accounts and Explanation	PR	Debit	Credit

Requirement 3 (Balance sheet presentation)

Requirement 4 (Adjustment to record Uncollectible Account Expense using the aging of accounts receivable)

Date	Accounts and Explanation	PR	Debit	Credit

Requirement 5 (Balance sheet presentation)

Requirement 6 (Days' sales in receivables)

Demonstration Problem #2

Will's Western Wear is a specialty clothing store. The accounting period of Will's Western Wear ends December 31. During 1999 and 2000, the business engaged in the following transactions:

1999
June 1   Loaned $18,000 to Leather Clothing, a supplier. Received a one-year 9% note.

July 1   Discounted the note received on June 1 at a local bank. The discount rate charged by the bank was 12%.

December 1   Loaned $10,000 to KPT International, a supplier. Received a four-months, 12% note.

2000
April 1   Collected the KPT International note at maturity.

June 1   The bank notified Will's Western Wear their note from Leather Clothing was dishonored.

September 1   All attempts to collect the Leather Clothing account were unsuccessful and it was written off (the company uses the allowance method).

Required:

1. Prepare the necessary journal entries to record the 1999 transactions on the books of Will's Western Wear.
2. Make any adjusting entries needed on December 31, 1999.
3. Record the 2000 entries.

Requirement 1 (1999 entries)

GENERAL JOURNAL

Date	Accounts and Explanation	PR	Debit	Credit

Requirement 2 (December 31, 1999 adjusting entries)

GENERAL JOURNAL

Date	Accounts and Explanation	PR	Debit	Credit

Requirement 3 (2000 entries)

GENERAL JOURNAL

Date	Accounts and Explanation	PR	Debit	Credit

SOLUTIONS

I. Matching

1. N	5. F	9. L	13. C	17. S
2. O	6. G	10. T	14. D	18. K
3. A	7. I	11. P	15. R	19. M
4. E	8. J	12. B	16. H	20. Q

II. Multiple Choice

1. C Writing off a specific account receivable using the allowance method takes the form of:

    Allowance for Uncollectible Accounts   XX
        Accounts Receivable   XX

    Both accounts involved are balance sheet accounts; accordingly, net income is not affected.

2. B Uncollectible Account Expense is estimated and recorded as an adjusting entry. It is a function of the operations of the business and is an operating expense.

3. D Failing to record the Uncollectible Accounts Expense also means that no increase in the Allowance for Uncollectible Accounts (contra accounts receivable) was recorded. Accordingly, expenses are understated and assets are overstated.

4. A Net Accounts Receivable is the result of netting the Accounts Receivable balance against its contra account, Allowance for Uncollectible Accounts.

5. C When Accounts Receivable and the Allowance are both reduced by $200, Net Accounts Receivable will be unchanged.
    [$22,500 - $1,500 = ($22,500 - $200) - ($1,500 - $200)]

6. C Allowance for Uncollectible Accounts is a companion account to Accounts Receivable and has a normal credit balance while Accounts Receivable has a normal debit balance. A contra account has two distinguishing characteristics: 1) it always has a companion account, and 2) its normal balance is opposite that of the companion account.

7. A A note receivable is an asset. An asset that will be converted to cash within one year is a current asset.

8. D Interest is a function of the amount advanced to the borrower, the interest rate, and the term of the loan.

9. C Discounting is done to get cash quickly for a note prior to its maturity date by selling the note to another entity. The entity buying the note will collect the maturity value and will pay less than this for the note when purchased.

10. C Of the items listed, all except "Accounts Receivable Expense" are acceptable account titles (descriptions) for the business's cost of extending credit to customers who do not pay.

III. Completion

1. matching (The direct write-off fails to match the business's cost of extending credit to customers who do not pay with the revenue generating the expense.)
2. operating
3. aging of accounts receivable (Aging the accounts focuses on estimating the appropriate balance in the contra account receivable account, Allowance for Uncollectible Accounts.)
4. percentage of sales (The percentage of sales method focuses on calculating the appropriate cost to match against sales in the current period as Uncollectible Accounts Expense.)
5. contingent (Other liabilities are the result of past transactions and will definitely require payment in the future.)
6. investing
7. acid-test (quick) ratio
8. one day's sales
9. maker, payee
10. from date of discount to maturity date

IV. Daily Exercises

1.

	Gross Accounts Receivable	Allowance for Bad Debt	Net Accounts Receivable	Bad Debt Expense
An account receivable is written off	-	-	0	0
An account receivable is reinstated	+	+	0	0
A customer pays his account receivable	-	0	-	0
1.5% of $900,000 in sales is estimated to be uncollectible	0	+	-	+
3% of $80,000 in accounts receivable is estimated to be uncollectible (the balance in the allowance account is a credit of $200)	0	+	-	+

2.

   A. interest = $3,000 × .12 × 3/12 = $90
      maturity value = $3,000 + $90 = $3,090

   B. interest = $10,000 × .09 × 90/360 = $225
      maturity value = $10,000 + $225 = $10,225

   C. maturity value = principal + interest
      interest = principal × rate × time
      $9,045 = P + (P × .06 × 30/360)
      P = $9,000
      interest = $45

   D. interest = principal × rate × time
      $320 = $4,000 × R × 6/12
      R = 8%
      maturity value = principal + interest
      maturity value = $4,000 + $320 = $4,320

3.

Cash		$165,090
Marketable Securities		61,200
Accounts Receivable	84,400	
Less: Allowance	5,270	79,130
Notes Receivable		18,000
Inventory		227,420
Prepaid Expenses		17,973
		$568,813

4. The acid-test ratio only uses those current assets that can be converted into cash quickly; therefore, the following would be included: Cash, Marketable Securities, Accounts Receivable (net), and Notes Receivable.

    For most businesses, Inventory is not considered a quick asset and prepaid expenses are never included.

5. When a previously written off receivable is collected, two entries are required. One entry re-instates the receivable, while the second entry records the collection.

Accounts Receivable	1,550	
Allowance for Uncollectible Accounts		1,550
To re-instate the Jones account		
Cash	1,550	
Accounts Receivable - Jones		1,550
To record collection of the Jones account		

6.

Accounts Receivable - Jones	1,550	
Bad Debt Expense		1,550
Cash	1,550	
Accounts Receivable		1,550

V. Exercises

1.

   a. Uncollectible Account Expense = .015 × $650,000 = $9,750

   b. Ending balance in Allowance for Uncollectible Accounts = $700 + $9,750 = $10,450

   c. Yes. The amount of Uncollectible Account Expense would be the same. However, the balance in the Allowance for Uncollectible Accounts would be different ($9,750 - 700 = $9,050).

2.

   a. The current balance in the Allowance account is $700 credit and the desired balance in the Allowance account is $11,000 credit. The Uncollectible Account Expense will be $11,000 - $700 = $10,300.

   b. The ending balance will be $11,000.

   c. Yes. It would require a credit of $11,700 to bring the balance in the Allowance account to a credit of $11,000; the corresponding debit is to the Uncollectible Account Expense. The ending balance in the Allowance account will be the same, $11,000.

3.

Cash	18,220.95	
Interest Expense		220.95
Note Receivable		18,000.00

maturity value = $18,000 + ($18,000 × .09 × 90/360) = $18,405

discount = $18,405 × .12 × 30/360 = $184.05

proceeds = $18,405 - $184.05 = $18,220.95

4.

Cash	5,982.30	
Interest Expense	17.70	
Notes Receivable		6,000

maturity value = $6,000 + ($6,000 × .06 × 120/360) = $6,120
discount = ($6,120 × .09 × 90/360) = $137.70
proceeds = $6,120 - 137.70 = $5,982.30

Note that in Exercises 3 and 4, the interest revenue or interest expense cannot be directly computed. It is the amount needed to balance the entry.

VI. Beyond the Numbers

In each case, the business should discount the note (sell it to the bank) as soon as possible, preferably upon receiving the note. Why? Assuming both notes are discounted upon receipt, the entries would be:

Exercise 3

Cash	18,122.85	
Interest Revenue		122.85
Note Receivable		18,000.00

(Maturity value is $18,540; therefore, the discount is $417.15 = $18,340 × 9% × 90/360; proceeds are $18,540 - $417.50 = 18,122.85.

Exercise 4

Cash	6,056.40	
Interest Revenue		56.40
Note Receivable		6,000.00

(Maturity value is $6,180; therefore, the discount is $123.60 = $6,180 × 9% × 120/360; proceeds are $6,120 - $123.60 = 6,056.40.

If you examine these entries carefully, you will see that in both cases interest has been earned without the holder (the business) keeping the note for even one day. In other words, when the discount rate is less than the interest rate, a business should sell the note as soon as possible, thereby maximizing the potential return.

VII. Demonstration Problems

Demonstration Problem #1

Requirement 1 (Write-off of uncollectible accounts)

Date	Accounts and Explanation	PR	Debit	Credit
12/31/X9	Allowance for Uncollectible Accounts		31,635	
	Accounts Receivable - Shen, Inc.			4,125
	Accounts Receivable - Brown Corporation			9,360
	Accounts Receivable – Gonzalez Products			7,140
	Accounts Receivable - APL Co.			10,010
	To write off uncollectible accounts.			

Requirement 2 (Adjustment to record Uncollectible Account Expense using the percentage-of-sales method)

Uncollectible Account Expense	198,750	
Allowance for Uncollectible Accounts		198,750

Net credit sales of 19X9 were $39,750,000. Uncollectible Account Expense for 19X9 is therefore $198,750 (39,750,000 × 0.5% = 198,750). An examination of the activity to date in the Uncollectible Account Expense and Allowance for Uncollectible Accounts reveals the effect of the entries made in Requirements 1 and 2.

Uncollectible Account Expense		Allowance for Uncollectible Accounts		Accounts Receivable	
(2) 198,750		(1) 31,635	Bal. 62,050	Bal. 3,125,000	(1) 31,635
Bal. 198,750			(2) 198,750	Bal. 3,093,565	
			Bal. 229,165		

Note that the Allowance account started at $62,050. In requirement 1, it was reduced by $31,635 when the uncollectible accounts were written off against the Allowance account. Note that prior to the 19X9, adjustment, the Allowance was down to $30,415 ($62,050 - $31,635 = $30,415). The Allowance was then adjusted upward to $229,165 in Entry 2, when the company recorded 19X9 Uncollectible Account Expense of $198,750.

Requirement 3 (Balance Sheet representation)

Accounts Receivable	3,093,565	
Less: Allowance for Uncollectible Accounts	229,165	2,864,400

Requirement 4 (Adjustment to record Uncollectible Account Expense using the aging of accounts receivable)

Uncollectible Account Expense	174,585	
Allowance for Uncollectible Accounts		174,585

When the aging of accounts receivable method is used, the adjustment brings Allowance for Uncollectible Accounts to the balance indicated by the aging schedule. Before adjustment, the balance in the allowance account was $30,415. The facts reveal that the desired balance in the allowance account should be set at $205,000. The difference between the unadjusted balance and the desired balance ($205,000 - $30,415 = $174,585) represents the amount of the adjustment and the amount of expense.

> **Study Tip:** When using the percentage of sales method, adjust for the estimate. When using accounts receivable as a basis for the estimate, adjust to the estimate (i.e., the estimate should be the balance in the allowance account after the adjusting entry is posted).

Requirement 5 (Balance Sheet representation)

Accounts Receivable	3,093,565	
Less: Allowance for Uncollectible Accounts	205,000	2,888,565

Requirement 6 (Days' Sales in receivable)

Sales in receivables = Average net Accounts Receivable ÷ One day's sales
One day's sales = Net sales ÷ 365 = $39,750,000 ÷ 365 = $108,904 (rounded)
Average net Accounts Receivable = ($2,742,107 + $2,888,565) ÷ 2 = $2,815,336
Days' sales in receivables = $2,815,336 ÷ $108,904 = 25.8 days

Demonstration Problem #2 Solved and Explained

Requirement 1 (1999 entries)

1999

June 1	Notes Receivable - Leather Clothing	18,000	
	Cash		18,000

This entry is necessary to record the loan transaction with the debtor Leather Clothing. A note receivable account is debited indicating that the debtor has signed a written promise to pay Will's Western Wear $18,000 plus interest, due in one year.

July 1	Cash	17,461.80	
	Interest Expense	538.20	
	Note Receivable - Leather Clothing		18,000

When a note receivable is discounted, the bank charges a discount. The discount is calculated by the bank based on the maturity value of the note, the bank's discount rate, and the length of time the bank holds the note until maturity. The maturity value is the amount the bank ultimately expects to receive when the note is collected. The $19,620 maturity value of the Leather Clothing note includes the principal of the note ($18,000) plus the interest required to be paid by the debtor (in this case, $1,620). The interest expense or interest revenue arising from the discounting transaction is derived by simply netting the proceeds actually received from the bank with the principal (or "face" amount) of the note. The proceeds will be the maturity value minus the bank's discount.

COMPUTATIONS:

Principal	$18,000
Plus: Interest ($18,000 × .09 × 12/12)	1,620
Maturity value	19,620
Less: Discount ($19,620 × .12 × 11/12)	2,158.20
Proceeds	17,461.80
Principal of note	$18,000.00
Less: Proceeds	17,461.80
Interest Expense	538.20

| Dec. 1 | Note Receivable - KPT International | 10,000 | |
| | Cash | | 10,000 |

This entry records the three-month loan to KPT International. Because the interest on the note is actually paid at maturity, and the note was held during two accounting periods, an adjusting entry will be necessary on December 31 to record one month of accrued interest.

Requirement 2 (December 31, 1999 adjusting entries)

| Dec. 31 | Interest Receivable | 100 | |
| | Interest Revenue | | 100 |

This entry records the interest earned on the note owed by KPT International for the month of December. Interest is earned on the note at $100 per month ($10,000 \times .12 \times 1/12$).

No adjusting entry is required for the discounted note receivable from Leather Clothing. However, the balance sheet should include a footnote concerning the contingent liability.

Requirement 3 (2000 entries)

2000
Apr. 1	Cash	10,400	
	Note Receivable		10,000
	Interest Receivable		100
	Interest Revenue		300

Note that although four months of interest was received by Will's Western Wear on April 1, only three months ($300) of the amount received was considered interest revenue in 2000. Because the note spanned two accounting periods, the December interest ($100) was accrued and, as a result, was reported as revenue in the year ending December 31, 1999.

| Jun. 1 | Accounts Receivable - Leather Clothing | 19,620 | |
| | Cash | | 19,620 |

Because Will's Western Wear remained contingently liable for the discounted note receivable, the bank charged the company's account for the maturity value of the note when the note was dishonored.

| Sept. 1 | Allowance for Uncollectible Accounts | 19,620 | |
| | Accounts Receivable - Leather Clothing | | 19,620 |

Under the allowance method, the balance in the accounts receivable is written off against the allowance account.

Chapter 9—Accounting for Merchandise Inventory, Cost of Goods Sold, and the Gross Margin

CHAPTER OVERVIEW

In Chapter 5 you learned about merchandising businesses—ones that purchase goods and resell them. When acquired, merchandise inventory (the goods) is a current asset which becomes an expense once the goods are sold. In this chapter the principles of internal control are applied to this very important asset. Specifically you will learn the techniques businesses use to determine the cost (i.e., value) of their ending inventory. The learning objectives for this chapter are to

1. Account for inventory by the perpetual and periodic systems.
2. Apply the inventory costing methods: specific unit cost, weighted average cost, FIFO, and LIFO.
3. Identify the income effects and the tax effects of the inventory costing methods.
4. Apply the lower-of-cost-or-market rule to inventory.
5. Determine the effects of inventory errors on cost of goods sold and net income.
6. Estimate ending inventory by the gross margin method.
7. Report inventory transactions on the statement of cash flows.

CHAPTER REVIEW

Objective 1 - Account for inventory by the perpetual and periodic systems.

The **perpetual inventory** system is used to keep a continuous record of each inventory item. With the perpetual system, the inventory item record shows quantities received, quantities sold, and the balance remaining on hand. With the **periodic inventory system**, inventory purchases are debited to the Purchases account, the quantity of ending inventory is counted and valued, and the cost of goods sold equation is used on the income statement.

Journal entries using the perpetual system differ from the entries made using the periodic system.

To record purchases:

Perpetual System			Periodic System		
Inventory	XX		Purchases	XX	
Accounts Payable		XX	Accounts Payable		XX

To record sales:

Accounts Receivable	XX		Accounts Receivable	XX	
Sales Revenues		XX	Sales Revenues		XX
Cost of Goods Sold	XX				
Inventory		XX			

When the perpetual system is used, Cost of Goods Sold is debited directly and Inventory is credited directly to transfer the cost of the unit sold from Inventory into Cost of Goods Sold. As a result, the balance in the Inventory account should approximate the actual goods on hand at any time. With a periodic system, however, the value of goods on hand cannot be determined by examining the ledger because only additions of inventory have been recorded in the Purchases account. Therefore, actual goods on hand can be determined only by a physical count or by estimating.

(Helpful hint: Review Exhibit 9-2 in your text.)

Whereas cost of goods sold is an account in the perpetual system, cost of goods sold is a calculation in a periodic system. The formula is: Beginning inventory + Net purchases - Ending inventory = Cost of goods sold. Net purchases is Purchases + Transportation charges - Discounts - Returns/allowances.

> **Study Tip**: This cost of goods formula is an important one to commit to memory. Just remember BI + NP – EI.

Sales revenue less cost of goods sold = **gross margin** (also called gross profit). Gross margin less operating expenses = net income. One challenge businesses face is determining the cost of inventory on hand. The basic formula is:

$$\text{Cost of inventory on hand} = \text{Quantity on hand} \times \text{Unit cost}$$

Quantity on hand is determined by a physical count of all the items of inventory the business owns. Determining unit cost, however, can be more complicated.

Objective 2 - Apply the inventory costing methods: specific unit cost, weighted average cost, FIFO, and LIFO.

Inventories are initially recorded at historical cost. Inventory cost is what the business pays to acquire the inventory. Inventory cost includes the invoice cost of the goods, less purchase discounts, plus taxes, tariffs, transportation, and insurance while in transit.

Determining unit costs is easy when costs remain constant. But prices frequently change. GAAP allows four different methods of assigning costs to each inventory item that is sold: 1) **specific unit cost**, 2) **weighted-average cost**, 3) **first-in, first-out**, and 4) **last-in, first-out**.

Specific unit costing (also called the **specific identification method**) is used by businesses whose inventory items are expensive or have "one-of-a-kind" characteristics—such as automobiles, jewelry, and real estate. Using specific unit cost to determine ending inventory is not practical for many businesses. When this is the case, the accountant has to make an assumption concerning the flow of costs through the inventory. Why is an assumption necessary? Because the actual (i.e., specific) unit cost of each item cannot be determined.

The three cost flow assumptions are **weighted average, FIFO, and LIFO.**

The **weighted-average cost method** is based on the average cost of all inventory items available for sale during the period. The weighted-average cost method requires the following computation:

$$\text{Average Unit Cost} = \frac{\text{Cost of Goods Available for Sale}}{\text{Number of Units Available for Sale}}$$

Cost of Goods Available for Sale = Beginning Inventory + Net Purchases
Ending Inventory = Number of Units Remaining × Average Unit Cost
Cost of Goods Sold = Cost of Goods Available for Sale - Ending Inventory

Under the **First-In, First-Out (FIFO)** method, the first costs into inventory are the first costs out to Cost of Goods Sold. Therefore, ending inventory reflects unit costs most recently incurred. If beginning inventory is 10 units at $4 each, 60 units were bought at $5 each, 80 more units were bought at $6 each, and there are 50 units left, the 50 remaining units would be assigned the $6 unit cost. Ending inventory would be $300.

Under the **Last-In, First-Out (LIFO)** method, the last costs into inventory are the first costs out to Cost of Goods Sold. Ending inventory is based on the oldest inventory unit costs. If beginning inventory is again 10 units at $4 each, 60 units were bought at $5 each, 80 more units were bought at $6 each, and there were 50 units left, 10 of the remaining units would be assigned the $4 unit cost and 40 would be assigned the $5 unit cost. Ending inventory would be $240 (10 × $4 + 40 × $5).

(Helpful hint: Review Exhibit 9-3 in your text.)

Objective 3 - Identify the income effects and the tax effects of the inventory costing methods.

Review Exhibit 9-4 in your text to be sure that you understand the income effects of the FIFO, LIFO, and weighted-average cost inventory methods.

When inventory costs are increasing:

	FIFO	Weighted-Average Cost	LIFO
Ending Inventory	Highest	Middle	Lowest
Cost of Goods Sold	Lowest	Middle	Highest
Gross Margin	Highest	Middle	Lowest:

When inventory costs are decreasing:

	FIFO	Weighted-Average Cost	LIFO
Ending Inventory	Lowest	Middle	Highest
Cost of Goods Sold	Highest	Middle	Lowest
Gross Margin	Lowest	Middle	Highest

Using LIFO to account for inventories has tax advantages when inventory costs are increasing. This is because using LIFO increases Cost of Goods Sold, and thus decreases Gross Margin and Operating Income. If Operating Income is smaller, total tax payments will be smaller. LIFO matches the most recent inventory costs (last into inventory, first out to Cost of Goods Sold) to revenue, but can result in unrealistic valuations of ending inventory on the balance sheet. The FIFO method presents an accurate ending inventory on the balance sheet but does not match current cost of inventory to revenue, since the current cost of inventory remains in ending inventory.

Generally, the inventory method used for tax purposes is the one that is used for financial reporting.

Different companies use different inventory methods to achieve a desired result. Notes to the financial statements disclose inventory accounting policies and may also report an alternative inventory amount. For example, if inventories are reported using LIFO in the financial statements, a firm may report inventories using FIFO in the notes to the financial statements. When this is done, substitute the FIFO amounts in place of the LIFO amounts for beginning and ending inventories to convert LIFO Cost of Goods Sold to FIFO Cost of Goods Sold. Note that net purchases will be the same for both methods.

LIFO vs. FIFO—some additional considerations:

a. Because LIFO results in the most recent costs reported on the income statement (as cost of goods sold), it presents the most recent cost/revenue relationship.
b. Because FIFO uses the most recent costs as ending inventory, it presents the most recent value for the asset on the balance sheet.
c. During periods of rising prices, FIFO results in inventory profits because the cost to replace a unit sold has risen.
d. Companies using LIFO can manage the income statement by timing inventory purchases at the end of the accounting period.
e. LIFO liquidation results when inventory quantities fall below the level of the previous period. If inventory costs are rising, the effect of LIFO liquidation is to shift lower cost units to cost of goods sold, resulting in higher net income.
f. FIFO and weighted-average are universally accepted whereas many countries do not permit LIFO valuations

As mentioned earlier, the perpetual system records each addition (purchase) and deletion (sale) of inventory. By so doing, an accurate up-to-date value for goods on hand is continually available.

Review Exhibit 9-7 in your text to understand how cost flows through an inventory record when a perpetual inventory system is used, assuming FIFO.

Four accounting concepts or principles directly impact merchandise inventory. The **consistency principle** states that the cost flow assumption used should be followed over time. The **disclosure principle** requires companies to tell the readers of the financial statements all information that would assist in making knowledgeable decisions about the company. The **materiality concept** requires companies to report significant events while allowing them more leeway in reporting insignificant (immaterial) events. Finally, **conservatism** dictates that no change to historical cost as the basis for inventory values be used when the value of the asset has risen. At the same time, a lower value can be used in certain circumstances.

Objective 4 - Apply the lower-of-cost-or-market rule to inventory.

The **lower-of-cost-or-market** rule (LCM) is a direct application of conservatism. Conservatism means that assets and income figures should not be overstated. Because the cost principle states that assets should be recorded at historical cost, the book value of assets is not reported at amounts higher than historical cost even if the value of the asset has increased.

Conservatism also directs accountants to decrease the reported value of assets that appear overvalued. The LCM rule requires that assets be reported on the financial statements at the lower of (1) historical cost or (2) market value (replacement cost). Thus, if inventory market value decreases below its historical cost, it should be written down to its market value. If ending inventory is written down, then cost of goods sold absorbs the impact of the write-down.

Once the value of inventory is written down to market, it is not written back up even if the market value subsequently increases.

Study Tip: When LCM is applied, the effect will always reduce asset value (on the balance sheet) and net income (on the income statement).

Objective 5 - Determine the effects of inventory errors on cost of goods sold and net income.

If the value of ending inventory is misstated, then cost of goods sold and net income will be misstated. Since the ending inventory for the current period becomes the beginning inventory for the next period, the errors will offset each other and total gross margin and net income for the two periods will be correct. Nevertheless, gross margin and net income for the individual periods will be misstated.

If ending inventory is overstated, then cost of goods sold is understated and net income is overstated. If ending inventory is understated, then cost of goods sold is overstated and net income is understated.

Study Exhibits 9-9 and 9-10 in your text carefully to familiarize yourself with the effect of inventory errors on 1) ending inventory, 2) cost of goods sold, and 3) net income.

Objective 6 - Estimate ending inventory by the gross margin method.

When a company wants an estimate of ending inventory, the **gross margin method** will calculate the amount quickly.

The gross margin (gross profit) method uses the historical gross margin rate to estimate cost of goods sold. Cost of goods sold is then subtracted from cost of goods available for sale to arrive at estimated ending inventory.

$$\text{Gross Margin Rate} = \frac{\text{Gross Margin}}{\text{Net Sales Revenue}}$$

To use the gross margin method, it is necessary to rearrange ending inventory and cost of goods sold in the cost of goods sold equation as follows:

Beginning Inventory
+ Net Purchases
= Cost of Goods Available for Sale
- Cost of Goods Sold
= Ending Inventory

Cost of goods sold will equal net sales minus the estimated gross margin (sales × gross margin rate) as illustrated in Exhibit 9-12 in your text.

Objective 7 - Report inventory transactions on the statement of cash flows.

Merchandise inventory has an obvious affect on both the income statement and balance sheet. On the income statement, inventory has a direct impact on cost of goods sold, the gross margin and net income. On the balance sheet, inventory can be one of the largest current assets. Inventory transactions are also reported on the statement of cash flows. Remember that the cash flows statement details cash inflows (receipts) and outflows (payments) for operating, investing, and financing activities. Inventory transactions are operating activities because they directly relate to the company's operations. The payments for inventory are reported as a cash outflow in the operating activities section. In addition, cash receipts from customers are reported as a cash inflow in the same section. Exhibit 9-12 in your text illustrates a typical operating activities section of a cash flows statement.

TEST YOURSELF

All the self-testing materials in this chapter focus on information and procedures that your instructor is likely to test in quizzes and examinations.

I. Matching   *Match each numbered term with its lettered definition.*

_____ 1. consignment
_____ 2. gross margin
_____ 3. materiality concept
_____ 4. consistency principle
_____ 5. gross margin percentage
_____ 6. inventory profit
_____ 7. specific unit cost method
_____ 8. First-In, First-Out (FIFO)

_____ 9. lower-of-cost-or-market rule
_____ 10. gross margin method
_____ 11. weighted-average cost method
_____ 12. Last-In, First-Out (LIFO)
_____ 13. periodic inventory system
_____ 14. perpetual inventory system
_____ 15. conservatism

A. inventory costing method in which the first costs into inventory are the first costs out to cost of goods sold
B. requires a company to perform strictly proper accounting only for items and transactions that are significant to the business's financial statements
C. the difference between net sales and cost of goods sold
D. a way to estimate inventory based on the cost of goods sold model: Beginning Inventory + Net Purchases = Cost of Goods Available for Sale. Cost of Goods Available for Sale - Cost of Goods Sold = Ending Inventory
E. the difference between gross margin figured on the FIFO basis and the gross margin figured on the LIFO basis
F. requires companies to use the same accounting methods and procedures from period to period
G. requires that an asset be reported in the financial statements at the lower of its historical cost or its market value
H. an inventory system in which the business does not keep a continuous record of the inventory on hand
I.   an inventory system in which the business keeps a continuous record for each inventory item to show the inventory on hand at all times
J. inventory costing method based on the average cost of inventory during the period
K. transfer of goods by the owner to another entity which, for a fee, sells the inventory on the owner's behalf
L. inventory costing method in which the last costs into inventory are the first costs out to cost of goods sold
M. inventory cost method based on the cost of particular units of inventory
N. Gross Margin divided by Net Sales Revenue
O. reporting items in the financial statements at amounts that lead to the gloomiest immediate financial results

II. Multiple Choice   *Circle the best answer.*

1. To determine the inventory count, a business will count all merchandise that:

    A. is physically present
    B. the business owns
    C. is physically presents plus merchandise shipped FOB destination
    D. is physically present plus merchandise shipped FOB shipping point

2. An automobile dealer will value inventory using which method?

    A. weighted-average   C. LIFO
    B. FIFO   D. specific unit cost

3. When prices are increasing, which inventory method will produce the highest ending inventory cost?

    A. weighted-average cost   C. LIFO
    B. FIFO   D. cannot be determined

4. When prices are decreasing, which inventory method will produce the lowest cost of goods sold?

    A. weighted-average cost   C. LIFO
    B. FIFO   D. cannot be determined

5. Which inventory method reports ending inventory costs on the balance sheet at a value that reflects current cost?

    A. weighted-average cost   C. LIFO
    B. FIFO   D. cannot be determined

6. Which of the followings can be used to estimate ending inventory?

    A. weighted-average cost   C. LIFO
    B. FIFO   D. gross margin

7. Cost of Goods Sold is debited directly using:

    A. only the perpetual inventory system   C. only the serial inventory system
    B. only the periodic inventory system   D. both the periodic and perpetual inventory systems

8. Closing entries to adjust inventory are used with:

    A. only the perpetual inventory system   C. only the serial inventory system
    B. only the periodic inventory system   D. both the periodic and perpetual inventory systems

9. To which of the following does the lower-of-cost-or-market rule apply?

   A. disclosure
   B. materiality
   C. conservatism
   D. consistency

10. To calculate the weighted-average unit cost:

   A. divide goods available for sale by ending inventory units
   B. divide goods available for sale by total units available for sale
   C. divide cost of goods sold by number of units sold
   D. divide cost of goods sold by number of units available for sale

III. Completion   *Complete each of the following.*

1. The largest current asset for most retailers is _____.
2. The largest single expense for most merchandisers is _____.
3. The inventory system that maintains continuous records of items in the inventory is called
   _____.
4. Which inventory system(s) require(s) a physical count of inventory? _____
   _____.
5. To calculate the gross margin percentage, _____ is divided by _____.
6. The lower-of-cost-or-market rule for inventory is an example of the _____
   principle.
7. Cash flows relating to inventory are reported in the _____ activities section of the
   cash flows statement.
8. During periods of rising prices, _____results in the highest cost of goods sold.
9. The _____method would not be appropriate for a retailer selling a large
   number of units each with low prices.
10. During periods of falling prices, _____results in the highest value for ending
   inventory.

IV. Daily Exercises

1. Through an error, the ending inventory was overstated by $3,000. Indicate the effect of this error on

   a. cost of goods sold

   b. the gross margin

   c. net income

   d. total current assets

2. Assume the per unit value of ending inventory is $11, and a current replacement cost per unit of $10. If the lower-of-cost-or-market rule is applied, indicate how the income statement and balance sheet will be affected.

3. A company purchases the following inventory:

    200 units at $6.00 each
    400 units at $6.50 each
    400 units at $6.60 each
    300 units at $6.70 each

    If 900 units are sold during the period, at what amount should ending inventory be stated assuming a FIFO cost assumptions.

4. Refer to the information in Daily Exercise #3 and apply a LIFO cost assumption.

5. Refer to the information in Daily Exercise #3 and apply a weighted-average assumption.

6. Given your answers to #3, #4, and #5 above, which assumption results in the lowest net income for the period? Which method results in the most realistic value of the inventory on the balance sheet?

V. Exercises

1. The following information is given for Teressa's Tile Co. for the month of August:

	Lbs. of tiles	Unit Cost
8/1 Inventory	600	$1.00
8/7 Purchase	800	1.10
8/13 Purchase	1,400	1.20
8/22 Purchase	1,400	1.25
8/29 Purchase	400	1.15

During the month, 3,800 pounds of tiles were sold.

A. How many tiles should be in the inventory at the end of August?

B. Using the weighted-average cost method, what are the cost of ending inventory and cost of goods sold?

C. Using the FIFO method, what are the cost of ending inventory and cost of goods sold?

D. Using the LIFO method, what are the cost of ending inventory and cost of goods sold?

2. The Brunnel Co.'s inventory was destroyed by a fire. The company's records show net sales of $360,000, beginning inventory of $80,000, net purchase of $300,000, and a gross margin rate of 40%. What is the estimated value of ending inventory?

3. Assume the following:

	X1	X2	X3
Beginning Inventory	$ 8,000	$15,000	$12,000
Net Purchases	45,000	50,000	55,000
Goods Available for Sale	53,000	65,000	67,000
Ending Inventory	15,000	12,000	8,000
Cost of Goods Sold	38,000	53,000	59,000

You discover the following errors:
   a. Ending inventory X1 was overstated by $6,000
   b. Ending inventory X2 was understated by $4,000

Considering these errors, recalculate cost of goods sold for all three years.

4. The following information is available for Gearty Co. for 19X9:

Beginning Inventory	$ 2,500
Ending Inventory	1,850
Operating Expenses	1,650
Cost of Goods Sold	15,975
Sales Discounts	255
Sales	21,500
Sales Returns and Allowances	165

Required:

1. What is net sales for 19X9?

2. What is gross profit for 19X9?

3. What is net income for 19X9?

4. What is the gross margin rate?

5. What is the inventory turnover rate?

5. The following information is given for Diane's Design 19X8:

Beginning Inventory	$ 12,250
Gross Margin	7,500
Operating Expenses	3,100
Purchase Returns & Allowance	600
Purchase Discounts	550
Purchases	39,250
Sales Discounts	500
Sales	51,500
Sales Returns & Allowances	1,700

Required

1. Compute net sales.

2. Compute net purchases.

3. Compute cost of goods sold.

4. Compute ending inventory.

5. Compute net income.

6. What is the inventory turnover rate?

7. What is the gross margin rate?

VI. Beyond the Numbers

Re-examine the facts presented in Exercise #1. A physical count was taken, and ending inventory was determined to be 700 pounds. In re-checking the sales, you verify that 3,800 pounds were sold. How would you explain the 100 pounds difference (800 pounds you expected to be on hand less the actual count of 700 pounds), and how would you "account" for it?

_____
_____
_____
_____
_____

VII. Demonstration Problems

Demonstration Problem #1

Nanearl's Beauty Supply has the following records relating to its August 19X9 inventory:

Date	Item	Quantity (units)	Unit Cost	Sale price
8/1	Beginning inventory	50	7	--
8/3	Purchase	80	8	--
8/9	Sale	90	--	14
8/11	Purchase	100	9	--
8/18	Sale	60	--	15
8/22	Purchase	40	10	--
8/28	Sale	60	--	18

Company accounting records indicate that the related operating expense for the month of August was $1,250.

Required:
1. Assume that Nanearl uses a periodic inventory system and a FIFO cost flow assumption, record the August 3 through August 28 transactions (omit explanations).
2. Assume Nanearl uses a perpetual inventory system and a FIFO cost flow assumption, record the August 3 through August 28 transactions (omit explanations).

Requirement 1 (Periodic Inventory System)

Date	Accounts and Explanation	PR	Debit	Credit

Requirement 2 (Perpetual Inventory System)

Date	Accounts and Explanation	PR	Debit	Credit

Demonstration Problem #2

Requirement 1

Refer to the information in Demonstration Problem #1. Assuming Nanearl uses a periodic system, complete the income statement columns below. (Round income statement figures to whole dollar amounts.)

Nanearl Beauty Supply

Income Statement

Month Ended August 31, 19X9

	LIFO	FIFO	Weighted Average
Sales revenue			
Cost of goods sold:			
Beginning inventory			
Net purchases			
Cost of goods available for sale			
Ending inventory			
Cost of goods sold			
Gross margin			
Operating expenses			
Operating income			

Requirement 2

Refer to Demonstration Problem #1, and assume the same facts in the problem *except* the company uses the perpetual inventory system. Complete the income statement below, through operating income. (Round income statement figures to whole dollar amounts.)

Nanearl Beauty Supply

Income Statement

Month Ended August 31, 19X9

	LIFO	FIFO	Weighted Average
Sales revenue			
Cost of goods sold			
Gross margin			
Operating expenses			
Operating income			

(Helpful hint: Before starting, think carefully about which income statement figures will change as a result of using the perpetual inventory system rather than the periodic inventory system. Those amounts that do not change can simply be transferred from your solution to Requirement #1.)

SOLUTIONS

I. Matching

1. K	5. N	9. G	13. H
2. C	6. E	10. D	14. I
3. B	7. M	11. J	15. O
4. F	8. A	12. L	

II. Multiple Choice

1.   B   Answer A does not include merchandise shipped FOB shipping point or exclude consignments; C includes merchandise shipped FOB destination and does not exclude consignments; D does not exclude consignments.

2.   D   Specific unit cost is appropriate for inventory items that may be identified individually like automobiles, jewels, and real estate.

3.   B   To obtain the highest ending inventory when prices are increasing it is necessary to have the most recent inventory costs on the balance sheet. The FIFO method accomplishes this.

4.   C   To obtain the lowest cost of goods sold when prices are decreasing it is necessary to have the newest inventory costs on the income statement. The LIFO method accomplishes this.

5.   B   LIFO assigns the most recent inventory costs to the income statement and older inventory cost to the balance sheet. FIFO, on the other hand, assigns the most recent inventory costs to the balance sheet and older inventory costs to the income statement.

6.   D   Of the items listed, only gross margin is an estimation technique. FIFO, LIFO, and weighted-average cost are techniques for establishing actual ending amounts, not estimates.

7.   A   Under the periodic inventory system, there is no Cost of Goods Sold general ledger account. Rather, cost of goods sold is a calculated amount. Accordingly, no entries can be made to it. Under the perpetual inventory system Cost of Goods Sold is a general ledger account and inventory purchases are debited directly to it.

8.   B   Since the perpetual inventory system will already reflect the correct end of period balance, no closing entries for Inventory are necessary. Recall that under the periodic inventory system, closing is necessary to remove the beginning balance and enter the ending balance in the Inventory account.

9.   C   LCM is an extension of the application of conservatism because it reduces the ending inventory value and therefore net income.

10.   B   The unit cost for the weighted-average method is calculated by dividing goods available for sale (beginning inventory + net purchases) by the total units available for sale.

III. Completion

1. merchandise inventory
2. Cost of Goods Sold
3. perpetual
4. Both systems require a physical count. In a perpetual inventory system this verifies that the inventory listed in the accounting records actually exists.
5. gross margin, net sales
6. conservatism (The LCM rule ensures that a business reports its inventory at its replacement cost if that is lower than its original cost. This rule ensures that assets are not overstated and that declines in inventory value are reported on the income statement in the period of the decline.)
7. operating
8. LIFO. (The oldest and therefore lower prices are used to value ending inventory.)
9. specific unit cost
10. LIFO (The oldest and therefore higher prices are used to value ending inventory.)

IV. Daily Exercises

1.
    a. if ending inventory is overstated, the cost of goods sold will be understated
    b. if cost of goods sold is understated, the gross margin will be overstated
    c. if the gross margin is overstated, then net income will be overstated
    d. if ending inventory is overstated, then total current assets will also be overstated

> **Study Tip:** The direction of the error in ending inventory value will also be the direction of the error in gross margin and net income.

2. When the $11 value is replaced with $10, the ending inventory value will decrease; therefore, cost of goods sold will increase and the gross margin and net income will decrease. The balance sheet will be affected because total assets will also decrease.

3. If 900 units were sold, there are 400 units on hand. Applying FIFO, the 400 units would be valued as followed:

   300 units at $6.70 each = $2,010
   100 units at $6.60 each = $660
   Total = $2,670

4. Applying LIFO, the 400 units would be valued as follows:

   200 units at $6.00 each = $1,200
   200 units at $6.50 each = $1,300
   Total = $2,500

5. Applying the weight-average cost, the 400 units would be valued as follows:

Cost of goods available for sale ÷ Total number of units available for sale
$8,450 ÷ 1,300 units = $6.50 per unit × 400 units = $2,600

6. The lowest net income will result if LIFO is used. Remember the Study Tip mentioned above—the lower the ending inventory, the lower the net income.

V. Exercises

1. A.

	Beginning inventory		600
+	Purchases*		4,000
	Pounds available for sale		4,600
-	Pounds sold		3,800
=	Ending inventory		800

*Sum of purchases on 8/7 (800), 8/13 (1,400), 8/22 (1,400), and 8/29 (400).

B.

8/1	600	pounds at	$1.00	$ 600
8/7	800		1.10	880
8/13	1,400		1.20	1,680
8/22	1,400		1.25	1,750
8/29	400		1.15	460
Goods available	4,600			$5,370

Average unit cost = 5,370 ÷ 4,600 = $1.167 (rounded)
Ending inventory = 800 pounds × $1.167 = $934
Cost of goods sold = 3,800 pounds × $1.167 = $4,435

C. Ending inventory will be the last 800 pounds purchased.

8/29	400 pounds at $1.15	$460
8/22	400 pounds at $1.25	500
	Ending inventory	$960

Cost of goods available for sale	$5,370
Less Ending inventory	(960)
Cost of goods sold	$4,410

D. Ending inventory will be the 800 pounds that have been in inventory the longest.

Beginning inventory	600 pounds at $1.00	$600
8/7	200 pounds at $1.10	220
Ending inventory		$820

Cost of goods available for sale	$5,370
Less Ending inventory	(820)
Cost of goods sold	$4,550

2.

	Beginning inventory	$ 80,000
+	Purchases	300,000
	Cost of goods available for sale	380,000
-	Cost of goods sold [$360,000 × (1-.40)]	216,000
=	Ending inventory	$164,000

3. For Xl, ending inventory decreases to $9,000, so cost of goods sold will increase to $44,000

For X2, beginning inventory decreases to $9,000, and ending inventory increases to $16,000, so:

	Beginning inventory	$ 9,000
+	Net purchases	50,000
	Goods available for sale	59,000
-	Ending inventory	16,000
=	Cost of goods sold	$43,000

For X3, beginning inventory increases to $16,000, so cost of goods sold increases to $63,000

4.

Requirement 1

Sales - Sales Returns & Allowances - Sales Discount = Net Sales
$21,500 - $165 - $255 = $21,080

Requirement 2

Net Sales - Cost of Goods Sold = Gross Profit (or Gross Margin)
$21,080 - $15,975 = $5,105

Requirement 3

Gross Margin - Operating Expenses = Net Income
$5,105 - $1,650 = $3,455

Requirement 4

Gross Margin ÷ Net Sales
$5,105 ÷ $21,080 = 24.2%

Requirement 5

Cost of Goods Sold ÷ Average Inventory
Average Inventory = ($2,500 + $1,850) ÷ 2 = $2,175
$15,975 ÷ $2,175 = 7.3 times

5.
Requirement 1

Sales - Sales Discounts - Sales Returns & Allowances = Net Sales
$51,500 - $500 - $1,700 = $49,300

Requirement 2

Purchases - Purchase Discounts - Purchase Returns & Allowances = Net Purchases
$39,250 - $550 - $600 = $38,100

Requirement 3

Net Sales - Cost of Goods Sold = Gross Margin
Cost of Goods Sold = $49,300 - $7,500 = $41,800

Requirement 4

Beginning Inventory + Net Purchase - Ending Inventory = Cost of Goods Sold
Therefore, Ending Inventory = Beginning Inventory + Net Purchase - Cost of Goods Sold
Ending Inventory = $12,250 + $38,100 - $41,800 = $8,550

Requirement 5

Gross Profit - Operating Expenses = Net Income
$7,500 - $3,100 = $4,400

Requirement 6

Inventory Turnover Rate = Cost of Goods Sold ÷ Average Inventory
Average Inventory = ($12,250 + $8,550) ÷ 2 = $10,400
Inventory Turnover Rate = $41,800 ÷ $10,400 = 4 times

Requirement 7

Gross Margin Rate = Gross margin ÷ Net sales
Gross Margin Rate = $7,500 ÷ $49,300 = 15.2%

VI. Beyond the Numbers

The 100-pound difference is called inventory shrinkage. Since the figure that appears on the balance sheet for ending inventory must represent the actual amount on hand (700 pounds), the shrinkage is accounted for by a larger cost of goods sold figure on the income statement. Possible explanations for the shrinkage are errors in the physical count, theft, and/or errors in recording purchases during the period. Internal control requires that the cause of the difference be investigated and appropriate corrective procedures taken.

VII. Demonstration Problems

Demonstration Problem #1 Solved and Explained

Requirement 1 (Periodic Inventory System)

Date	Accounts and Explanation	PR	Debit	Credit
8/3	Purchases		640	
	Account Payable			640
8/9	Account Receivable		1,260	
	Sales			1,260
8/11	Purchases		900	
	Account Payable			900
8/18	Account Receivable		900	
	Sales			900
8/22	Purchases		400	
	Account Payable			400
8/28	Account Receivable		1,080	
	Sales			1,080

These six journal entries are pretty straightforward. With a periodic system, the Purchase account is debited as merchandise for resale is acquired, but is not affected when goods are sold.

> **Study Tip**: In a periodic system, the cost flow assumption (in this case FIFO) is irrelevant as far as these transactions are concerned. It becomes important only when you need to determine the value of ending inventory.

Requirement 2 (Perpetual Inventory System)

Date	Accounts and Explanation	PR	Debit	Credit
8/3	Inventory		640	
	Account Payable			640
8/9	Account Receivable		1,260	
	Sales			1,260
	Cost of Goods Sold		670	
	Inventory			670
	(50 × $7 + 40 × $8)			
8/11	Inventory		900	
	Account Payable			900
8/18	Account Receivable		900	
	Sales			900
	Cost of Goods Sold		500	
	Inventory			500
	(40 × $8 + 20 × $9)			
8/22	Inventory		400	
	Account Payable			400
8/28	Account Receivable		1,080	
	Sales			1,080
	Cost of Goods Sold		540	
	Inventory			540
	(60 × $9)			

In a perpetual system, goods for resale are debited to the Inventory account. When a sale occurs, the entry is identical to those recorded in a periodic system. However, a second entry is required for each sale. This entry transfers the cost of the sale from the Inventory account to a Cost of Goods Sold account. The amount of the entry is determined by the cost flow assumption used. In this problem, FIFO is assumed. Therefore, the cost of each sale is assigned using the oldest costs in the inventory. For instance, the 8/9 sale was 90 units. How much did these units cost the business? Assuming FIFO, 50 of the units cost $7 each (these are the units from the beginning inventory, i.e., the first units (oldest) in the inventory), and the next 40 units (90 - 50) cost $8 each (the purchase on 8/3). This same analysis applies to the 8/18 and 8/28 sales. The details are provided following each entry.

Demonstration Problem #2

Requirement 1

Nanearl Beauty Supply
Income Statement
Month Ended August 31, 19X9

	LIFO		FIFO		Weighted Average	
Sales revenue		$3,240		$3,240		$3,240
Cost of goods sold:						
Beginning inventory	350		350		350	
Net purchases	1,940		1,940		1,940	
Cost of goods available for sale	2,290		2,290		2,290	
Ending inventory	430		580		509	
Cost of goods sold		1,860		1,710		1,781
Gross margin		1,380		1,530		1,459
Operating expenses		1,250		1,250		1,250
Operating income		$ 130		$ 280		$ 209

Computations:

Sales Revenue:

Sale Date	Quantity	Price	Total
8/9	90	$14	$1,260
8/18	60	15	900
8/28	60	18	1,080
	210		$3,240

Sales revenue is unaffected by the firm's method of accounting for inventory costs. Quantity × Price = Total.

Beginning inventory: 8/1 quantity (50 units) × unit cost ($7) = $350

Purchase Date	Quantity	Price	Total
8/3	80	$8	$ 640
8/11	100	9	900
8/22	40	10	400
	220		$1,940

Computation for beginning inventory, purchases, and goods available for sale are identical under the three methods.

	Beginning inventory in units	50
+	Total August purchases in units	220
	Units available for sale	270
-	Units sold	210
=	Ending inventory in units	60

Valued at LIFO:

Purchase Date	Quantity	Price	Total
Beginning inventory	50	$7	$350
8/3	10	8	80
	60		$430

LIFO attains the best matching of current expense with current revenue. The most recently acquired costs (the last items in) are deemed sold first (the first ones out). Logically, ending inventory should consist of the oldest layers of cost.

Valued at FIFO:

Purchase Date	Quantity	Price	Total
8/22	40	$10	$400
8/11	20	9	180
	60		$580

FIFO reports the ending inventory at its most recent cost. The oldest costs are expensed as cost of goods sold. Note that net income under FIFO is larger than that reported under LIFO. In a period of rising prices, LIFO will generally produce a lower net income. The potential tax savings achieved under a LIFO valuation has made it an increasingly popular valuation method in recent years.

Valued at weighted-average cost:

Purchase Date	Quantity	Price	Total
Beginning inventory	50	$7	$ 350
Purchases in August	220	Various	1,940
	270		$2,290

$2,290 inventory cost / 270 units = $8.48 per unit (rounded)

60 ending inventory units × $8.48 weighted-average cost per unit = $508.80 (rounded to $509)

The weighted-average cost method reports ending inventory and produces operating income that falls between the results of FIFO and LIFO. It is not used as a valuation method by as many firms as LIFO and FIFO.

Requirement 2

Nanearl Beauty Supply
Income Statement
Month Ended August 31, 19X9

	LIFO	FIFO	Weighted Average
Sales revenue	$3,240	$3,240	$3,240
Cost of goods sold	1,830	1,710	1,746
Gross margin	1,410	1,530	1,494
Operating expenses	1,250	1,250	1,250
Operating income	$ 160	$ 280	$ 244

Computations:

Sales—same as Demonstration Problem #1

Cost of Goods Sold:
Remember, in a perpetual system cost of goods sold is an account balance, not a calculation. Therefore, to arrive at the correct amount, you have to trace through each purchase and sale to determine which cost figures have been transferred from Inventory to Cost of Goods Sold, as follows:

LIFO:

Date	Quantity	Price		Total
8/9 Sale	80	$8	$640	
	10	7	70	
				$ 710
8/18 Sale	60	9		540
8/28 Sale	40	10	400	
	20	9	180	
				580
		Cost of goods sold, LIFO		$1,830
	40	7	280	
	20	9	180	
		Ending inventory, LIFO		$ 460*

*Note that this amount is not the same as LIFO periodic.

FIFO:

Date	Quantity	Price		Total
8/9 Sale	50	$ 7	$350	
	40	8	320	
				670
8/18 Sale	40	8	320	
	20	9	180	
				500
8/28 Sale	60	9		540
		Cost of goods sold, FIFO		$1,710
	40	10	400	
	20	9	180	
		Ending inventory, FIFO		$580**

**Note that this is the same as FIFO periodic.

Weighted-average cost:

This is even more complicated because it requires you to re-calculate a new average each time there is an addition to inventory (for this reason it is referred to as a moving weighted-average system).

8/9   Sale

50 units at $7 per unit = $350
80 units at $8 per unit = 640
130                    $990

Average unit cost   = $990 = $7.615 per unit, therefore
                        130

90 units × $7.615 = $ 685.35

8/18   Sale

40 units at $7.615 per unit = $304.60 (from above)
100 units at $9 per unit   =   900.00
140                        $1,204.60

Average unit cost   = $1,204.60 = $8.604 per unit, therefore
                           140

60 units × $8.604 = $ 516.84

8/28   Sale

80 units at $8.604 per unit = $688.32 (from above)
40 units at $10 per unit   =   400.00
120                       $1,088.32

Average unit cost   = $1,088.32 = $9.069 per unit, therefore
                           120

60 units × $9.069 = $ 544.14

Cost of goods sold, weighted-average cost $1,746.33

Ending inventory = 60 units × $9.069 = $544.14***

***Note that this amount is not the same as weighted-average periodic.

Chapter 10—Accounting for Plant Assets, Intangible Assets, and Related Expenses

CHAPTER OVERVIEW

In Chapter 7, you were introduced to the principles of internal control. In Chapters 7, 8, and 9, you saw how companies maintain control over three very important current assets: cash, receivables, and inventories. In this chapter, we continue the discussion of internal control with specific application to non-current assets, also called long-lived assets. Long-lived assets include things such as equipment, buildings, natural resources, and intangible assets. The learning objectives for the chapter are to

1. Determine the cost of a plant asset.
2. Account for depreciation.
3. Select the best depreciation method for income tax purposes.
4. Account for the disposal of a plant asset.
5. Account for natural resource assets and depletion.
6. Account for intangible assets and amortization.
7. Report plant asset transactions on the statement of cash flows.

CHAPTER REVIEW

Objective 1 - Determine the cost of a plant asset.

Business assets are classified as current or long-lived (long-term) assets. Current assets are considered to be useful for one year or less. Long-lived assets are expected to be useful longer than a year. Plant assets (also called fixed assets) are long-lived assets such as land and equipment. Plant assets are tangible; that is, they have physical form.

The cost of a plant asset is the purchase price plus any other amount paid to acquire it and make it ready for use.

The **cost of land** includes the purchase price, brokerage commission, survey fees, legal fees, transfer taxes, back property taxes, costs to grade or clear the land, and costs to demolish or remove any unwanted buildings or other structures.

The **cost of an existing building** includes the purchase price, brokerage commission, taxes, and any expenditure to repair or renovate the building to make it ready for use.

The **cost of machinery and equipment** includes the purchase price less any discounts, plus transportation charges, transportation insurance, commissions, and installation costs.

Improvements to land are not part of the cost of land because the usefulness of the improvement decreases over time. Such improvements include roads, paving, fencing, driveways, parking lots, and lawn sprinkler systems. Improvements to land should be recorded in a separate asset account. The cost of improvements to leased assets is called **leasehold improvements**. **Construction in progress** refers to assets a company has begun building but not yet finished. **Capital leases** refer to plant assets a company does not own which are being leased over an extended period of time.

Interest costs incurred during the time a plant asset is being constructed are considered a necessary cost to "acquire" the asset and are therefore capitalized (i.e., debited to the asset account.) The amount of interest capitalized is the lesser of the interest cost based on average accumulated construction expenditure or the actual interest cost on the borrowed money during the period.

When a company purchases a group of assets for one single amount (also known as a **group purchase** or a **basket purchase**), the total cost of the assets is allocated to individual assets by the relative-sales-value method. To use the **relative-sales-value method**, it is necessary to:

1. Determine the market value of each asset by appraisal of the assets.
2. Sum the individual asset market values to obtain the total market value of all assets that have been acquired.
3. Calculate a ratio of the market value of each individual asset to the total market value of all assets (item 1 divided by item 2).
4. Multiply the ratio for each asset (from item 3) by the total purchase price paid for the assets. The resulting amounts will be considered the cost of each of the assets in the basket purchase.

Capital expenditures are expenditures that significantly affect an asset by 1) increasing the asset's productive capacity, 2) increasing the asset's efficiency, or 3) extending the asset's useful life. Capital expenditures are debited to an asset account:

Asset   XX
    Cash   XX

Revenue expenditures are those that maintain the existing condition of an asset or restore an asset to good working order. Revenue expenditures are debited to an expense account:

Expense Account   XX
    Cash   XX

Many expenditures related to plant assets are repairs to the assets. **Extraordinary repairs** are capital expenditures, while ordinary repairs are revenue expenditures. Review Exhibit 10-2 in your text.

Depreciation is the process of allocating a plant asset's cost to expense over the useful life of the asset. Note that depreciation is based on an asset's cost, and that depreciation is not in any way related to cash. A contra account called Accumulated Depreciation is used to record the total amount of a plant asset's cost that has been recorded as depreciation expense. The adjusting journal entry to record depreciation is:

Depreciation Expense   XX
    Accumulated Depreciation   XX

To measure depreciation, it is necessary to determine the plant asset's cost, estimated useful life, and estimated residual value (salvage value or scrap value).

Estimated useful life is the length of service a business expects from the plant asset. Useful life may be expressed as a length of time, units of output, or other measures. For example, a computer may be expected to be useful for four years, while a printing press might be expected to print one billion sheets of paper over its useful life. Note that the useful life of an asset is an estimate of the usefulness of an asset and is not necessarily related to the physical life. For example, an asset such as a computer may become obsolete (not economically useful) long before it physically deteriorates.

Estimated residual value is the expected cash value of an asset at the end of its useful life. It is also called scrap or salvage value.

The **depreciable cost** of an asset is its cost minus residual value.

Objective 2 - Account for depreciation.

1. The **straight-line (SL) depreciation method** allocates the depreciable cost of a plant asset to depreciation expense in equal amounts per period over the life of the asset. The formula for straight-line depreciation is:

$$\text{Depreciation expense} = \frac{\text{cost - residual value}}{\text{useful life}}$$

Recall that the adjusting entry to record depreciation expense is:

Depreciation Expense   XX
    Accumulated Depreciation   XX

As accumulated depreciation increases each year, the remaining **book value of the asset** (cost - accumulated depreciation) declines. The final book value of an asset will be its residual value.

(See Exhibit 10-5.)

2. The **units-of-production (UOP) depreciation method** allocates the cost of an asset to depreciation expense based on the output that the asset is expected to produce. The formula for units-of-production depreciation is:

$$\text{UOP depreciation per unit of output} = \frac{\text{cost - residual value}}{\text{useful life in units}}$$

With UOP, the total depreciation expense in a period is:

Depreciation Expense = UOP depreciation per unit of output $\times$ units of output in the period

While the straight-line method could be used for any plant asset, the UOP method is not appropriate for all assets. Rather, it is used for assets where the life is a function of use rather than time. (For example, an airplane where flying hours is a more accurate measure of life compared with years.)

(See Exhibit 10-6.)

> **Study Tip:** Of the three methods discussed in this section, units of production is the only one which ignores time in the formula.

3. The **double-declining-balance (DDB) method** is an accelerated depreciation method. **Accelerated depreciation** simply means that a larger portion of an asset's cost is allocated to depreciation expense in the early years of an asset's life, and a smaller portion is allocated to depreciation expense toward the end of the asset's useful life.

To compute double-declining-balance depreciation:

    a. Compute the straight-line depreciation rate per year:

$$(1 \div \text{Useful life in years}) = X\%$$

    b. Multiply the straight-line depreciation rate per year by 2 (double it) to obtain the double-declining-balance rate:

$$\text{DDB rate} = (1 \div \text{Useful life in years}) \times 2$$

    c. Multiply the asset's beginning book value for a period (remember that book value equals cost minus accumulated depreciation) times the DDB rate. Book value will decrease each period, therefore depreciation expense will decrease each period. Note that the residual value of the asset is ignored until the net book value of the asset approaches the asset's residual value.

$$\text{Depreciation Expense} = \text{DDB rate} \times \text{book value}$$

    d. When the net book value of the asset approaches the asset's residual value, adjust the year's depreciation so that the remaining book value of the asset is equal to the residual value. The final year's depreciation amount will be equal to:

Book value at the beginning of the year - Residual value

Depreciation is no longer recorded after the book value of the asset is reduced to the residual value, even if the asset is still in use.

Study Exhibit 10-7 in your text to familiarize yourself with the double-declining-balance method.

Study Tips: Some important points to remember:
1. You never depreciate below the estimated salvage value.
2. Units-of-production ignores time.
3. Double-declining-balance ignores salvage value initially.
4. Double-declining-balance uses book value, while the other methods use depreciable cost.

Study Tip: The method used does not determine the total amount of the asset's cost to recognize as depreciation expense over the asset's life. Rather, the method determines the amount of the total to allocate each accounting period. Regardless of method, accumulated depreciation will be the same when the asset is fully depreciated.

Objective 3 - Select the best depreciation method for income tax purposes.

Although depreciation is a noncash expense, the amount of depreciation recorded affects the amount of income tax a business pays. Higher depreciation expense will reduce taxable income, and therefore income tax payments. Using an accelerated depreciation method will increase depreciation expense in the early years of an asset's life. This will decrease taxable income and income taxes, but only initially. The cash available to the business increases because tax payments are reduced.

Review Exhibit 10-10 in your text to see how accelerated depreciation reduces taxes and increases the cash flows of a business.

For federal income tax purposes, the IRS has in place a **Modified Accelerated Cost Recovery System** (**MACRS**, pronounced "makers"). MACRS ignores both residual value and estimated useful life, and simply assigns assets to one of eight life classes, most of which (but not all) are based on double-declining balance.

If a plant asset is held for only part of the year, partial year depreciation is computed by multiplying the full year's depreciation by the fraction of the year that the asset is held.

If a company finds that a change is warranted in its estimate of a plant asset's useful life, it computes revised annual depreciation this way:

$$\frac{\text{Book value - Residual value}}{\text{Remaining life}}$$

If an asset becomes fully depreciated (i.e., book value = residual value) but remains in use, both the asset and contra asset account should remain in the ledger until the business disposes of the asset.

Objective 4 - Account for the disposal of a plant asset.

With the possible exception of land, eventually a plant asset will no longer serve the needs of the business. The business will generally dispose of the asset by junking it, selling it, or exchanging it. The simplest accounting entry occurs when a company junks an asset. If the asset is fully depreciated with no residual value, the entry to record its disposal is:

Accumulated Depreciation—Asset	XX	
Asset		XX

If the asset is not fully depreciated, a loss is recorded for the remaining book value:

Accumulated Depreciation—Asset	X	
Loss on Disposal of Asset	X	
Asset		XX

These entries have the effect of removing the asset from the books.

When an asset is sold, the first step is to update depreciation for the partial year of service. Depreciation is recorded from the beginning of the accounting period to the date of the sale:

Depreciation Expense	XX	
Accumulated Depreciation—Asset		XX

The second step is to compute the remaining book value:

Book Value = Cost - Accumulated Depreciation

If cash received is greater than the remaining book value, a gain is recorded:

Cash	XX	
Accumulated Depreciation—Asset	XX	
Asset		XX
Gain on Sale of Asset		XX

If cash received is less than the remaining book value, a loss is recorded:

Cash	XX	
Loss on Sale of Asset	XX	
Accumulated Depreciation—Asset	XX	
Asset		XX

Note that gains will increase income and losses will decrease income. Therefore, both gains and losses are listed on the income statement.

When plant assets are exchanged or traded in, the balance for the old asset must be removed from the books and the replacement asset must be recorded.

Internal control dictates that plant assets be safeguarded by:

1. Assigning responsibility for custody of the assets.
2. Separating custody of assets from accounting for the assets.

Study Tip: This item is a cornerstone of internal control in almost every area.

3. Setting up security measures; for instance, armed guards and restricted access to plant assets to prevent theft.
4. Protecting assets from the elements (rain, snow, etc.).
5. Having adequate insurance against fire, storm, and other casualty losses.
6. Training operating personnel in the proper use of the asset.
7. Keeping a regular maintenance schedule.

In addition, companies will set up subsidiary records for each plant asset with detailed information about it.

Objective 5 - Account for natural resource assets and depletion.

Depletion expense is that portion of the cost of **natural resources** used up in a particular period. It is computed in the same way as UOP depreciation (refer to Objective 2 for the UOP formula). The appropriate entry is:

Depletion Expense	XX	
Accumulated Depletion		XX

Objective 6 - Account for intangible assets and amortization.

Intangible assets are assets that have no physical substance. They include patents, copyrights, trademarks, brand names, franchises, leaseholds, and goodwill. The acquisition cost of an intangible asset is recorded as:

Intangible Asset	XX	
Cash		XX

The cost of intangible assets is expensed through **amortization** over the asset's useful life up to a maximum of 40 years. Amortization is usually computed on a straight-line basis, similar to straight-line depreciation. Amortization is recorded as:

Amortization Expense	XX	
Intangible Asset		XX

Note that the book value of the intangible asset is reduced directly. There is no Accumulated Amortization account. Additionally, the residual value of most intangible assets is zero. Finally, the useful life of many amortizable assets is much shorter than the legal life of such assets—for example, copyrights.

One important type of intangible asset is **goodwill**. Goodwill is recorded only when another company is acquired. The amount of goodwill, if any, is equal to the difference between the price paid for the acquired company and the market value of the acquired company's net assets (assets - liabilities):

Goodwill = Price Paid - Market Value of Net Assets

If the purchase price paid is less than the market value of the acquired company's net assets, there is no goodwill.

For most companies, research and development (R&D) costs are recorded as expenses when incurred.

Objective 7 - Report plant asset transactions on the statement of cash flows.

The statement of cash flows will reflect the acquisition of plant assets and the sale of plant assets. The purchase and sale of plant assets are investing activities. Cash inflows result when plant assets are sold for cash while cash outflows result when plant assets are purchased for cash. See Exhibit 10-14.

TEST YOURSELF

All the self-testing materials in this chapter focus on information and procedures that your instructor is likely to test in quizzes and examinations.

I. Matching   *Match each numbered term with its lettered definition.*

_____ 1. accelerated depreciation
_____ 2. extraordinary repairs
_____ 3. double-declining-balance
_____ 4. franchises and licenses
_____ 5. relative-sales-value method
_____ 6. straight-line depreciation
_____ 7. capitalized interest
_____ 8. units-of-production
_____ 9. amortization
_____ 10. copyright

_____ 11. depletion
_____ 12. goodwill
_____ 13. leasehold improvements
_____ 14. capital lease
_____ 15. intangible asset
_____ 16. revenue expenditure
_____ 17. patent
_____ 18. trademarks
_____ 19. MACRS
_____ 20. capitalize

A. the exclusive right to reproduce and sell a book, musical composition, film, or other work of art
B. a method of depreciation for federal income tax purposes
C. that portion of a natural resource's cost that is used up in a particular period
D. an accelerated method of depreciation that computes annual depreciation by multiplying the asset's decreasing book value by a constant percentage, which is two times the straight-line rate
E. repair work that generates a capital expenditure
F. privileges granted by a private business or a government to sell a product or service in accordance with specified conditions
G. excess of the cost of an acquired company over the sum of the market value of its net assets
H. an asset with no physical form
I. a cost a renter incurs to improve rented facilities
J. costs incurred to maintain an asset
K. a grant from the federal government giving the holder the exclusive right to produce and sell an invention
L. an allocation technique for identifying the cost of each asset purchased in a group for a single amount
M. a depreciation method that writes off a relatively large amount of an asset's cost nearer the start of its useful life than does the straight-line method
N. an allocation of cost that applies to intangible assets
O. a lease which covers an extended period of time
P. depreciation method in which an equal amount of depreciation expense is assigned to each year (or period) of asset use
Q. interest cost incurred while an asset is being constructed
R. distinctive identifications of a product or service
S. a depreciation method in which a fixed amount of depreciation is assigned to each unit of output produced by the plant asset
T. to include a related cost as part of an asset's cost

II. Multiple Choice *Circle the best answer.*

1. All of the following are intangible assets except:

   A. patent
   B. brand name
   C. equipment
   D. goodwill

2. Which of the following long-lived assets is *not* depreciated?

   A. delivery truck
   B. equipment
   C. machinery
   D. coal mine

3. The cost of equipment includes all of the following except:

   A. sales tax
   B. repairs that occur one year after installation
   C. freight charges
   D. installation costs

4. Depreciation expense for an asset is the same every year. The depreciation method is:

   A. double-declining-balance
   B. MACRS
   C. straight-line
   D. units-of-production

5. A depreciation method that is not related to specific periods of time is:

   A. double-declining-balance
   B. MACRS
   C. straight-line
   D. units-of-production

6. You are computing depreciation for the first year of an asset's life. Which depreciation method ignores time?

   A. double-declining-balance
   B. MACRS
   C. straight-line
   D. units-of-production

7. Which of the following methods result in the same amount of depreciation each period?

   A. double-declining-balance
   B. units-of-production
   C. straight-line
   D. MACRS

8. Which depreciation method will usually result in the lowest income tax expense in the first year of an asset's life?

   A. double-declining-balance
   B. MACRS
   C. straight-line
   D. units-of-production

9. The depreciable cost of an asset equals:

    A. cost - salvage value   C. cost - residual value
    B. cost - accumulated depreciation   D. cost - the current year's depreciation expense

10. Depletion is computed using which of the following depreciation methods?

    A. double-declining-balance   C. straight-line
    B. MACRS   D. units-of-production

11. The cost of repairing a gear on a machine would probably be classified as:

    A. capital expenditure   C. intangible asset
    B. extraordinary repair expense   D. revenue expenditure

12. Which of the following costs should be capitalized?

    A. gas and oil for a delivery van   C. research and development costs for new products

    B. repainting the interior of the sales floor   D. the cost of borrowing money to construct a new shopping center

III. Completion *Complete each of the following.*

1. Two distinguishing characteristics of plant assets are that they are _____ and _____.
2. Depreciation is defined as _____.
3. Depreciation is a _____ expense.
4. Most companies use _____ depreciation for tax purposes.
5. The maximum time period over which an intangible asset can be amortized is _____ years.
6. When two or more assets are purchased in a group, the total cost of the assets is allocated to individual assets by the _____ method.
7. To calculate depreciation, you must know the following four items: 1)_____, 2)_____, 3)_____, and 4)_____.
8. Depreciation is an example of the _____ principle.
9. _____ relates to natural resources, while _____ relates to intangible assets.
10. _____ is used to depreciate assets for federal tax purposes.
11. Proceeds from the sale of plant assets are listed in the _____ activities section of the statement of cash flows.
12. The most widely used depreciation method for financial statements is _____.
13. Costs related to plant assets can be classified as either _____ expenditures or _____ expenditures.

IV. Daily Exercises

1. On August 20, 19X9, Aaron Callow, owner of Callow Catering, purchased a new commercial-sized grill and oven for the business. The new equipment carried an invoice price of $9,700 plus a 6% sales tax. In addition, the purchaser was responsible for $460 of freight charges. The sale was subject to 3/15, n/45 discount/credit terms. Upon receipt of the new equipment, Callow paid $925 to have the oven installed and connected. To finance this purchase, Callow borrowed $11,000 from the bank for 90 days at 10% interest. Callow paid the invoice within 15 days, earning the 3% discount.

   Classify each of the following costs as revenue or capital expenditures.

Cost	Classification
a) $9,700 (equipment)	_____
b) $582 (sales tax)	_____
c) $460 (freight)	_____
d) $291 (discount)	_____
e) $925 (installation)	_____
f) $275 (interest on loan)	_____

2. Based on your answer from #1, calculate the fully capitalized cost of the new equipment.

3. Review the information in Daily Exercise #1 above, and calculate depreciation for 1999, using both the straight-line and the double-declining balance method. The equipment is estimated to have a six-year life with a $1,000 residual value.

4. On January 7, 1999, Peterson Petroleum purchased a producing oil field for $68,000,000. Peterson estimated the oil field contained approximately 100,000,000 barrels of crude oil. When all the oil had been extracted, the property would be abandoned. By the end of the year, Peterson had extracted 8,400,000 barrels of oil. Calculate the depletion expense for the year and record the necessary adjusting entry.

5. Review the facts in question 4 above and assume the property was purchased on July 10, 1999. How would the answer change given the later purchase date?

V. Exercises

1. A company buys Machines X, Y, and Z for $150,000. The market values of the machines are $60,000, $72,000, and $108,000, respectively. What cost will be allocated to each machine?

2. Edward's Equipment Co. purchased a machine for $36,000 on January 4, 1999. Edward expects the machine to produce 25,000 units over five years and then expects to sell the machine for $11,000. Edward produced 7,000 units the first year and 9,000 units the second year. Compute the depreciation expense for 1999 and 2000. Round your answer to the nearest dollar.

	1999	2000
Straight-line	_____	_____
Units-of-production	_____	_____
Double-declining-balance	_____	_____

3. On January 8, 1999, Nancy Company purchased used equipment for $12,500. Nancy expected the equipment to remain in service for four years. She depreciated the equipment on a straight-line basis with $500 salvage value. On April 30, 2001, Nancy sold the equipment for $2,000. Record depreciation expense for the equipment for the four months ended April 30, 2001, and also record the sale of the equipment.

Date	Account and Explanation	PR	Debit	Credit

4. On July 1, 19X9, Nan Company purchased Tucket Company for $2,800,000 cash. The market value of Tucket's assets was $3,600,000, and Tucket had liabilities of $1,600,000.

   a. Compute the cost of the goodwill purchased by Nan Company.

   b. Record the purchase by Nan Company.

Date	Account and Explanation	PR	Debit	Credit

   c. Record the amortization of the goodwill on 12/31/X9, assuming a useful life of 40 years.

Date	Account and Explanation	PR	Debit	Credit

VI. Beyond the Numbers

Evaluate the following statement: "I do not see any problems in paying for next year's budgeted capital expenditures. We have estimated we will need approximately $110,000 for new equipment and we have more than three times that amount in our depreciation reserves (accumulated depreciation) at the moment."

VII. Demonstration Problems

Demonstration Problem #1

On January 1, 1997, Bradbeer, Inc. purchased three pieces of equipment. Details of the cost, economic life, residual value, and method of depreciation are shown below:

Equipment	Cost	Useful Life	Residual Value	Depreciation Method
A	$24,000	6 yrs	$3,000	straight-line
B	16,000	40,000 units	1,000	units-of-production
C	18,000	5 yrs	4,000	double-declining-balance

Required:

1. Prepare a schedule computing the depreciation expense for each piece of equipment over its useful life.
2. Prepare the journal entry to record the disposal of Equipment A. Assume that it has been depreciated over its useful life, and that it cannot be sold or exchanged (it is being scrapped).
3. Prepare the journal entry to record the sale of Equipment B for $1,000. Assume that it has been depreciated over its useful life.

Requirement 1 (Schedule of depreciation)

	A	B	C
Asset cost			
Less: Residual value			
Depreciable cost			

Equipment A
Schedule of Depreciation Expense
(Straight-Line Method)

Year	Depreciable Cost	Depreciable Rate	Depreciation Expense
1997			
1998			
1999			
2000			
2001			
2002			

Equipment B
Schedule of Depreciation Expense
(Units-of-production)

Year	Depreciable Cost	Units Produced	Depreciation Expense
1997		12,400	
1998		10,750	
1999		11,230	
2000		6,100	

Equipment C
Schedule of Depreciation Expense
(Double-Declining-Balance)

Year	Book Value × Rate	Depreciation Expense	Book Value
1997			
1998			
1999			
2000			
2001			

Requirement 2 (Journal entry—Equipment A)

Date	Account and Explanation	PR	Debit	Credit

Requirement 3 (Journal entry—Equipment B)

Date	Account and Explanation	PR	Debit	Credit

Demonstration Problem #2

Requirement 1

On April 5, 1991, Mandy Manufacturing Company purchased a machine for $18,000. Its estimated useful life was 10 years with no salvage value. Additional expenses were made for transportation, $500; and installation costs, $900. On January 10, 1998, repairs costing $8,000 were made, increasing the efficiency of the machine and extending its useful life to four years beyond the original estimate. On December 1, 1999, some worn-out parts were replaced for $300. The company closes its books on December 31 and uses the straight-line method.

Required:

Present journal entries to record the following:
1. the purchase of the machine
2. payment of transportation and installation costs
3. depreciation for 1991
4. the repair on January 10, 1998
5. depreciation for 1998
6. the repair on December 1, 1999
7. depreciation for 1999

Date	Account and Explanation	PR	Debit	Credit

SOLUTIONS

I. Matching

1. M	5. L	9. N	13. I	17. K
2. E	6. P	10. A	14. O	18. R
3. D	7. Q	11. C	15. H	19. B
4. F	8. S	12. G	16. J	20. T

II. Multiple Choice

1. C Equipment is a tangible asset.

2. D A coal mine is a natural resource and as such is depleted, not depreciated.

3. B The cost of equipment includes all amounts paid to acquire the asset and to ready it for its intended use. Repairs to equipment indicate that it is in use and therefore should not be included as part of the equipment's cost.

4. C Straight-line depreciation is the only method of depreciation that results in the same amount of depreciation every year. The other methods listed are accelerated (double-declining-balance) or can result in differing amounts of depreciation each year (UOP and MACRS).

5. D Units-of-production depreciation is based on the number of units produced by the depreciable asset. The other methods listed all depend on time in the depreciation calculation.

6. D Of all the methods listed, only unit-of-production ignores time in the depreciation calculation.

7. C Straight-line depreciation is the only method of depreciation that results in the same amount of depreciation every year.

8. A The depreciation method that will result in the lowest income tax in the first year is the method that results in the largest depreciation deduction. Double-declining balance gives the largest deduction in the asset's first year.

9. A & C Item B equals the asset's book value. Item D has no significance.

10. D Both depletion and units-of-production follow the general formula: (cost - residual value) / useful life in units.

11. D Capital expenditures are those that increase capacity or efficiency of the asset or extend its useful life. Revenue expenditures merely maintain an asset in its existing condition or restore the asset to good working order.

12. D The interest cost on the loan should be capitalized while the shopping center is being developed. The other costs are revenue expenditures and should be debited to expense accounts.

III. Completion

1. long-lived, tangible (The physical form (tangibility) of plant assets provides their usefulness.)

2. a systematic allocation of an asset's cost to expense (Depreciation is not a method of asset valuation.)

3. noncash (Cash is expended either at the acquisition of a plant asset or over time as the asset is paid for. The debit to Depreciation Expense is balanced by a credit to Accumulated Depreciation, not Cash.)

4. accelerated (MACRS) (Accelerated depreciation methods cause larger depreciation deductions in the first years of an asset's life. The larger deductions result in lower taxable income and lower taxes.)

5. 40

6. relative-sales-value (The need to depreciate each asset separately makes it necessary to allocate the purchase price by some reasonable manner.)

7. cost; estimated useful life; estimated residual value; depreciation method (Order is not important.)
8. matching (Matching means to identify and measure all expenses incurred during the period and to match them against the revenue earned during that period.)
9. depletion; amortization
10. MACRS (Modified Accelerated Cost Recovery System)
11. investing
12. straight-line
13. capital; revenue (Order not important.)

IV. Daily Exercises
1.
    a. capital expenditure
    b. capital expenditure
    c. capital expenditure
    d. (capital expenditure)

> **Study Tip**: The discount is in parentheses because it represents a reduction in the cost of the equipment.

    e. capital expenditure
    f. revenue expenditure

> **Study Tip**: The interest on the loan does not qualify as a capital expenditure. Generally, interest is capitalized only on self-constructed assets, and then only during the period it takes to construct the asset.

2. $11,376
Given the answers in part 1, the calculation is $9,700 + 582 + 460 - 291 + 925. The accounts would appear as follows:

Grill/Oven		Interest Expense	
9,700	291	275	
582			
460			
925			
Bal. 11,376			

3. Straight-Line   =   (Cost - Residual Value) ÷ Life
               =   ($11,376 (from #2 above) - $1,000) ÷ 6 years
               = $1,729 per year (rounded)
$1,726 × 4/12   = $575 (rounded)

Double-Declining Balance   =   Book Value × Rate
Rate = 1/6 × 2 = 1/3
$11,376 × 1/3 × 4/12 = $1,264

> **Study Tip:** For assets placed in service during the year, depreciation is calculated to the nearest whole month.

4. For natural resources, the most appropriate method is units of production.

    UOP = (Cost - Residual Value) ÷ Estimated Total Production
         = \$68,000,000 ÷ 100,000,000 barrels
         = \$0.68 per barrel
    \$0.68 x 8,400,000 barrels = \$5,712,000

| 12/31/99 | Depletion Expense | 5,712,000 | |
| | Accumulated Depletion | | 5,712,000 |

5. Assuming a later purchase date, the answer would be the same. Why? Units of production ignores time in the formula; only actual production is relevant.

V. Exercises

1. Machine X = [\$60,000 / (\$60,000 + \$72,000 + \$108,000)] × \$150,000 = \$37,500
    Machine Y = [\$72,000 / (\$60,000 + \$72,000 + \$108,000)] × \$150,000 = \$45,000
    Machine Z = [\$108,000 / (\$60,000 + \$72,000 + \$108,000)] × \$150,000 = \$67,500
    (Proof: \$37,500 + \$45,000 + \$67,500 = \$150,000)

2.

	1999	2000
Straight-line	5,000	5,000
Units-of-production	7,000	9,000
Double-declining-balance	14,400	8,640

Straight-line = (\$36,000 - \$11,000) / 5 years = \$5,000

Units-of-production = (36,000 - 11,000) / 25,000 units = \$1.00 per unit
     1999 = \$7,000 × \$1.00 = \$7,000
     2000 = \$9,000 × \$1.00 = \$9,000

Double-declining-balance:
     DDB rate = (1 / 5) × 2 = .40
     1999 = .40 × \$36,000 = \$14,400
     Book value = \$36,000 - \$14,400 = \$21,600
     2000 = .40 × \$21,600 = \$8,640

3.

Annual depreciation = (\$12,500 - \$500) / 4 = \$3,000
Accumulated depreciation 1/1/01 = 2 years @ \$3,000 per year = \$6,000

4/30	Depreciation Expense	1,000	
	Accumulated Depreciation		1,000
	Dep. for 4 months (4 / 12 × 3,000) = 1,000		

4/30	Cash		2,000	
	Loss on Sale of Asset		3,500	
	Accumulated Depreciation		7,000	
	Equipment			12,500
	Loss = Cash + Accumulated. Dep. - Cost			

Because cash received ($2,000) is less than book value ($12,500 - $7,000 = $5,500), there is a loss of $3,500 ($5,500 - $2,000) on the sale.

4.

A.

Purchase price for Tucket		$2,800,000
Market value of Tucket	3,600,000	
Less: Tucket's liabilities	1,600,000	
Market value of Tucket's net assets		2,000,000
Goodwill		$800,000

B.

Date	Account and Explanation	PR	Debit	Credit
7/1	Assets		3,600,000	
	Goodwill		800,000	
	Liabilities			1,600,000
	Cash			2,800,000

C.

Date	Account and Explanation	PR	Debit	Credit
12/31	Amortization expense		10,000	
	Goodwill			10,000
	1/ 40 × $800,000 = $20,000 × 1/2 = $10,000			

VI. Beyond the Numbers

The person making the statement is confused about depreciation reserves (i.e., accumulated depreciation). There is no cash involved in accounting for depreciation; therefore, the balance in accumulated depreciation does not represent any money available for future use. The balance in accumulated depreciation represents the amount of the related assets' cost that has been recognized as an expense because of the assets' loss of usefulness to the business.

VII. Demonstration Problems

Demonstration Problem #1 Solved and Explained

	A	B	C
Asset cost	$24,000	$16,000	$18,000
Less: Residual value	3,000	800	4,000
Depreciable cost	$21,000	$15,200	$14,000

Study Tip: Under the double-declining-balance method, the residual value is not considered until the book value approaches residual value.

Equipment A
Schedule of Depreciation Expense
(Straight-Line Method)

Year	Depreciable Cost	Depreciable Rate	Depreciation Expense
1997	$21,000	1/6	$3,500
1998	21,000	1/6	3,500
1999	21,000	1/6	3,500
2000	21,000	1/6	3,500
2001	21,000	1/6	3,500
2002	21,000	1/6	3,500
		Total	$21,000

The book value of the equipment after 2002 is $3,000 (cost - accumulated depreciation = $24,000 - $21,000 = $3,000).

Equipment B
Schedule of Depreciation Expense
(Units-of-Production)

Year	Depreciable Cost	Units Produced	Depreciation Expense
1997	$15,000	12,400	$ 4,650*
1998	15,000	10,750	4,031
1999	15,000	11,230	4,211 (rounded)
2000	15,000	6,100	2,108 (rounded)**
		Total	$15,000

*The per-unit cost is $0.38 ($15,000 / 40,000 units = $0.375).
The book value after 2000 is $800 ($16,000 - $15,200 = $800).
**The original production estimate for the equipment was 40,000 units. The actual production over the life of the equipment was 40,480. Assuming the original estimates (for total production and residual value) are reasonable, the 2000 depreciation should be based on 5,620 units, the number required to total 40,000 units.

Study Tip: The depreciable cost is not affected by the method used. The method simply determines how the depreciable cost will be spread over the asset's life.

Equipment C
Schedule of Depreciation Expense
(Double-Declining-Balance)

Year	Book Value × Rate	Depreciation Expense	Book Value
1997	.40 × 18,000	7,200	$11,800
1998	.40 × 11,800	4,720	7,080
1999	.40 × 7,080	2,832	4,248
2000	4,248 - 4,000	248	4,000
2001		0	4,000

The straight-line depreciation rate for an asset with useful life of five years is 1/5 per year, or 20%. Double the straight-line rate is 2/5, or 40%. This rate does not change from 1997 through 2001.

Study Tip: The most frequent error made by students in applying double-declining-balance deals with the residual value. Unlike units-of-production, with DDB, the residual value is not taken into account until the final years (in this example, the fourth year) of the asset's life.

Depreciation expense for Equipment C in the fourth year is not $1,699 ($4,248 × .40) because in the fourth year depreciation expense is the previous year's book value less the residual value ($4,248 - $4,000 = $248). As the asset is fully depreciated at the end of the fourth year, there is no depreciation recorded for the fifth year.

Requirement 2 (Journal entry—Equipment A)

Date	Account and Explanation	PR	Debit	Credit
	Accumulated Depreciation—A		21,000	
	Loss on Disposal of Equipment		3,000	
	Equipment A			24,000

When fully-depreciated assets cannot be sold or exchanged, an entry removing them from the books is necessary upon disposal. The entry credits the asset account and debits its related Accumulated Depreciation account. If the fully depreciated asset has no residual value, no loss on the disposal occurs. In most cases, however, it will be necessary to record a debit to a Loss on Disposal account to write off the book value of a junked asset. There can never be a gain on the junking or scrapping of an asset.

Requirement 3 (Journal entry—-Equipment B)

Date	Account and Explanation	PR	Debit	Credit
	Cash		1,000	
	Accumulated depreciation—B		15,000	
	Equipment B			16,000

A gain is recorded when an asset is sold for a price greater than its value. A loss is recorded when the sale price is less than book value. In this case, Equipment B and its related Accumulated Depreciation account are removed from the books in a manner similar to Equipment A. The book value of the asset is $1,000. As this equals the selling price, no gain or loss results.

Demonstration Problem #2 Solved and Explained

Date	Account and Explanation	PR	Debit	Credit
1.	Machine		18,000	
	Cash			18,000
2.	Machine		500	
	Cash			500
	Transportation cost.			
	Machine		900	
	Cash			900
	Installation cost.			

Both the transportation and installation costs are debited to the Machine account because they are necessary costs incurred to place the asset in service. Therefore, the total cost basis for the machine is $19,400, not $18,000.

3.	Depreciation Expense—Machine		1,455	
	Accumulated Depreciation			1,455

($19,400 (see above) / 10 = 1,940 × 9/12 = $1,455)

Since the asset was acquired and placed in service early in April, the first year's depreciation is 9/12 of the company's financial period. Thereafter, annual depreciation is $1,940.

4.	Machine		8,000	
	Cash (or Accounts Payable)			8,000

This is clearly a capital expenditure because the machine will last past its original life estimate. Therefore, the cost should be reflected in an asset account, not in an expense account.

5.	Depreciation Expense—Machine		1,973	
	Accumulated Depreciation			1,973

Accumulated depreciation through 12/31/97 is $13,095. For 1991, depreciation is $1,455; 1992 to 1997 is equal to $1,940 per year × 6 = $11,640. $1,455 + $11,640 = $13,095.

Therefore, on 1/10/98 book value is $6,305 ($19,400 - $13,095). The $8,000 debit in entry (4) increases book value to $14,305, and now life is four years more than the original life estimate. As of 1/10/98, the machine is 6 years, 9 months old. The revised life estimate is now 14 years. Therefore, as of 1/10/98, the asset has 7 years, 3 months of life left (14 years - 6 years, 9 months). To calculate the new depreciation amount, divide book value ($14,305) by remaining life (7.25 years) or $1,973 per year (rounded).

6.	Repair Expense		300	
	Cash			300

This is clearly a revenue expenditure—one necessary to maintain the asset.

7.	Depreciation Expense		1,973	
	Cash			1,973

See explanation for #5 above.

Chapter 11—Current Liabilities and Payroll Accounting

CHAPTER OVERVIEW

Beginning with Chapter 7, you have learned about internal control—procedures designed to safeguard assets. These procedures were applied to cash in Chapter 7. Thereafter, additional assets were introduced: receivables (Chapter 8), inventory (Chapter 9), and long-term assets (Chapter 10). In this chapter we continue to focus on the balance sheet, but switch to the other side of the accounting equation and examine liabilities, specifically current liabilities and payroll. Long-term liabilities are examined in Chapter 15. The learning objectives for this chapter are to

1. Account for current liabilities of known amount.
2. Account for current liabilities that must be estimated.
3. Identify and report contingent liabilities.
4. Compute payroll amounts.
5. Make basic payroll entries.
6. Use a payroll system.
7. Report current liabilities on the balance sheet.

CHAPTER REVIEW

Liabilities are obligations to transfer assets (for example, to make cash payments for purchases on account) or to provide services in the futures (for example, to earn unearned revenue). Current liabilities are due within one year or within the company's operating cycle if it is longer than one year. Long-term liabilities are those not classified as current.

Objective 1 - Account for current liabilities of known amount.

Current liabilities include liabilities of a known amount and liabilities that are estimated.

Current liabilities of a known amount are:

Accounts payable: amounts owed to suppliers for goods or services purchased on account.

Short-term notes payable: notes due within one year. Companies issue notes payable to borrow cash, to purchase inventory, or to purchase plant assets. Interest expense and interest payable must be accrued at the end of the accounting period.

Suppose a company acquires a plant asset and issues a note payable. The entry is:

Plant Asset	XX	
Notes Payable, Short-Term		XX

Interest expense and interest payable are recorded at the end of the accounting period with this entry:

Interest Expense	XX	
Interest Payable		XX

When the note is paid off at maturity, the entry is:

Notes Payable, Short-Term	XX	
Interest Payable	XX	
Interest Expense	XX	
Cash		XX

Notes payable are often issued at a discount. This means that the borrower repays the interest and receives cash in an amount equal to the face value of the note less the discount. The entry is:

Cash	XX	
Discount on Notes Payable		XX
Notes Payable, Short-Term		XX

Discount on Notes Payable is a contra account to Notes Payable, Short-Term. The balance sheet will report the liability as:

Current liabilities:

Notes payable, short-term	$ XXX
Less: discount on- notes payable	XX
Notes payable, short-term, net	$ XXX

Accrued interest is computed on the face value of the note. Since discounting a note effectively means that the interest has been paid in advance, there is no interest payable. Instead, the Discount is reduced. The entry is:

Interest Expense	XX	
Discount on Notes Payable		XX

Reducing Discount on Notes Payable increases the net liability of the Note Payable.

When the note is paid off, two entries are required. First, the balance of interest expense is recorded:

Interest Expense	XX	
Discount on Notes Payable		XX

Second, the payment is recorded:

Notes Payable, Short-Term	XX	
Cash		XX

Other current liabilities: sales taxes payable, accrued expenses, unearned revenues, payroll liabilities, the current portion of long-term debt, and contingent liabilities of a known amount (such as contingent liabilities arising from notes discounted and guaranteed notes).

Most states tax retail sales. Sales tax is usually collected in addition to the price of an item. Retailers are actually collecting the tax for the government, and therefore Sales Tax Payable is a current liability.

Sales taxes may be accounted for in one of two ways:

1. Recorded the tax separately for daily sales:

Cash	XX	
Sales Revenue		XX
Sales Tax Payable		XX

2. Record sales including the taxes collected:

Cash	XX	
Sales Revenue		XX

At the end of each month, an adjusting entry is made to correct the Sales Revenue and Sales Tax Payable accounts:

Sales Tax Payable	XX	
Cash		XX

In either case, when the taxes are paid to the government the entry is:

Sales Tax Payable	XX	
Cash		XX

Some long-term liabilities, such as notes, bonds, or mortgages are paid in installments. The current portion of long-term debt is the amount of that debt that is payable within one year. It is reported in the current liabilities section of the balance sheet. The remainder is reported in the long-term liabilities section of the balance sheet.

Accrued expenses such as interest payable and payroll items are current liabilities. Unearned revenues occur when a company receives cash from customers before earning the revenue. As goods are delivered or services are rendered, revenue is recorded. Unearned revenue is recorded as:

Cash	XX	
Unearned Revenue		XX

As the unearned revenue is earned, it is recorded as:

Unearned Revenue	XX	
Revenue		XX

Objective 2 - Account for current liabilities that must be estimated.

Current liabilities that are estimated include warranties payable, vacation pay liability, and income tax payable (for a corporation).

Recall that the matching principle requires that expenses be matched with revenues. A company can reasonably estimate, often as a percentage of sales, the amount of warranty expense that will be incurred as a result of defective products. Estimated Warranty Payable is a current liability, recorded as:

| Warranty Expense | XX | |
| Estimated Warranty Payable | | XX |

It is important to remember that when a repair or replacement occurs within the warranty period, the Estimated Warranty Payable (rather than Warranty Expense) is debited.

Most companies provide paid vacations to their employees. The matching principle dictates that the amount of vacation employees have earned be recorded in the period when it was earned and not in a subsequent period when the employee actually takes the time off with pay. Therefore, the company needs to accrue the **estimated vacation pay liability** each period, as follows:

| Vacation Pay Expense | XX | |
| Estimated Vacation Pay Liability | | XX |

When an employee takes time off with pay, the liability account is debited as follows:

| Estimated Vacation Pay Liabilities | XX | |
| Cash | | XX |

Unlike sole proprietorships and partnerships, corporations must pay taxes on the income. On a regular basis throughout the year, corporations send in payments to the government, recorded as follows:

| Income Tax Expense | XX | |
| Cash | | XX |

At the end of the year, the corporation must accrue the taxes owed, but not yet paid, as follows:

| Income Tax Expense | XX | |
| Income Tax Payable | | XX |

The liability will be removed when the company remits a check to the government.

Objective 3 - Identify and report contingent liabilities.

A **contingent liability** is a potential liability that depends on a future event that may occur as the result of a past transaction. Contingent liabilities may be difficult to estimate, as in lawsuits, where the amounts are determined by the courts. The disclosure principle requires companies to keep outsiders informed of relevant information about the company.

Some companies report contingent liabilities on the balance sheet after total liabilities, but with no amount listed. An explanatory note usually accompanies a short presentation. Other companies simply report contingent liabilities in supplementary notes only. Contingent liabilities are not required to be presented on the balance sheet. If it is probable that a loss will occur and the amount can be reasonably estimated, then an actual liability should be recorded. If recorded, it will appear as a liability on the balance sheet and as a loss on the income statement.

Accounting for both current liabilities and contingent liabilities can pose ethical challenges for the business. Because some current liabilities must be estimated (which means the related expense is also estimated), someone may attempt to manipulate the amount of the estimate in an attempt to manipulate the amount of reported net income. In addition, someone may choose to overlook, or underestimate, the amount of a contingent liability. External auditors are particularly concerned with unreported liabilities and want to ensure that the financial statements are accurate.

Review the Decision Guidelines following the contingent liability discussion in your text.

Objective 4 - Compute payroll amounts.

Gross pay is the total amount an employee earns before taxes and deductions. Net pay is the amount of the payroll check the employee receives. Some payroll deductions from gross pay are required, such as federal or state income taxes and FICA (Social Security tax), and others are optional, such as union dues and insurance premiums. The amount of income tax withheld is determined by the amount earned, and the number of withholding allowances claimed by the employee (this information is supplied to the business when the employee completes a W-4 form—see Exhibit 11-5 in your text), and the employee's marital status.

FICA taxes are subdivided into two parts: the Social Security tax (providing retirement, disability, and survivor benefits), and the Medicare tax (health insurance). The amount of FICA tax paid is determined by the current FICA tax rate and, in the case of Social Security, the maximum annual earning limit. There is no earning limit for the Medicare tax.

The amounts withheld from gross pay are liabilities that occur in the course of compensating employees.

In addition to taxes withheld from employees' earnings, the employer is responsible for payment of the employer's share of FICA taxes, state and federal unemployment taxes. These amounts are expenses to the employer, not payroll deductions. Employers pay FICA tax equal to the amount withheld from employees.

Objective 5 - Make basic payroll entries.

The following example shows how payroll entries are made:

Suppose that when you graduate, you get a job that pays $3,000 per month, and you are paid monthly. Assume also that your employer pays $200 per month for your health insurance and $100 per month for your pension. Your pay stub reports the following:

Gross pay	$3,000
FICA (assuming an 8% rate)	240
Income Taxes (given)	450
Net Pay	$2,310

Your employer's entry to record salary expense is:

Salary Expense	3,000	
Employee Income Tax Payable		450
FICA Tax Payable		240
Salary Payable to Employee		2,310

Your employer would record payroll expense as:

Payroll Tax Expense	428	
FICA Tax Payable (a matching amount)		240
State Unemployment Tax Payable		162
(3,000 x 5.4%)		
Federal Unemployment Tax Payable		24
(3,000 x .8%)		

Finally, your employer would record fringe benefits expense:

Health Insurance Expense	200	
Pension Expense	100	
Employee Benefit Payable		300

Objective 6 - Use a payroll system.

A **payroll system** includes these components:

1. **A payroll register**
2. **A payroll bank account**
3. **Payroll checks**
4. **An earnings record for each employee**

1. The payroll register lists individual earnings and deductions for employees as well as totals. Computerized systems may also compute employer payroll tax expense such as FICA and federal and state unemployment. The payroll register is the source document for recording the payroll. (See Exhibit 11-7.)
2. The company deposits money in the payroll bank account exactly to cover net pay.

3. Most companies issue payroll checks which list gross pay, deductions, and net pay. Using the example in the previous section, the entry your employer makes when your check is distributed to you is:

Salary Payable	2,310	
Cash (Payroll account)		2,310

Assume that you are the only employee of your company. Then payroll taxes are remitted to the government, the entry is:

Employee Income Tax Payable	450	
FICA Tax Payable	480	
State Unemployment Tax Payable	162	
Federal Unemployment Tax Payable	24	
Cash (Regular account)		1,116

Note that the FICA Tax Payable amount ($480) includes both the amount withheld from your paycheck ($240) and the amount recorded by your employer as payroll tax expense ($240).

When your employer remits the payments for your health insurance and pension, the entry is:

Employee Benefit Payable	300	
Cash (Regular account)		300

4. Employers maintain earnings records (see Exhibit 11-10) which are used in preparing payroll tax returns (Form 941—see Exhibit 11-9) and tax statements (W-2 forms) for employees.

When employees are eligible to receive post-retirement benefits (usually medical insurance), companies are required by FASB to accrue the expense each period. These benefits are another example of accrued liabilities.

Internal Control and Payroll

Special controls for payroll accounting are necessary because of the large number of transactions and the number of different parties involved. These controls are designed to maintain an efficient system while, at the same time, safeguarding payroll disbursements. Efficiency is achieved when separate bank accounts are maintained for payroll checks, while payroll disbursements are safeguarded through the separation of duties related to personnel (hiring and firing) and payroll (check distribution, time cards, employee identification cards, etc.)

Objective 7 - Report current liabilities on the balance sheet.

At the end of the fiscal year, liabilities are reported on the balance sheet. The year-end payroll liability is the amount of payroll expense still unpaid. Study Exhibits 11-12 and 11-13 in your text to review how current liabilities are reported on the balance sheet and the categories of current liabilities.

TEST YOURSELF

All the self-testing materials in this chapter focus on information and procedures that your instructor is likely to test in quizzes and examinations.

I. Matching   *Match each numbered term with its lettered definition.*

_____ 1. 941
_____ 2. commission
_____ 3. FICA tax
_____ 4. W-2
_____ 5. gross pay
_____ 6. net pay
_____ 7. W-4
_____ 8. contingent liabilities

_____ 9. discounting a note payable
_____ 10. short-term note payable
_____ 11. unemployment compensation tax
_____ 12. withheld income tax
_____ 13. postretirement benefits
_____ 14. overtime
_____ 15. fringe benefits

A. a liability which may arise in the future
B. a borrowing arrangement in which the bank subtracts the interest amount from the note's face value and the borrower receives the net amount
C. benefits which an employee will receive after retirement
D. the form submitted to the federal government reconciling the employer's liability for withheld income and FICA taxes
E. a form submitted by each employee indicating the employee's marital status and number of withholding allowances claimed
F. employee compensation computed as a percentage of the sales that the employee has made
G. employee compensation, like health and life insurance and retirement pay, which the employee does not receive immediately in cash
H. a form summarizing each employee's annual gross wages and deductions
I. income taxes that are deducted from employees' gross pay and remitted to the government
J. the amount of employee compensation that the employee actually takes home
K. note payable due within one year, a common form of financing
L. excess hours worked for which a premium is earned
M. payroll tax paid by employers to the government, for the purpose of paying benefits to people who are out of work
N. Social Security tax which is withheld from employees' pay and matched by the employer
O. the total amount of salary, wages, commissions, or any other employee compensation before taxes and other deductions are taken out

II. Multiple Choice   *Circle the best answer.*

1. Which of the following is *not* a current liability?

   A. Warranties
   B. Pension Expense

   C. Unearned Revenue
   D. Vacation Liability

2. Interest on a discounted note payable is recorded:

   A. at maturity
   B. at the end of the accounting period
   C. in monthly payments
   D. when the note is discounted

3. Which of the following is probably a contingent liability?

   A. Interest Payable
   B. Notes Payable
   C. Lawsuit Claims
   D. Income Tax Payable

4. The major expense of most service organizations is:

   A. Payroll
   B. Interest Expense
   C. Cost of Goods Sold
   D. Rent Expense

5. A contingent liability becomes a real liability when:

   A. a loss is probable but cannot be estimated
   B. a loss is possible
   C. a loss is probable and can reasonably be estimated
   D. a loss can be reasonably estimated

6. Which of the following has a maximum amount an employee must pay in a year?

   A. Federal income tax
   B. Medicare tax
   C. State income tax
   D. Social Security tax

7. Which of the following is *not* a component of a payroll?

   A. payroll checks
   B. payroll register
   C. payroll petty cash fund
   D. earnings records

8. Which of the following is *not* a control for safeguarding cash in a payroll system?

   A. separating hiring duties from the paycheck disbursement duties
   B. requiring employees to wear identification badges
   C. maintaining two payroll bank accounts
   D. having employees punch a time clock

9. Which of the following is *not* required to calculate federal withholding tax?

   A. marital status
   B. withholding allowances
   C. social security number
   D. amount of gross pay

10. Which of the following is *not* an estimated liability?

    A. warranties
    B. post-retirement benefits
    C. vacation pay
    D. notes payable

III. Completion   *Complete each of the following statements.*

1. Estimating the warranty expense is an example of the _____ principle.
2. Discount on Notes Payable is a(n) _____ account.
3. Listing a contingent liability is an example of the _____ principle.
4. To calculate the amount to withhold for income taxes, the following information is required: _____, _____, _____, and
   _____.
5. The W-2 reports the _____.
6. The W-4 is completed by the _____ and indicates the _____.
7. Withheld federal income taxes and FICA taxes are reported to the government on the _____ form, which is submitted _____.
8. FICA is an acronym for the _____.
9. The account title Payroll Tax Expense reflects which specific payroll taxes? _____
   _____.
10. For a contingent liability to be recorded, FASB requires that the liability be both _____ and _____.

IV. Daily Exercises

1. Indicate whether each of the following is paid by the employee (deducted from his gross pay), paid by the employer, or both.

	Paid by employee	Paid by employer
Charitable contributions	_____	_____
Social Security tax	_____	_____
Federal income tax	_____	_____
Unemployment tax	_____	_____
Union dues	_____	_____
Medicare tax	_____	_____

2. Indicate whether each of the following liabilities is a known amount (K) or an estimated amount (E).

_____ A. Accounts Payable	_____ G. Sales Tax Payable
_____ B. Short-term Notes Payable	_____ H. Liability for Vacation Pay
_____ C. Property Taxes Payable	_____ I. Postretirement Benefits
_____ D. Warranty Liability	_____ J. Interest Payable
_____ E. Salaries Expense	_____ K. Pension Premium Payable
_____ F. Income Taxes Payable	

3. Record the following transactions:
   a. On December 1, a used truck is purchased for $12,000, and a six-month, 12% note payable is issued.

b. Adjust for interest as of December 31, the close of the fiscal year.

c. The payment of the note on June 1.

4. Review the facts in Daily Exercise #3 above but assume the company signed a note for $12,720 with the interest included in the face value of the note. Record the December 1, December 31, and June 1 entries.

5. If a company has net sales of $4,200,000, and past experience indicates estimated warranty expense to be 2.5% of net sales, record the adjusting entry for the warranty liability. Assume a customer returns an item covered by the warranty the following month, and the company uses $75 in parts and $20 in labor to repair the item, present a journal entry to record the repair.

V. Exercises

Make journal entries for each of the following independent transactions or groups of transactions.

1. A company borrows $12,000 on August 1 giving a 9%, one-year note payable.

GENERAL JOURNAL

Date	Accounts and Explanation	PR	Debit	Credit

Record an adjusting entry on December 31 for the note in #1.

GENERAL JOURNAL

Date	Accounts and Explanation	PR	Debit	Credit

2. A company discounts a $20,000, 120-day note payable to the bank at 12% on 10/2/X1.

GENERAL JOURNAL

Date	Accounts and Explanation	PR	Debit	Credit

3. A company receives $13,580 when it discounts a four-month note payable at 9%.

GENERAL JOURNAL

Date	Accounts and Explanation	PR	Debit	Credit

4. The entry to adjust sales revenue and record 6% sales tax on sales of $31,800 (including sales tax) made during the month of August.

GENERAL JOURNAL

Date	Accounts and Explanation	PR	Debit	Credit

5. Suzy Simmons earns $10.00 per hour with time and a half for more than 40 hours per week. During the second week of the new year, she worked 48 hours. Suzy's payroll deductions include federal income tax at 15%, state income tax at 6%, Social Security tax at 6%, Medicare at 1.5%, and a contribution to United Giving of $15.00 per week.

GENERAL JOURNAL

Date	Accounts and Explanation	PR	Debit	Credit

VI. Beyond the Numbers

Review the information in Exercises 1 and 2 above and, for each note record all the transactions as they would appear on the books of the payee (the bank) for the life of each note.

GENERAL JOURNAL

Date	Accounts and Explanation	PR	Debit	Credit

VII. Demonstration Problems

Demonstration Problem #1

Green Stems, Inc. is a small flower shop that employs three people. Glen Green is the store's salesperson, and Rose Pinard and Janice Flowers are part-time employees. Prior to the current pay period, Glen has earned $62,400, Rose has earned $6,800, and Janice has earned $4,400. For the month of December, 19X9, Glen's gross salary was $5,800. Rose worked 55 hours, 40 of them at her regular wage of $10.00 per hour, and the remaining 15 hours at time and a half for overtime. Janice worked 35 hours, all at her regular rate of $10.00 per hour.

Assume the following additional facts:

Medicare rate = 1.5%
Social Security rate = 6.0% on a base of $65,000
Federal unemployment rate = .8% on a base of $7,000
State unemployment rate = 5.4% on a base of $7,000

Individual income tax withholding:

	Federal	State
Glen Green	$1,725.00	$315.00
Rose Pinard	90.00	28.00
Janice Flowers	26.00	12.00

Voluntary monthly withholding:

Glen Green	$20 (United Giving)
Rose Pinard	$10 (U.S. Savings Bonds)

Fringe benefits:
The company contributes to a pension plan an amount equal to 6% of gross income.

Required:

1. Compute the gross and net pay of each employee for the month of December.
2. Record the following payroll entries that Green Stems, Inc. would make for:
   a. Expense for employee salary, including overtime pay
   b. Employer payroll taxes
   c. Expense for fringe benefits
   d. Payment of cash to employees
   e. Payment of all payroll taxes
   f. Payment for fringe benefits and voluntary withholdings
3. What was the total payroll expense incurred by Green Stems, Inc. for the month of December? How much cash did the business actually spend on its payroll including all costs incurred beyond the cost of the gross payroll?

Requirement 1

	Gross Pay
Glen Green	
Rose Pinard	
Janice Flowers	
Total Gross Pay	

	Net pay		
Explanation	Green	Pinard	Flowers

Requirement 2

GENERAL JOURNAL

Date	Accounts and Explanation	PR	Debit	Credit

Requirement 3

<u>Total December Payroll</u>

<u>Total Cash Spent in December</u>

Demonstration Problem #2

The following events occurred in December Vega Del Toro Corporation:

1. On December 1, borrowed $15,000 from the bank, signing a six-month note at 9% interest.
2. On December 16, purchased equipment and signed a one-year, non-interest bearing note payable for $10,000. The cash price of the equipment was $9,100.
3. During December a competitor filed a lawsuit against the company alleging violation of antitrust regulations. If the company loses the suit, it is estimated damages will exceed $1 million.
4. The December payroll totaled $45,000, which will be paid on January 10. Employees accrue vacation benefits at the rate of 2% of monthly payroll. (Ignore payroll deductions and the employer's payroll tax expense.)
5. Sales for the month amounted to 700 units at $200 each, subject to a retail sales tax of 5%. Each unit carries a 90-day warranty requiring the company to repair or replace the unit if it becomes defective during the warranty period. The estimated cost to the company to honor the warranty is $45, and past experience has shown that approximately 3% of the units will be returned during the warranty period.

Required:

1. Record the external transactions and, where appropriate, the required adjusting entry at December 31. See the format on the next page.
2. Based on your entries in Requirement 1, present the current liability section of the balance sheet.

Requirement 1 (Journal entries)

Date	Accounts and Explanation	PR	Debit	Credit

Requirement 2 (Current liability section of balance sheet)

SOLUTIONS

I. Matching

1. D	5. O	9. B	13. C
2. F	6. J	10. K	14. L
3. N	7. E	11. M	15. G
4. H	8. A	12. I	

II. Multiple Choice

1.   B   Of the items listed, all are liabilities that are due within one year except for pensions which are an expense.

2.   D   The note payable is discounted (interest is taken out) when the loan is made. The bank subtracts the interest from the note's face amount and the borrower receives the net amount.

3.   C   A contingent liability is not an actual liability. It is a potential liability that depends on a future event arising out of a past transaction. Of the items listed, all except "lawsuit claims" are real liabilities.

4.   A   Recall that Cost of Goods Sold is the largest expense for a merchandising business. The efforts of employees are a significant part of doing business in service companies and, accordingly, Payroll is often the major expense.

5.   C   The FASB says to record an actual liability when 1) it is probable that the business has suffered a loss, and 2) its amount can be reasonable estimated.

6.   D   The Social Security tax has an upper limit that is set by law.

7.   C   Of the items listed, all are components of a payroll except for the "payroll petty cash fund" which is a nonexistent item.

8.   B   Of the items listed, only B is not a control for safeguarding cash in a payroll system.

9.   C   Federal income taxes are based on gross earnings, marital status, and number of withholding allowances.

10.   D   Notes payable are a known liability, all the others are estimated.

III. Completion

1. matching (Matching means to identify and measure all expenses incurred during the period and to "match" them against the revenue earned during that period.)
2. contra liability (It has a debit balance.)
3. disclosure (providing relevant information to outsiders)
4. gross earnings, marital status, number of withholding allowances claimed, length of pay period
5. yearly gross wages and deductions

6. employee; number of withholding allowances claimed
7. 941; quarterly
8. Federal Insurance Contribution Act
9. FICA and federal and state unemployment taxes
10. probable; reasonably estimated

IV. Daily Exercises

1.

	Paid by employee	Paid by employer
Charitable contributions	x	
Social Security tax	x	x
Federal income tax	x	
Unemployment tax		x
Union dues	x	
Medicare tax	x	x

(You may also be aware of employers who match charitable contributions of their employees.)

2.

K	A. Accounts Payable	K	G. Sales Tax Payable
K	B. Short-term Notes Payable	E or K	H. Liability for Vacation Pay
E or K	C. Property Taxes Payable	E	I. Postretirement Benefits
E	D. Warranty Liability	K	J. Interest Payable
K	E. Salaries Expense	E	K. Pension Premium Payable
E or K	F. Income Taxes Payable		

3.

Truck	12,000	
Note Payable		12,000
Interest Expense	120	
Interest Payable		120
($12,000 x 12% x 1/12)		
Note Payable	12,000	
Interest Payable	120	
Interest Expense	600	
Cash		12,720

4.

Truck	12,000	
Discount on Notes Payable	720	
Note Payable		12,720
Interest Expense	120	
Discount on Notes Payable		120
Notes Payable	12,720	
Interest Expense	600	
Discount on Note Payable		600
Cash		12,720

5.

Warranty Expense	105,000	
Estimated Warranty Payable		105,000
($4,200,000 x 2.5%)		
Estimated Warranty Payable	95	
Parts Inventory		75
Wage Expense		20

Study Tip: Note the cost of the employee's time to repair the item is included in the total debit to the estimated warranty payable account.

V. Exercises

1.

GENERAL JOURNAL

Date	Accounts and Explanation	PR	Debit	Credit
	Cash		12,000	
	Note Payable			12,000

Adjusting entry on December 31:

GENERAL JOURNAL

Date	Accounts and Explanation	PR	Debit	Credit
	Interest Expense		450	
	Interest Payable			450

2.

GENERAL JOURNAL

Date	Accounts and Explanation	PR	Debit	Credit
	Cash		19,200	
	Discount on Note Payable		800	
	Note Payable			20,000
	Discount = 20,000 x .12 x 120/360			

3.

GENERAL JOURNAL

Date	Accounts and Explanation	PR	Debit	Credit
	Cash		13,580	
	Discount on Note Payable		420	
	Note Payable			14,000
	Discount = Note Payable x .09 x 4 months			
	Cash + Discount = Note Payable			
	9,000 + (NP x .09 x 4/12) = NP			
	Note Payable = 14,000			

4.

GENERAL JOURNAL

Date	Accounts and Explanation	PR	Debit	Credit
	Sales Revenue		1,800	
	Sales Tax Payable			1,800
	Sales + Sales Tax = 31,800			
	Sales Tax = .06 x Sales			
	Sales = 30,000			

5.

GENERAL JOURNAL

Date	Accounts and Explanation	PR	Debit	Credit
	Wage Expense		520.00	
	Federal Income Tax Payable			87.00
	State Income Tax Payable			31.20
	Social Security Tax Payable			31.20
	Medicare Tax Payable			7.80
	United Giving Payable			15.00
	Wage Payable			355.80
	Wage Expense = (40 hrs x $10) + (8 hrs x $10 x 1.5)			
	= 400 + 120 = 520			

VI. Beyond the Numbers

1.

Date	Accounts and Explanation	PR	Debit	Credit
8/1	Note Receivable		12,000	
	Cash			12,000
12/31	Interest Receivable		450	
	Interest Earned			450
8/1	Cash		13,080	
	Note Receivable			12,000
	Interest Receivable			450
	Interest Earned			630

2.

Date	Accounts and Explanation	PR	Debit	Credit
10/2	Note Receivable		20,000	
	Discount on Notes Receivable			800
	Cash			19,200
12/31	Discount on Notes Receivable		600	
	Interest Earned			600
1/30	Cash		20,000	
	Note Receivable			20,000
	Discount on Notes Receivable		200	
	Interest Earned			200

Study Tip: If it is a Note Payable to the maker, then it must be a Note Receivable to the payee. Similarly, if it is a Discount on Notes Payable to the maker, then it is a Discount on Notes Receivable to the payee. The latter would be a contra-asset account.

VII. Demonstration Problems

Demonstration Problem #1 Solved and Explained

Requirement 1

	Gross Pay	
Glen Green	$5,800	(Salary)
Rose Pinard	625	(40 hrs x 10 + 15 overtime hrs x $15)
Janice Flowers	350	(35 hrs x $10 per hr.)
Total Gross Pay	$6,775	

Gross pay represents an employee's total earnings before any amounts (for taxes, contributions, and so on) are deducted from the employee's paycheck.

Net pay

Explanation	Green	Pinard	Flowers
Gross pay	5,800.00	625.00	350.00
Less:			
Federal tax	1,725.00	90.00	26.00
State tax	315.00	28.00	12.00
Withheld Social Security tax			
($2,600 x .06)	156.00		
($625 x .06)		37.50	
($350 x .06)			21.00
Medicare tax (1.5%)	87.00	9.38	5.25
Voluntary Contributions:			
United Giving	20.00		
U.S. Savings Bonds		10.00	
Net pay	3,497.00	450.12	285.75

Social Security taxes withheld from wages are subject to a base of $65,000. Wages earned below the base are taxed at 6%, amounts over the base rate are not subject to the tax. Since Pinard and Flowers have cumulative earnings of $6,800 and $4,400, respectively, all of their December wages are subject to the 6% tax. Prior to December, Green's cumulative earnings totaled $62,400. As a result, only $2,600 ($65,000 - $62,400) of the $5,800 earned in December is subject to the Social Security tax. The remaining $3,200 earned by Green exceeds the base and is therefore not subject to the tax. There is no earnings limit to the Medicare tax.

Requirement 2

GENERAL JOURNAL

Date	Accounts and Explanation	PR	Debit	Credit
a.	Sales Salary Expense		5,800	
	Office Salary Expense		975	
	Employee Federal Income Tax Payable			1,841
	(1,725 + 90 + 26)			
	Employee State Income Tax Payable			355
	(315 + 28 + 12)			
	Social Security Tax Payable			214.50
	(156 + 37.50 + 21)			
	Medicare Tax Payable			101.63
	(87 + 9.38 + 5.25)			
	United Giving Contribution Payable			20.00
	U.S. Savings Bonds Payable			10.00
	Salary Payable to Employees			4,232.87

b.	Payroll Tax Expense		350.23	
	Social Security Tax Payable			214.50
	(156 + 37.50 + 33)			
	Medicare Tax Payable			101.63
	(87 + 9.38 + 5.25)			
	State Unemployment Tax Payable			29.70
	(200 + 350) x .054			
	Federal Unemployment Tax Payable			4.40
	(200 + 350) x .008			

The cost of payroll to an employer will often exceed the actual compensation earned by employees by a substantial amount. The employer must match the employee contribution to FICA tax, as well as pay both the federal and state unemployment taxes. In addition numerous fringe benefits (often in the form of pension contributions and medical and life insurance) can greatly increase the cost of payroll.

Note that in many cases, the company does not incur an expense for a tax or voluntary contribution, but rather acts merely as a collector for the federal or state government (or as a collector for another third party). The only taxes and other collections or payments that ultimately result in an expense to the business are those paid by the business, such as employer FICA tax (both Social Security and Medicare), federal and state unemployment tax, and pension contribution.

Current Month's Compensation Subject to Tax

	Green	Pinard	Flowers
FICA: Social Security			
$65,000 base - $62,400	2,600		
$65,000 base - $6,800		625	
$65,000 base - $4,400			350
FICA: Medicare	5,250	625	350
State Unemployment Tax			
$7,000 - $62,400	none		
$7,000 - $6,800		200	
$7,000 - $4,400			350
Federal Unemployment Tax			
$7,000 - $62,400	none		
$7,000 - $6,800		200	
$7,000 - $4,400			350

Note that Pinard earned compensation of $625, and only the amount of earnings below the $7,000 base is subject to the unemployment taxes. Since her earnings after being paid for December total $7,675, only her wages under the base ($7,000 - $6,800) are subject to the taxes.

GENERAL JOURNAL

Date	Accounts and Explanation	PR	Debit	Credit
c.	Pension Expense (5,800 + 625 + 350) x .06		406.50	
	Employee Benefit Payable			406.50
d.	Salary Payable to Employees		4,232.87	
	Cash			4,232.87
e.	Employee Federal Income Tax Payable		1,841.00	
	Employee State Income Tax Payable		355.00	
	Social Security Tax Payable (214.50 + 214.50)		429.00	
	Medicare Tax Payable (101.63 + 101.63)		203.26	
	State Unemployment Tax Payable		29.70	
	Federal Unemployment Tax Payable		4.40	
	Cash			2,862.36
	United Giving Contribution Payable		20.00	
	U.S. Savings Bonds Payable		10.00	
	Employee Benefit Payable		406.50	
	Cash			436.50

Requirement 3

The total cost of the payroll includes gross salaries and wages plus all additional costs to the employer in the form of either fringe benefits or payroll related taxes paid by the employer. Summarized in entries (a) to (c) above, total December payroll for Green Stems, Inc. totaled $7,531.73 computed as follows:

Total December Payroll

Gross wages:	
Sales salary	$5,800.00
Office salary	975.00
Payroll tax expense (entry b)	350.23
Pension fringe benefit (entry c)	406.50
	7,531.73

Total cash spent by the business is also $7,531.73, as summarized by entries (d) to (f).

Demonstration Problem #2 Solved and Explained

Requirement 1

1. 12/1   Cash   15,000

                  Notes Payable   15,000

    12/31   Interest Expense   112.50

                  Interest Payable   112.50

The company needs to accrue interest expense for December, calculated as follows:

$$\$15,000 \times .09 \times 1/12 = \$112.50$$

2. 12/16   Equipment   9,100

                  Discount on Notes Payable   900

                        Notes Payable   10,000

Since the cash price of the equipment on the purchase date is $9,100, the $900 difference is clearly the interest expense contained in the face of the note. This amount is debited to a Discount account.

    12/31   Interest Expense   37.50

                  Discount on Notes Payable   37.50

Since the $900 discount applies to the life of the note (one year), a portion needs to be transferred to interest expense for December, calculated as follows:

$$\$900 \times 15/360 = \$37.50$$

3. No entry required. However, the footnotes to the balance sheet should contain information about this lawsuit. This is an example of a contingent liability.

4. 12/31   Salary Expense   45,000

                  Salary Payable   45,000

              Vacation Pay Expense   900

                  Estimated Vacation Pay Liability   900

The matching principle requires that the additional expense of vacation pay be included with December's other expenses. The calculation is $45,000 × .02 = $900. As employees claim their vacation pay, the entry is:

              Estimated Vacation Pay Liability   XX

                  Cash   XX

(Of course, vacation pay is subject to taxes just as salaries are.)

5.   Accounts Receivable   147,000
                 Sales   140,000
                 Sales Tax Payable   7,000

12/31   Warranty Expense   945
                 Estimated Warranty Liability   945

The warranty expense is based on the cost to the company of repairing or replacing each unit. Therefore, the estimate is calculated as follows:

Unit sales × estimate × cost to repair/replace
700 × .03 × $45 = $945

Study Tip: Estimating warranty expense is another example of the matching principle.

Requirement 2 (Current liability section of balance sheet)

Notes Payable ($15,000 + $10,000)	$25,000.00	
Less: Discount on Notes Payable ($900 - $37.50)	862.50	$24,137.50
Interest Payable		112.50
Salaries Payable		45,000.00
Vacation Pay Liability		900.00
Sales Tax Payable		7,000.00
Warranty Liability		945.00
Total Current Liabilities		$78,095.00

Chapter 12—Accounting for Partnerships

CHAPTER OVERVIEW

In Chapter 1 you were introduced to the three legal forms of business organization: sole proprietorships, partnerships, and corporation. Since then, the focus has been on either sole proprietorships or corporations. We now turn our attention to the third type, partnerships. This topic can be covered in one chapter because the differences are not all that great and most of the topics covered so far apply to all three forms. The learning objectives for this chapter are to

1. Identify the characteristics of a partnership.
2. Account for partner's initial investments in a partnership.
3. Allocate profits and losses to the partners by different methods.
4. Account for the admission of a new partner to the business.
5. Account for the withdrawal of a partner from the business.
6. Account for the liquidation of a partnership.
7. Prepare partnership financial statements.

CHAPTER REVIEW

Objective 1 - Identify the characteristics of a partnership.

A **partnership** is an association of two or more persons who are co-owners of a business for profit. Partners frequently draw up a **partnership agreement**, also called **articles of partnership**. This agreement is a contract between the partners which sets forth the duties and rights of each partner.

The **characteristics of a partnership** are:

1. **Limited life**. The addition or withdrawal of a partner dissolves the partnership.
2. **Mutual agency**. Every partner has the authority to obligate the business to contracts within the scope of regular business operations.
3. **Unlimited liability**. If the partnership cannot pay its debts, the partners are personally responsible for payment.
4. **Co-ownership**. Assets of the business become the joint property of the partnership.
5. **No partnership income taxes**. The net income of a partnership is divided among the partners, who individually pay income taxes on their portions of the partnership's income.
6. **Partners' owner's equity accounts**. Separate owner's equity accounts will be set up for each partner, both a Capital account and Withdrawal account.

Exhibit 12-2 in your text summarizes the advantages and disadvantages of partnerships.

Objective 2 - Account for partner's initial investments in a partnership.

Partners may invest assets and liabilities in a business. The simplest investment to account for is cash:

Cash	XX	
Partner's Name, Capital		XX

Assets other than cash are recorded at their current market value. Suppose Craine invests land in a partnership. The land cost $60,000 several years ago and has a current market value of $95,000. The correct entry on the partnership's books is:

Land	95,000	
Craine, Capital		95,000

Objective 3 - Allocate profits and losses to the partners by different methods.

If there is no partnership agreement, or the agreement does not specify how profits and losses are to be divided, then the partners share profits and losses equally. If the agreement specifies a method for sharing profits, but not losses, then losses are shared in the same manner as profits.

Several methods exist to allocate profits and losses. Partners may share profits and losses according to a stated fraction or percentage. If the partnership agreement allocates 2/3 of the profits and losses to Chang, and 1/3 to Estrada, then the entry to record the allocation of $60,000 of income is:

Income Summary	60,000	
Chang, Capital		40,000
Estrada, Capital		20,000

The partnership agreement may provide that profits and losses be allocated in proportion to the partner's capital contributions to the business. To find the income allocated to a particular partner, use this formula:

$$\text{Income allocated to a partner} = \frac{\text{Partner's capital}}{\text{Total capital}} \times \text{Net income}$$

Suppose Chang and Estrada have the capital balances listed below:

Chang, Capital	240,000
Estrada, Capital	160,000
Total Capital balances	400,000

Partnership income of $60,000 will be allocated as follows:

Chang:	(240,000 / 400,000) 60,000 =	36,000
Estrada:	(160,000 / 400,000) 60,000 =	24,000
Total income allocated to partners		60,000

The entry to record the allocation of profits is:

Income Summary	60,000	
Chang, Capital		36,000
Estrada, Capital		24,000

Sharing of profits and losses may also be allocated based on a combination of capital contributions, service to the business, and/or interest on capital contributions. The important point to remember is to follow the exact order of allocation specified by the partnership agreement.

When a loss occurs the process does not change. Simply follow the terms of the agreement (or divide the loss equally in the absence of an agreement) in the order specified.

Partners generally make periodic withdrawals of cash from a partnership. If Estrada withdraws $5,000 from the partnership, the entry is:

Estrada, Drawing	5,000	
Cash		5,000

The drawing accounts must be closed to the capital accounts at the end of the period. If Estrada's $5,000 withdrawal is the only withdrawal during the period, the closing entry is:

Estrada, Capital	5,000	
Estrada, Drawing		5,000

Objective 4 - Account for the admission of a new partner to the business.

Remember that a partnership is dissolved when a new partner is added or an existing partner withdraws. Often a new partnership is immediately formed to replace the old partnership. CPA firms and law firms often admit new partners and have existing partners retire during the course of a year.

A new partner may be admitted into an existing partnership either by purchasing a present partner's interest or by investing in the partnership. The new partner must be approved by all the current partners in order to participate in the business.

When **purchasing a partnership interest**, the new partner pays the old partner directly, according to the terms of the purchase agreement. The purchase transaction has no effect on the partnership's books. The only entry the partnership will make is to close the old partner's capital account and open the new partner's capital account:

Old Partner, Capital	XX	
New Partner, Capital		XX

A person may also be admitted to a partnership by directly **investing in the partnership**. This investment can be a simple investment, and is recorded as:

Cash and Other assets	XX	
New Partner, Capital		XX

The new partner's interest in the business will equal:

$$\text{New partner's interest} = \frac{\text{New partner's capital}}{\text{Total capital}}$$

Note that sharing of profits and losses is determined by the new partnership agreement, and not by the proportion of total capital allotted to the new partner .

Successful partnerships frequently require incoming partners to pay a **bonus** to existing partners. In this situation, the incoming partner will pay more for a portion of the partnership interest than the amount of capital he receives. The difference, which is a bonus to the existing partners, is computed by a three-step calculation:

1) Total capital before new partner's investment
    + New partner's investment
    = Total capital after new partner's investment

2) New partner's capital = Total capital after new partner's investment new partner's interest in the partnership

3) Bonus to existing partners = New partner's investment - New partner's capital

The entry on the partnership books to record the transaction is:

Cash	XX	
New Partner, Capital		XX
Old Partners, Capital		XX

Note that the bonus paid by the new partner is credited to the old partners' Capital account. The allocation of the bonus to existing partners is based on the partnership agreement of the existing partners.

In some cases, a potential new partner may bring substantial future benefits to a partnership, such as a well-known reputation. In this situation, the existing partners may offer the newcomer a partnership share that includes a bonus. The calculation is similar to the calculation for a bonus to the existing partners:

1) Total capital before new partner's investment
    + New partner's investment
    = Total capital after new partner's investment

2)   New partner's capital = Total capital after new partner's investment
           New partner's interest in the partnership

3)   Bonus to new partner = New partner's investment - New partner's
           investment

The entry on the partnership books to record the transaction is:

Cash and Other Assets	XX	
Old Partners, Capital	XX	
New Partner, Capital		XX

Note that the bonus paid to the new partner is debited to the old partners' Capital accounts. The allocation of the bonus to the new partner is based on the partnership agreement of the existing partners.

Objective 5 - Account for the withdrawal of a partner from the business.

Partners may **withdraw from a partnership** due to retirement, partnership disputes, or other reasons. The withdrawing partner may sell his or her interest or may receive the appropriate portion of the business directly from the partnership in the form of cash, other partnership assets, or notes.

The first step is to determine whether the partnership assets are to be valued at book value or market value. If assets are to be valued at market value, they must be revalued, often by an independent appraiser. Increases in asset values are debited to asset accounts and credited to the partners capital accounts (according to the profit-and-loss sharing ratio). Decreases in asset values are debited to the partners' capital accounts and credited to asset accounts. The revalued assets then become the new book value of the assets.

A partner may withdraw from a partnership at book value, at less than book value, or at more than book value. (Remember that book value may or may not be equal to current market value, depending upon whether the assets have been revalued or not.) A partner willing to withdraw at less than book value may be eager to leave the partnership. A partner withdrawing at more than book value may be collecting a bonus from the remaining partners, who may be eager to have the partner withdraw.

Withdrawal at book value is recorded as:

Withdrawing Partner, Capital	XX	
Cash, Other Assets, or Note Payable		XX

Withdrawal at less than book value is recorded by:

Withdrawing Partner, Capital	XX	
Cash, Other Assets, or Note Payable		XX
Remaining Partners, Capital		XX

When a partner withdraws at less than book value, the difference between the withdrawing partner's capital and the payment to the withdrawing partner is allocated to the remaining partners based on the new profit-and-loss ratio.

Withdrawal at more than book value is recorded by:

Withdrawing Partner, Capital	XX	
Remaining Partners, Capital	XX	
Cash, Other Assets, or Note Payable		XX

When a partner withdraws at more than book value, the difference between the payment to the withdrawing partner and the withdrawing partner's capital is allocated to the remaining partners based on the new profit-and-loss ratio.

The death of a partner also dissolves the partnership. The books are closed to determine the deceased partner's capital balance on the date of death. Settlement with the partner's estate is made according to the partnership agreement. The entry is:

Deceased Partner, Capital	XX	
Liability Payable to Estate		XX

Objective 6 - Account for the liquidation of a partnership.

Liquidation is the process of going out of business and involves three basic steps:

1. Selling the partnership assets and allocating gains or losses to the partners' capital accounts based on the profit-and-loss ratio.
2. Paying the partnership liabilities.
3. Distributing the remaining cash to the partners based on their capital balances.

When selling assets, gains result in credits (increases) to partners' capital accounts. Losses result in debits (decreases) to partners' capital accounts.

The general worksheet for liquidation of a partnership is:

	Cash	+	Noncash Assets	=	Liabilities	+	Capital	
Balances before sale of assets	XX		XX		XX		XX	
Sale of assets and sharing of							XX	if gain
gains and (losses)	XX		(XX)				(XX)	if loss
Balances after sale of assets	XX		-0-				XX	
Payment of liabilities	(XX)				(XX)			
Balances after payment of liabilities	XX		-0-		-0-		XX	
Disbursement of cash to partners	(XX)						(XX)	
Ending balances	-0-		-0-		-0-		-0-	

Occasionally, allocation of losses on the sale of assets results in a capital deficiency for one or more partners. The deficient partner should contribute personal assets to eliminate the deficiency. If not, the deficiency must be allocated to the remaining partners.

Objective 7 - Prepare partnership financial statements.

Partnership financial statements are similar to the financial statements of a proprietorship. The exceptions are that a partnership income statement includes a section showing the division of net income to the partners, and the owners' equity section of the balance sheet includes accounts for each partner.

TEST YOURSELF

All the self-testing materials in this chapter focus on information and procedures that your instructor is likely to test in quizzes and examinations.

I. Matching   *Match each numbered term with its lettered definition.*

_____ 1. partnership agreement or articles of partnership
_____ 2. capital deficiency
_____ 3. unlimited personal liability
_____ 4. Dissolution
_____ 5. Liquidation
_____ 6. mutual agency
_____ 7. bonus
_____ 8. limited partner
_____ 9. general partner

A. a contract among partners specifying such things as the name, location, and nature of the business; the name, capital investment, and the duties of each partner; and the method of sharing profits and losses by the partners
B. a debit balance in a partner's capital account
C. ending of a partnership
D. the ability of every partner to bind the business to a contract within the scope of the partnership's regular business operations
E. the process of going out of business
F. when partnership (or a proprietorship) cannot pay its debts with business assets, the partners (or the proprietor) must use personal assets to meet the debt
G. a partner in a limited partnership whose liability is unlimited
H. a partner in a limited partnership whose liability is limited
I. results when assets contributed (or withdrawn) do not equal the amount credited (or debited) to a partner's capital account

II. Multiple Choice   *Circle the best answer.*

1. Which of the following provisions will *not* be found in the partnership agreement?

   A. liquidation procedures
   B. profit-and-loss ratio
   C. withdrawals allowed to partners
   D. dividends payable to partners

2. Which of the following does *not* result in dissolution of a partnership?

   A. addition of a new partner
   B. withdrawal of a partner
   C. marriage of a partner
   D. death of a partner

3. Assets and liabilities contributed by a partner to a partnership are recorded at:

   A. expected future value
   B. fair market value
   C. original cost
   D. book value

4. Profits and losses are usually shared by partners according to

  A. verbal agreements
  B. the balance in partners' equity accounts
  C. partners' personal wealth
  D. the partnership agreement

5. When a partner takes money out of the partnership, the partner's:

  A. drawing is credited
  B. drawing is debited
  C. capital is debited
  D. capital is credited

6. A new partner may be admitted to a partnership:

  A. only by investing in the partnership
  B. only by purchasing a partner's interest
  C. by purchasing common stock of the partnership
  D. either by investing in the partnership or by purchasing a partner's interest

7. In a partnership liquidation, a gain from the sale of assets is allocated to the:

  A. payment of partnership liabilities
  B. partners based on their capital balances
  C. partner with the lowest capital balance
  D. partners based on their profit-and-loss ratio

8. If a partner has a debit balance in his capital account and is personally insolvent, then the other partners:

  A. absorb the deficiency based on their personal wealth
  B. absorb the deficiency based on their capital balances
  C. absorb the deficiency based on their profit-and-loss ratio
  D. sue the insolvent partner's spouse

9. ABC partnership shares profits and losses in a 5:4:3 ratio respectively. This means:

  A. partner A receives 5/12 of the profits
  B. partner A receives 5/9 of the profits
  C. partner B receives 1/4 of the profits
  D. partner C receives 1/3 of the profits

10. In a limited partnership, which of the following is false?

  A. there must be more than one partner
  B. there must be at least one general partner
  C. all partners have unlimited liability
  D. some partners have limited liability

III. Completion   *Complete each of the following statements.*

1. If the partnership agreement does not specify a profit-and-loss ratio, profits and losses are allocated _____.

2. The five characteristics of a partnership are: 1) _____,
   2) _____, 3) _____,
   4) _____, and 5) _____.

3. The difference between a partnership and sole proprietorship is that a partnership has _____ owners, while a sole proprietorship has _____ owner.

4. _____ refers to the ability of any partner to contract on behalf of the partnership.

5. A _____ occurs when a new partner is admitted or an existing partner leaves a partnership.

6. A partnership undergoes _____ when it ceases operations and settles all its affairs.

7. A debit balance in a partner's capital account is called _____.

8. The steps in liquidating a partnership are:

1)_____

2)_____

3)_____

4)_____

9. A partner with limited liability is called a _____.

10. When liquidating, cash is distributed to the partners according to the _____.

IV. Daily Exercises

1. Two sole proprietors, Wells Co. and Bank Co., decide to form a partnership called Wells Bank. Wells will contribute the following to the proprietorship:

Cash	8,000
Inventory	7,200
Equipment	11,700
Liabilities	6,100

The current market value of the equipment is $9,000 and the current market value of the inventory is $7,600. Record the journal entry to reflect Wells' investment.

Accounts and Explanation	Debit	Credit

2. The ACE partnership reported $45,000 net income its first year of operations If the partners neglected to agree on the distribution of profits, how much should partners A, C, and E receive?

3. Refer to the information in Daily Exercise #2 above, but assume the partners agreed to a $12,000 per partner salary allowance, with any balance divided 3:2:1 among A, C, and E. Calculate the amount owed to each partner.

4. Review the information in Daily Exercises #3 above, but assume the first year resulted in net income of $6,000. Calculate the amount A, C, and E should receive.

5. Record the journal entry for Daily Exercise #4 above.

Accounts and Explanation	Debit	Credit

6. A partnership has decided to liquidate. After selling the assets and paying the debts, $9,000 in liabilities remain outstanding. To whom should the creditors look for payment?

7. Assume the same information in Daily Exercise #5, except the partnership is a limited partnership. How would your answer change?

V. Exercises

1. Lewis and Clark formed a partnership. Lewis contributed cash of $9,000 and land with a fair market value of $65,000 that had cost $14,000. The partnership also assumed Lewis's note payable of $24,000. Clark contributed $20,000 in cash, equipment with a fair market value of $14,000 that had cost $22,000, and the partnership assumed his accounts receivable of $3,200.

Make journal entries to show each partner's contribution to the business.

Date	Accounts and Explanation	PR	Debit	Credit

2. Price and Cost formed a partnership. Price invested $75,000 and Cost invested $50,000. Price devotes most of his time on the road developing the business, while Cost devotes some of his time to managing the home office and the rest of his time watching television. They have agreed to share profits as follows:

- The first $50,000 of profits is allocated based on the partner's capital contribution.
- The next $50,000 of profits is allocated 3/4 to Price and 1/4 to Cost based on their service to the partnership.
- Any remaining amount is allocated equally.

A. If the partnership profits are $110,000, how much will be allocated to Price, and how much will be allocated to Cost?

B. If the partnership has a loss of $70,000, how much will be allocated to Price, and how much will be allocated to Cost?

C. If the partnership profits are $62,000, how much will be allocated to Price, and how much will be allocated to Cost?

A.

	Price	Cost	Total

B.

	Price	Cost	Total

C.

	Price	Cost	Total

3. Keith and Vince are partners in a landscaping business. Their capital balances are $24,000 and $16,000 respectively. They share profits and losses equally. They admit Amy to a one-fourth interest with a cash investment of $8,000. Make the journal entry to show the admission of Amy to the partnership.

Date	Accounts and Explanation	PR	Debit	Credit

4. Anne, Barbara, and Cathy are partners with capital balances of $15,000, $45,000, and $30,000 respectively. They share profits and losses equally. Barbara decides to retire.

A. Make the journal entry to show Barbara's retirement if she is allowed to withdraw $25,000 in cash.

Date	Accounts and Explanation	PR	Debit	Credit

B. Make the journal entry to show Barbara's retirement if she is allowed to withdraw $45,000 in cash.

Date	Accounts and Explanation	PR	Debit	Credit

C. Make the journal entry to show Barbara's retirement if she is allowed to withdraw $55,000 in cash.

Date	Accounts and Explanation	PR	Debit	Credit

5. The following balance sheet information is given for Three Ts Company:

Cash	16,000	Liabilities	28,000
Noncash assets	56,000	Tom, Capital	6,000
		Tran, Capital	24,000
		Tony, Capital	14,000
Total assets	72,000	Total liabilities and capital	72,000

Tom, Tran, and Tony use a profit and loss ratio of 3:4:1, respectively. Assume that any partner with a deficit in his or her capital account is insolvent.

Prepare the journal entries for liquidation assuming the noncash assets are sold for $20,000.

Date	Accounts and Explanation	PR	Debit	Credit

VI. Beyond the Numbers

Review the information in Exercises 5. Assume all information is the same except Tom is a limited partner. Prepare journal entries to record the liquidation.

Date	Accounts and Explanation	PR	Debit	Credit

VII. Demonstration Problems

Demonstration Problem #1

The partnership of Russell and Stoner is considering admitting Wayne as a partner on April 1, 1999. The partnership general ledger includes the following balances on that date:

Cash	40,000	Total liabilities	50,000
Other assets	85,000	Russell, Capital	25,000
		Stoner, Capital	50,000
Total assets	125,000	Total liabilities and capital	125,000

Russell's share of profit and losses is 1/3 and Stoner's share is 2/3.

Required:

1. Assume that Wayne pays Stoner $75,000 to acquire Stoner's interest of the business, and that Russell has approved Wayne as a new partner.

   a. Prepare the journal entries for the transfer of partner's equity on the partnership books.
   b. Prepare the partnership balance sheet immediately after Wayne is admitted as a partner.

2. Suppose Wayne becomes a partner by investing $75,000 cash to acquire a one-fourth interest in the business.

   a. Prepare a schedule to compute Wayne's capital balance. Record Wayne's investment in the business.
   b. Prepare the partnership balance sheet immediately after Wayne is admitted as a partner.

Requirement 1

a. (Journal entry)

Date	Accounts and Explanation	PR	Debit	Credit

b.

Russell, Stoner, and Wayne
Balance Sheet
April 1, 1999

Requirement 2

a. Computation of Wayne's capital balance:

(Journal entry)

Date	Accounts and Explanation	PR	Debit	Credit

b. (Balance Sheet)

Russell, Stoner, and Wayne
Balance Sheet
April, 1999

Demonstration Problem #2

The partnership of B, T, and U is liquidating. The partnership agreement allocated profits to the partners in the ratio of 3:2:1. In liquidation, the noncash assets were sold in a single transaction for $120,000 on August 31, 1999. The partnership paid the liabilities the same day. The partnership accounts are presented at the top of the liquidation schedule which follows.

1. Complete the schedule summarizing the liquidation transactions. See the format on the next page. You may wish to refer to the partnership liquidation exhibits in the text. Assume that U invests cash of $4,000 in the partnership in partial settlement of any capital account deficiency. This cash is distributed to the other partners. The other partners must absorb the remainder of the capital deficiency.
2. Journalize the liquidation transactions.
3. Post the liquidation entries.

Requirement 1 (Summary of liquidation transactions)

	Cash	+	Noncash Assets	=	Liabilities	+	Capital B (1/2)	+	T (1/3)	+	U (1/6)
Balance before sale of assets	30,000		240,000		120,000		90,000		50,000		10,000
a) Sale of assets and sharing of loss											
Balances											
b) Payment of liabilities											
Balances											
c) U's investment of cash to share part of his deficiency											
Balances											
d) Sharing of deficiency by remaining partners in ratio of 3/5 to 2/5											
Balances											
e) Distribution of cash to partners											
Balances											

Requirement 2 (Journal entries to record the liquidation transactions)

a.

Date	Accounts and Explanation	PR	Debit	Credit

b.

Date	Accounts and Explanation	PR	Debit	Credit

c.

Date	Accounts and Explanation	PR	Debit	Credit

d.

Date	Accounts and Explanation	PR	Debit	Credit

e.

Date	Accounts and Explanation	PR	Debit	Credit

Requirement 3 (Post the liquidation transactions)

Cash	
30,000	

Noncash Assets	
240,000	

Liabilities	
	120,000

B, Capital	
	90,000

T, Capital	
	50,000

U, Capital	
	10,000

SOLUTIONS

I. Matching

1. A	5. E	9. G
2. B	6. D	
3. F	7. I	
4. C	8. H	

II. Multiple Choice

1. D Dividends are distributions of earnings paid by corporations to their shareholders. It is a term that is strictly applicable to corporate accounting and as such cannot apply to partnership accounting.

2. C The marriage of a partner is an event of the partner's personal life and has no direct bearing on the partnership entity. All of the other items listed cause a dissolution of the partnership.

3. B Using fair market value is appropriate to accurately measure exactly what each partner is bringing into the partnership.

4. D The partnership agreement can specify the distribution of profits and losses in any manner to which the partners have agreed.

5. B Withdrawing money from the partnership requires a credit to cash which is balanced with a debit to the partner's Drawing account. The balance of the partner's Drawing account will be closed to his Capital account at the end of the period.

6. D Of the items listed, answer C "purchasing common stock of the partnership" is inappropriate since partnerships do not have stock; answers A and B are incorrect because of the use of the word "only" in the answers.

7. D Gains and losses incurred in liquidation are distributed as are any other gains and losses, in accordance with the partnership agreement.

8. C The deficiency in a partner's capital account balance is distributed as if it were a loss, in accordance with the partnership agreement.

9. A To determine a partner's fractional share, create a denominator by summing the integers (5 + 4 + 3 = 12) and use the partner's ratio as the numerator. Thus, A receives 5/12, B receives 4/12 or 1/3, and C receives 3/12 or 1/4.

10. C The key distinction is the limitation of liability by at least one of the partners, who is identified as a limited partner.

III. Completion

1. equally
2. limited life, mutual agency, unlimited liability, co-ownership of property, no partnership income taxes
3. two or more, one
4. mutual agency
5. dissolution
6. liquidation
7. deficit
8. close the books, sell the assets, pay the debts, distribute the cash (order is important)
9. limited partner
10. the balance in the capital accounts (*not* the profit/loss ratio)

IV. Daily Exercises

1.

Cash	8,000	
Inventory	7,600	
Equipment	9,000	
Liabilities		6,100
Wells, Capital		18,500

Assets contributed are recorded at their current market value. Wells's net investment is $18,500, the difference between the value of the assets ($8,000 + $7,600 + $9,000) less the liabilities.

2. Each partner receives an equal share. When the partners fail to specify, the distribution of profits (and losses) is always equal.

3.

	Partners			Amount
	A	C	E	45,000
Salary Allowance	12,000	12,000	12,000	(36,000)
Balance				9,000
3:2:1	4,500	3,000	1,500	(9,000)
	16,500	15,000	13,500	0

Proof: $16,500 + $15,000 + $13,500 = $45,000

Study Tip: After the calculating, always verify the individual amounts sum back to the original amount.

4.

		Partners		Amount
	A	C	E	6,000
Salary Allowance	12,000	12,000	12,000	(36,000)
Balance				(30,000)
3:2:1	(15,000)	(10,000)	(5,000)	(30,000)
	(3,000)	2,000	7,000	6,000

Proof: $-3,000 + $2,000 + $7,000 = $6,000

5.

A, Capital	3,000	
Income Summary	6,000	
C, Capital		2,000
E, Capital		7,000

6. The partnership's creditors can look to any of the partners for payment. In a general partnership, each partner has unlimited personal liability for partnership's debts. Creditors would be wise to enforce their claims against the partner with the largest net worth.

7. In a limited partnerships, two classes of partners exist—general and limited. The liability of a limited partner extends only to the amount invested. The fact that liabilities remain after all the assets have been sold and the cash proceeds distributed to creditors indicates the limited partners' obligations have been met. Therefore, the creditors can look only to the general partner(s) for payment.

V. Exercises

1.

GENERAL JOURNAL

Date	Accounts and Explanation	PR	Debit	Credit
	Land		65,000	
	Cash		9,000	
	Notes Payable			24,000
	Lewis, Capital			50,000
	Cash		20,000	
	Equipment		14,000	
	Account Receivable		3,200	
	Clark, Capital			37,200

2.

A.

	Price	Cost	Total
Total net income			110,000
Sharing of first $50,000 of net income, based on capital contribution:			
Price (75,000/125,000 50,000)	30,000		
Cost (50,000/125,000 50,000)		20,000	
Total			50,000
Net income remaining for allocation			60,000
Sharing of the next $50,000 based on service:			
Price (3/4 50,000)	37,500		
Cost (1/4 50,000)		12,500	
Total			50,000
Net income remaining for allocation			10,000
Remainder shared equally:			
Price (1/2 10,000)	5,000		
Cost (1/2 10,000)		5,000	
Total			10,000
Net income remaining for allocation			-0-
Net income allocated to the partners	72,500	37,500	110,000

B.

	Price	Cost	Total
Total net income (loss)			(70,000)
Sharing of first $50,000 of net income (loss), based on capital contribution:			
Price (50,000/125,000 50,000)	(30,000)		
Cost (50,000/125,000 50,000)		(20,000)	
Total			(50,000)
Net income (loss) remaining for allocation			(20,000)
Sharing of the remainder based on service:			
Price (3/4 20,000)	(15,000)		
Cost (1/4 20,000)		(5,000)	
Total			(20,000)
Net income (loss) remaining for allocation			-0-
Net income (loss) allocated to the partners	(45,000)	(25,000)	(70,000)

C.

	Price	Cost	Total
Total net income			62,000
Sharing of first $50,000 of net income, based on capital contribution:			
Price (50,000/125,000 50,000)	30,000		
Cost (50,000/125,000 50,000)		20,000	
Total			50,000
Net income remaining for allocation			12,000
Sharing of the remainder based on service:			
Price (3/4 12,000)	9,000		
Cost (1/4 12,000)		3,000	
Total			12,000
Net income remaining for allocation			-0-
Net income allocated to the partners	39,000	23,000	62,000

3. Total new partnerships equity is $48,000 ($24,000 + $16,000 + $8,000). One fourth of $48,000 is $12,000.

Date	Accounts and Explanation	PR	Debit	Credit
	Cash		8,000	
	Keith, Capital [1/2 (12,000 - 8,000)]		2,000	
	Vince, Capital		2,000	
	Amy, Capital [1/4 (24,000 + 16,000 + 8,000)]			12,000

4.

A.

Date	Accounts and Explanation	PR	Debit	Credit
	Barbara, Capital		45,000	
	Cash			25,000
	Anne, Capital			10,000
	Cathy, Capital			10,000

B.

Date	Accounts and Explanation	PR	Debit	Credit
	Barbara, Capital		45,000	
	Cash			45,000

C.

Date	Accounts and Explanation	PR	Debit	Credit
	Barbara, Capital		45,000	
	Anne, Capital		5,000	
	Cathy, Capital		5,000	
	Cash			55,000

5.

Date	Accounts and Explanation	PR	Debit	Credit
	Cash		20,000	
	Tom, Capital		13,500	
	Tran, Capital		18,000	
	Tony, Capital		4,500	
	Noncash assets			56,000

Loss on sale = 36,000 (56,000 - 20,000). Therefore,

Tom = 36,000 × 3/8 = 13,500
Tran = 36,000 × 4/8 = 18,000
Tony = 36,000 × 1/8 = 4,500

	Liabilities		28,000	
	Cash			28,000
	Tran, Capital		6,000	
	Tony, Capital		1,500	
	Tom, Capital			7,500

Tom's deficit = 7,500 (6,000 - 13,500)
Tran = 4/5 × 7,500 = 6,000
Tony = 1/5 × 7,500 = 1,500

	Tony, Capital		8,000	
	Cash			8,000
	Tran's balance = 0 (24,000 - 18,000 - 6,000 = 0)			

VI. Beyond the Numbers

Date	Accounts and Explanation	PR	Debit	Credit
	Cash		20,000	
	Tom, Capital		6,000 *	
	Tran, Capital		24,000 **	
	Tony, Capital		6,000	
	Noncash Assets			56,000

* Because Tom is a limited partner, the amount of loss he must absorb is limited to the balance in his capital account.

** After debiting Tom's account for $6,000, the remaining loss is distributed between Tran and Tony, as follows:

Tran = 30,000 × 4/5 = 24,000
Tony = 30,000 × 1/5 = 6,000

	Liabilities		28,000	
	Cash			28,000
	Tony, Capital		8,000	
	Cash			8,000

VII. Demonstration Problems

Demonstration Problem #1 Solved and Explained

Requirement 1

a. July 1   Stoner, Capital   50,000   Debit closes Stoner's account
                      Wayne, Capital   50,000 Credit opens Wayne's account
              To transfer Stoner's equity in the partnership to Wayne.

Note that the book value of Stoner's capital account ($50,000) is transferred, not the price Wayne paid ($75,000) to buy into the business. Since the partnership received no cash from the transaction, the entry would be the same no matter what Wayne paid Stoner for the interest.

b.

Russell and Wayne
Balance Sheet
April 1, 1999

Cash	40,000	Total liabilities	50,000
Other assets	85,000	Russell, Capital	25,000
		Wayne, Capital	50,000
Total assets	$125,000	Total liabilities and capital	$125,000

Requirement 2

a. Computation of Wayne's capital balance:
    Partnership capital before Wayne is admitted
         (25,000 + 50,000) $ 75,000
    Wayne's investment in the partnership   75,000
    Partnership capital after Wayne is admitted $150,000
    Wayne's capital in the partnership
         (100,000 1/4) $ 37,500

Date	Accounts and Explanation	PR	Debit	Credit
April 1	Cash		75,000	
	Wayne, Capital			37,500
	Russell, Capital (1/3 of $37,500)			12,500
	Stoner, Capital (2/3 of $37,500)			25,000
	To admit Wayne as a partner with a one-fourth interest in the business.			

Note that Russell's capital account increased by $12,500 and Stoner's capital account increased by $25,000. These amounts represent Russell and Stoner's proportionate share of the $37,500 amount by which Wayne's $75,000 payment exceeded his $37,500 capital account credit. When a partner is admitted by investment in the partnership, often the investment exceeds the new partner's capital account credit, and the original partners share proportionately in the difference.

b.

Russell, Stoner, and Wayne
Balance Sheet
April, 1999

Cash (40,000 + 75,000)	$115,000	Total liabilities	$ 50,000
Other assets	85,000	Russell, Capital	37,500
		Stoner, Capital	75,000
		Wayne, Capital	37,500
Total assets	$200,000	Total liabilities and capital	$200,000

Points to Remember

1. Partners may specify any profit or loss sharing method they desire. Common arrangements include:

   a. Sharing equally - unless the partners agree otherwise, profits and losses are required by law to be divided equally
   b. Sharing based on a stated fraction
   c. Sharing based on capital contributions
   d. Sharing based on salaries and interest
   e. Sharing based on a combination of the above and/or other factors

> **Study Tip:** Be alert to problems requiring an allocation of profits and losses when the capital account balances are given for each partner, but nothing is specified about the sharing method. When the sharing method is not specified, each partner receives an equal share.

2. New partners are often admitted to established partnerships. Technically, a new partnership is formed to carry on the former partnership's business, and the old partnership ceases to exist (it is dissolved). Although the old partnership dissolves, the business is not normally terminated, nor are the assets liquidated.

> **Study Tip:** Be sure you can distinguish between the admission of a partner by purchase of a partner's interest (Requirement 1) and admission by making a direct investment in the proprietorship (Requirement 2).

Demonstration Problem #2 Solved and Explained

Requirement 1 (Summary of liquidation transactions)

	Cash	+	Noncash Assets	=	Liabilities	+	Capital B (1/2)	+	T (1/3)	+	U (1/6)
Balance before sale of assets	30,000		240,000		120,000		90,000		50,000		10,000
a) Sale of assets and sharing of loss	120,000		(240,000)				(60,000)		(40,000)		(20,000)
Balances	150,000		-0-		120,000		30,000		10,000		(10,000)
b) Payment of liabilities	(120,000)				(120,000)						
Balances	30,000		-0-		-0-		30,000		10,000		(10,000)
c) U's investment of cash to share part of his deficiency	4,000										4,000
Balances	34,000		-0-		-0-		30,000		10,000		(6,000)
d) Sharing of deficiency by remaining partners in ratio of 3/5 to 2/5							(3,600)		(2,400)		6,000
Balances	34,000		-0-		-0-		26,400		7,600		-0-
e) Distribution of cash to partners	(34,000)						(26,400)		(7,600)		
Balances	-0-		-0-		-0-		-0-		-0-		-0-

Requirement 2 (Journal entries to record the liquidation transactions)

a.

Date	Accounts and Explanation	PR	Debit	Credit
	Cash		120,000	
	B, Capital [(240,000 - 120,000) 3/6]		60,000	
	T, Capital [(240,000 - 80,000) 2/6]		40,000	
	U, Capital [(200,000 - 80,000) 1/6]		20,000	
	Noncash Assets			240,000
	To record the sale of noncash assets in liquidation, and to distribute loss to partners.			

b.

Date	Accounts and Explanation	PR	Debit	Credit
	Liabilities		120,000	
	Cash			120,000
	To pay liabilities in liquidation.			

c.

Date	Accounts and Explanation	PR	Debit	Credit
	Cash		4,000	
	U, Capital			4,000
	T's contribution to pay part of the capital deficiency in liquidation.			

After posting the entries above, U's capital account reveals a $6,000 deficiency, indicated by its debit balance:

U, Capital			
Loss on sale 20,000		Bal.	10,000
		Investment	4,000
Bal. 6,000			

d.

Date	Accounts and Explanation	PR	Debit	Credit
	B, Capital ($6,000 3/5)		3,600	
	T, Capital ($4,000 2/5)		2,400	
	U, Capital			6,000
	To allocate U's capital deficiency to the other partners in their profit and loss ratios.			

Prior to U's withdrawal from the partnership, the partners shared profits and losses as follows:

Ratio: B   3 = 1/2
        T   2 = 1/3
        U   1 = 1/6

The remaining partners are required to absorb the deficiency left by a partner who is unable to contribute sufficient capital to cover the deficiency. After a $4,000 contribution, U's deficiency was reduced to $6,000. Note that between B and T, profits and losses are shared in the ratio of 3 to 2 (or 60% and 40%). As a result, U's uncovered deficiency is allocated to B and T by reducing their capital accounts by $3,600 ($6,000÷60%) and $2,400 ($6,000÷40%), respectively.

e.

Date	Accounts and Explanation	PR	Debit	Credit
	B, Capital		26,400	
	T, Capital		7,600	
	Cash			34,000
	To distribute cash to partners on liquidation of partnership.			

Requirement 3 (Post the liquidation transactions)

Cash

Bal.	30,000	Payment of liabilities	120,000 (b)
(a) Sale of assets 120,000			
(c) U's contribution	4,000		
Bal.	34,000	Final distribution	34,000 (e)
Bal.	0		

Noncash Assets

Bal. 240,000	240,000 (a)		

Liabilities

(b) 120,000	Bal. 120,000		

B, Capital

(a) Loss of sale	60,000	Bal.	90,000
(c) Loss on U	3,600		
Final distribution	26,400	Bal.	26,400
		Bal.	0

T, Capital

(a) Loss on sale	40,000	Bal.	50,000
(d) Loss on U	2,400		
(e) Final distribution	7,600	Bal.	7,600
		Bal.	0

U, Capital

(a) Loss on sale	20,000	Bal.	10,000
		Investment	4,000 (c)
Bal.	6,000	Bal.	6,000 (d)
		Bal.	0

Chapter 13—Corporate Organization, Paid-In Capital, and the Balance Sheet

CHAPTER OVERVIEW

In Chapter 12 you learned about the partnership form of organization. In this chapter, we begin an in-depth discussion of the corporate form of organization. Because the corporate form is more complex than either sole proprietorships or partnerships, our discussion of corporations continues in Chapter 14, 15, and 16. Therefore, an understanding of the topics in this chapter is important before continuing to the next chapter. The learning objectives for this chapter are to

1. Identify the characteristics of a corporation.
2. Record the issuance of stock.
3. Prepare the stockholders' equity section of a corporation balance sheet.
4. Account for cash dividends.
5. Use different stock values in decision making.
6. Evaluate a company's return on assets and return on stockholders' equity.
7. Account for a corporation's income tax.

CHAPTER REVIEW

Objective 1 - Identify the characteristics of a corporation.

1. A corporation is a **separate legal entity** chartered and regulated under state law. The owners' equity of a corporation is held by stockholders as shares of stock.
2. A corporation has **continuous life**. A change in ownership of the stock does not affect the life of the corporation.
3. **Mutual agency of owners is not present** in corporations. A stockholder cannot commit a corporation to a binding contract (unless that stockholder is also an officer of the corporation).
4. Stockholders have **limited liability**. That is, they have no personal obligation for the debts of the corporation.
5. **Ownership and management are separated**. Corporations are controlled by boards of directors who appoint officers to manage the business. Boards of directors are elected by stockholders. Thus, stockholders are not obligated to manage the business; ownership is separate from management.
6. **Corporations pay taxes**: state franchise taxes and federal and state income taxes. Corporations pay dividends to stockholders who then pay personal income taxes on their dividends. This is considered double taxation of corporate earnings.

Exhibit 13-1 in your text summarizes the advantages and disadvantages of a corporation.

Corporations come into existence when a **charter** is obtained from a relevant state official. **Bylaws** are then adopted. The stockholders elect a **board of directors**, who appoint the officers of the corporation. (Review Exhibit 13-2 in your text.)

Owners receive **stock certificates** for their investment. The basic unit of investment is a **share**. A corporation's outstanding stock is the shares of its stock that are held by stockholders. Stockholders' equity is reported differently than owners' equity of a proprietorship or a partnership because corporations must report the sources of their capital. These sources are **paid-in or contributed capital** from sale of stock, and **retained earnings**. Generally, paid-in capital is not subject to withdrawal. Retained Earnings is the account that at any time is the sum of earnings accumulated since incorporation, minus any losses, and minus all dividends distributed to stockholders. Revenues and expenses are closed into Income Summary and then Income Summary is closed to Retained Earnings. To close net income, debit Income Summary and credit Retained Earnings. To close net loss, debit Retained Earnings and credit Income Summary.

Stockholders have four basic **rights**:

1. to participate in management by voting their shares,
2. to receive a proportionate share of any dividend,
3. to a proportionate share of the remaining assets after payment of liabilities in the event of liquidation, and
4. to maintain a proportionate ownership in the corporation (**preemptive right**).

Stock may be **common** or **preferred** and have a **par value** or **no-par value**. **Par value** is an arbitrary value that a corporation assigns to a share of stock. Different classes of common or preferred stock may also be issued. Each class of common or preferred stock is recorded in a separate general ledger account. Preferred stockholders receive their dividends before common stockholders and take priority over common stockholders in the receipt of assets if the corporation liquidates.

The corporate charter specifies the number of shares a corporation is authorized to issue. The corporation is not required to issue all the stock it is authorized to issue.

Exhibit 13-6 in your text compares common stock, preferred stock, and long-term debt.

Objective 2 - Record the issuance of stock.

If a corporation sells common stock for a cash receipt equal to the par value, the entry to record the transaction is:

Cash	XX	
Common Stock		XX

Par value is usually set low enough so that stock will not be sold below par. A corporation usually sells its common stock for a price above par value, that is, at a premium. The **premium** is also paid-in capital, but is recorded in a separate account called **Paid-In Capital in Excess of Par Value**. A premium is not a gain, income, or profit to the corporation. A corporation cannot earn a profit or incur a loss by buying or selling its own stock. The entry to record stock issued at a price in excess of par value is:

Cash	XX	
Common Stock		XX
Paid-in Capital in Excess of Par - Common Stock		XX

If no-par common stock has no stated value, the entry is the same as for a cash selling price equal to par value (above). Accounting for no-par common stock with a **stated value** is identical to accounting for par-value stock. When a corporation receives non-cash assets as an investment, the assets are recorded by the corporation at their current market value.

Accounting for preferred stock follows the same pattern as accounting for common stock. The difference is that instead of the word "Common," the word "Preferred" will appear in the titles of the general ledger accounts.

Occasionally a corporation will receive a donation such as land or some other asset. The donated asset is recorded at its current market value. If the donation is received from a governmental agency, the account Donated Capital is credited. Donated Capital is a separate category of Paid-in Capital and is listed on the balance sheet. If the donation is received from someone other than a governmental agency, the account credited is Revenue from Donations and reported as Other Revenue on the income statement.

Objective 3 - Prepare the stockholders' equity section of a balance sheet.

Preferred stock always appears before common stock in the stockholders' equity section of the balance sheet.

The format of the stockholders' equity section of the balance sheet is:

Stockholders' Equity	
Paid-in capital:	
Preferred stock, $ par, number of shares authorized,	
number of shares issued	XX
Paid-in capital in excess of par - preferred stock	XX
Common stock, $ par, number of shares authorized,	
number of shares issued	XX
Paid-in capital in excess of par - common stock	XX
Donated capital	XX
Total paid-in capital	XX
Retained earnings	XX
Total stockholders' equity	XX

> **Study Tip:** Review the Decision Guidelines *Reporting Stockholders' Equity on the Balance Sheet* in your text.

A **dividend** is a distribution of cash to the stockholders of a corporation. A corporation must have Retained Earnings and sufficient cash in order to declare a dividend. A dividend must be declared by the board of directors before the corporation can pay it. Once a dividend has been declared, it is a legal liability of the corporation.

On the **date of declaration** the board also announces the **date of record** and the **payment date**. Those owning the shares on the date of record will receive the dividend. The payment date is the date the dividends are actually mailed.

Objective 4 - Account for cash dividends.

When a dividend is declared, this entry is recorded:

Retained Earnings	XX	
Dividends Payable		XX

Dividends Payable is a current liability.

The date of record falls between the declaration date and the payment date and requires no journal entry. The dividend is usually paid several weeks after it is declared. When it is paid, this entry is recorded:

Dividends Payable	XX	
Cash		XX

Preferred stockholders have priority over common stockholders for receipt of dividends. In other words, common stockholders do not receive dividends unless the total declared dividend is sufficient to pay the preferred stockholders first.

Preferred stock usually carries a stated percentage rate or a dollar amount per share. Thus, if par value is $50 per share, "5% preferred" stockholders receive a $2.50 ($50 × 5%) annual dividend. Stockholders holding "$3 preferred" stock would receive a $3 annual cash dividend regardless of the par value of the stock. The dividend to common stockholders will equal:

Common dividend = Total dividend - Preferred dividend

A dividend is passed when a corporation fails to pay an annual dividend to preferred stockholders. Passed dividends are said to be in arrears. **Cumulative preferred stock** continues to accumulate annual dividends until the dividends are paid. Therefore, a corporation must pay all dividends in arrears to cumulative preferred stockholders before it can pay dividends to other stockholders.

Dividends in arrears are not liabilities, but are disclosed in notes to the financial statements. Preferred stock is considered cumulative unless it is specifically labeled as noncumulative. Noncumulative preferred stock does not accumulate dividends in arrears.

Convertible preferred stock can be exchanged by the holder for another class of stock. Suppose you have 200 shares of preferred stock and each share can be converted to four shares of common stock. If the market value of 800 shares of common stock exceeds the market value of 200 shares of convertible preferred stock, conversion would be to your advantage.

The entry to record conversion, assuming that the par value of the preferred stock is greater than the par value of the common stock, is:

Preferred stock	XX	
Common stock		XX
Paid-in capital in excess of par -		
common stock		XX

Objective 5 - Use different stock values in decision making.

Market value (market price) is the price at which a person could buy or sell a share of the stock. Daily newspapers report the market price of many publicly traded stocks.

Sometimes preferred stock can be redeemed by the corporation for a stated amount per share. This amount, which is set when the stock is issued, is called **redemption value**.

Preferred stock may also be issued with a **liquidation value**. This is the amount the corporation agrees to pay preferred stockholders if the company liquidates. Dividends in arrears are added to liquidation value to determine the amount to be paid if liquidation occurs.

Book value is the amount of stockholders' equity per share of stock. If only common stock is outstanding:

$$\textbf{Book value} = \frac{\textbf{Total stockholders' equity}}{\textbf{Number of shares outstanding}}$$

If both preferred and common stock are outstanding, preferred stockholders equity must be calculated first. If preferred stock has no redemption value, then total preferred equity in the equation below is equal to the balance in Preferred Stock plus Paid-in Capital in Excess of Par-Preferred. If preferred stock has a redemption value, then total preferred equity in the equation below equals the total redemption value (redemption value per share × number of preferred shares).

$$\textbf{Preferred book value} = \frac{\textbf{Total preferred equity + Dividends in arrears}}{\textbf{Number of preferred shares outstanding}}$$

$$\textbf{Common book value} = \frac{\textbf{Total equity - (Total preferred equity + Dividends in arrears)}}{\textbf{Number of common shares outstanding}}$$

Objective 6 - Evaluate a company's return on assets and return on stockholders' equity.

1. $\textbf{Rate of return on total assets} = \dfrac{\underline{\textbf{Net income + Interest expense}}}{\textbf{Average total assets}}$

The return on total assets (or return on assets) measures how successfully the company was in using its (average) assets to earn a profit.

2. $\textbf{Rate of return on common stockholders' equity} = \dfrac{\underline{\textbf{Net income - Preferred dividends}}}{\textbf{Average common stockholders' equity}}$

The denominator, average common stockholders' equity, is equal to total stockholders' equity minus preferred equity.

The rate of return on common stockholders' equity also measures profitability of the company. The return on equity should always be higher than the return on assets.

Objective 7 - Account for a corporation's income tax.

Because corporations have a distinct legal identity (they have the right to contract, to sue, and be sued--just as individuals have these rights), their income is taxed just like individuals. However, unlike individuals, the amount of tax actually paid will differ from the expense incurred for the period (for individuals, these amounts are generally the same). The difference results from the following:

Income tax expense is calculated by multiplying the applicable tax rate times the amount of pre-tax accounting income as reported on the income statement, while **income tax payable** is calculated by multiplying the applicable tax rate times the amount of taxable income as reported on the corporate tax return. Because these results will differ, a third account, **Deferred Income Tax**, is used to reconcile the entry, as follows:

Income Tax Expense	XX	
Income Tax Payable		XX
Deferred Income Tax		XX
(When the expense is greater than the liability.)		

Income Tax Expense	XX	
Deferred Income Tax	XX	
Income Tax Payable		XX
(When the expense is less than the liability.)		

TEST YOURSELF

All the self-testing materials in this chapter focus on information and procedures that your instructor is likely to test in quizzes and examinations.

Matching   *Match each numbered term with its lettered definition.*

_____ 1. authorized stock
_____ 2. book value
_____ 3. chairperson of the board
_____ 4. convertible stock
_____ 5. cumulative stock
_____ 6. legal capital
_____ 7. revenue from donations
_____ 8. liquidation value
_____ 9. market value
_____ 10. outstanding stock
_____ 11. stated value
_____ 12. preferred stock
_____ 13. stockholders' equity
_____ 14. retained earnings
_____ 15. deferred income tax

_____ 16. board of directors
_____ 17. bylaws
_____ 18. charter
_____ 19. common stock
_____ 20. deficit
_____ 21. dividends
_____ 22. limited liability
_____ 23. paid-in capital
_____ 24. par value
_____ 25. preemptive right
_____ 26. premium on stock
_____ 27. contributed capital
_____ 28. income tax expense
_____ 29. income tax payable

A. an account which reconciles the difference between income tax expense and income tax payable
B. a corporation's capital that is earned through profitable operation of the business
C. a corporation's capital from investments by the stockholders
D. a debit balance in the retained earnings account
E. a group elected by the stockholders to set policy for a corporation and to appoint its officers
F. another term for paid-in capital
G. the account created when a corporation receives a gift from a donor who receives no ownership interest in the company
H. a stockholder's right to maintain a proportionate ownership in a corporation
I. an arbitrary amount assigned to a share of stock
J. an elected person on a corporation's board of directors who is usually the most powerful person in the corporation
K. the portion of stockholders' equity that cannot be used for dividend
L. distributions by a corporation to its stockholders
M. means that the most that a stockholder can lose on his investment in a corporation's stock is the cost of the investment
N. owners' equity of a corporation
O. similar to par value
P. preferred stock that may be exchanged by the stockholders, if they choose, for another class of stock in the corporation
Q. preferred stock whose owners must receive all dividends in arrears before the corporation pays dividends to the common stockholders
R. pre-tax accounting income times the tax rate
S. shares of stock in the hands of stockholders
T. stock that gives its owners certain advantages such as the priority to receive dividends and the priority to receive assets if the corporation liquidates

U. the amount that a corporation agrees to pay a preferred stockholder per share if the company liquidates
V. the amount of owners' equity on the company's books for each share of its stock
W. taxable income times the tax rate
X. the constitution for governing a corporation
Y. the document that gives the state's permission to form a corporation
Z. the excess of the issue price of stock over its par value
AA. the most basic form of capital stock
BB. the price for which a person could buy or sell a share of stock
CC. the maximum number of shares of stock a corporation may issue

II. Multiple Choice   *Circle the best answer.*

1. The corporate board of directors is:

   A. appointed by the state
   B. elected by management
   C. elected by the stockholders
   D. appointed by corporate officers

2. A stockholder has no personal obligation for corporation liabilities. This is called:

   A. mutual agency
   B. limited agency
   C. transferability of ownership
   D. limited liability

3. Stated value has the same meaning as:

   A. market value
   B. par value
   C. book value
   D. redemption value

4. A stock certificate shows all of the following except:

   A. additional paid-in capital
   B. stockholder name
   C. par value
   D. company name

5. The ownership of stock entitles common stockholders to all of the following rights except:

   A. right to receive guaranteed dividends
   B. voting right
   C. preemptive right
   D. right to receive a proportionate share of assets in a liquidation

6. When a corporation declares a cash dividend:

   A. liabilities decrease, assets decrease
   B. assets decrease, retained earnings decreases
   C. assets decrease, retained earnings increases
   D. liabilities increase, retained earnings decrease

7. When a corporation pays a cash dividend:

    A. liabilities decrease, assets increase
    B. assets decrease, retained earnings decreases
    C. liabilities decrease, assets decrease
    D. retained earnings decrease, liabilities increase

8. When a company issues stock in exchange for assets other than cash, the assets are recorded at:

    A. market value   C. book value
    B. original cost   D. replacement cost

9. Dividends Payable is a(n):

    A. expense   C. paid-in capital account
    B. current liability   D. stockholders' equity account

10. Dividends in arrears on preferred stock are reported:

    A. on the balance sheet   C. on the income statement
    B. as a reduction of retained earnings   D. as a footnote to the financial statements

III. Completion   *Complete each of the following.*

1. Every corporation issues _____ stock.
2. The corporation's constitution is called the _____.
3. Preferred stockholders have preference over common stockholders in _____ _____ and _____.
4. Dividends are declared by _____.
5. Taxable income times the applicable tax rate equals _____.
6. Stockholders' equity minus preferred equity equals _____.
7. The date of _____ determines who receives the dividend.
8. The date of _____ establishes the liability to pay a dividend.
9. The price at which a share of stock is bought or sold is called the _____ value.
10. Corporations come into existence when a _____ is approved by the _____ government.

IV. Daily Exercises

1. Arrange the following stockholders' equity items in the correct sequence.

   Donated capital
   Common stock
   Paid-in capital in excess of par - preferred
   Retained earnings
   Preferred stock
   Paid-in capital in excess of par - common

2. Assets donated to a corporation are recorded at their current market value. However, the account credited is determined by the source of the donation. Which two accounts could be credited and what circumstances dictate which to use? How are both reported on the financial statements?

3. A company issues 40,000 shares of common stock for $30 per share. Record this transaction (omit explanation) assuming

   a. the stock had a par value of $1 per share
   b. the stock had no par value, but a stated value of $1 per share
   c. the stock had no par or stated value

4. On September 10, the board of directors declares an annual dividend of $30,000 payable on October 30 to stockholders of record on September 30. Make the journal entries to record the declaration date, record date, and payment date.

5. Refer to the information in Daily Exercise #4 and assume the company has 4,000 shares of $50 par, 4% preferred stock issued and 10,000 shares of $1 par common stock. The preferred stock is non-cumulative and this is the first dividend the corporation has declared since the stock was issued four years ago. Calculate the amount due to each class of shareholder.

6. Refer to the information in Daily Exercise #5, but assume the preferred stock is cumulative. Calculate the amount due each class of shareholder.

V. Exercises

1. The charter of Berger Corporation authorizes the issuance of 25,000 shares of preferred stock and 300,000 shares of common stock. During the first year of operation, Berger Corporation completed the following stock-issuance transactions:

March 1   Issued 40,000 shares of $1 par common stock for cash of $15 per share.
March 10   Issued 5,000 shares of 6%, no-par preferred stock with stated value of $50 per share. The issue price was cash of $60 per share.
March 28   Received inventory valued at $25,000 and equipment with a market value of $60,000 in exchange for 2,000 shares of $1 par common stock.

Prepare the journal entries for March 1, 10, and 28.

2. Review the information in Exercise #1 and assume retained earnings has a balance of $95,000. Prepare the stockholders' equity section of the Berger Corporation balance sheet at the end of the first year.

3. Coles Corporation has 2,000 shares of $50 par, cumulative, 8% preferred stock outstanding. There were no dividends in arrears at the end of 1996, and no dividends were paid in 1997 or 1998. Coles also has 10,000 shares of $5 par common stock outstanding.

   A. If Coles pays a total of $60,000 in dividends in 1999, how much will each class of stockholders receive?

   B. If Coles pays a total of $20,000 in dividends in 1999, how much will each class of stockholders receive?

4. The balance sheet of Winter House Corporation reports total stockholders' equity of $719,500, consisting of the following:

   a. Redeemable preferred stock; redemption value $22,000; 400 shares issued and outstanding
   b. Common stockholders' equity, 15,500 shares issued and outstanding.
   c. Winter House has paid preferred dividends for the current year and there are no dividends in arrears.

   Compute the book value per share of the preferred stock and the common stock.

5. Natural Fibers Corporation reported pre-tax income of $242,000 on their income statement and $186,000 taxable income on their tax return. Assuming a corporate tax rate of 35%, present the journal entry to record Natural Fibers taxes for the year.

Date	Accounts and Explanation	PR	Debit	Credit

VI. Beyond the Numbers

Using the information in Daily Exercise #5 and #6, state the effect (increase, decrease, no effect), as of 12/31 on the return on assets, return on stockholders' equity, and book value in each situation. Assume preferred's redemption value is its par value.

VII. Demonstration Problems

Demonstration Problem #1

On January 1, 1999, California authorized Video Productions, Inc. to issue 100,000 shares of 6%, $25 par preferred stock and 1,000,000 shares of common stock with a $1 par value. During January, the company completed the following selected transactions related to its stockholders' equity:

1/10   Sold 50,000 shares of common stock at $15 per share.
1/11   Issued 6,000 shares of preferred stock for cash at $25 per share.
1/17   Issued 20,000 shares of common stock in exchange for land valued at $420,000.
1/24   An old building and small parcel of land was donated to the corporation by a town for a future office site that would employ 60 people. The site value was $125,000; the building was worthless.
1/27   Sold 2,000 shares of preferred stock at $31 a share.
1/31   Earned a small profit for January and closed the $3,800 credit balance of Income Summary into the Retained Earnings account.

Required

1. Record the transactions in the general journal.
2. Post the journal entries into the equity accounts provided.
3. Prepare the stockholders' equity section of Video Productions, Inc. balance sheet at Jan 31, 1999.
4. Compute the book value per share of the preferred stock and the common stock. The preferred stock has a liquidation value of $30 per share. No dividends are in arrears.

Requirement 1 (journal entries)

Date	Accounts and Explanation	PR	Debit	Credit

Requirement 2 (postings)

Requirements 3 (Stockholders' equity section)

Video Productions, Inc.
Balance Sheet - Stockholders' Equity Section
January 31, 1999

Requirement 4 (book value per share)

Demonstration Problem #2

Wilcox Corporation has the following capital structure: 5,000 shares of $25 par, 4% preferred stock authorized and outstanding, and 100,000 authorized shares of $2 par common stock, 20,000 shares issued. During years X1 through X4, the corporation declared the following dividends:

X1	$0
X2	2,000
X3	40,000
X4	120,000

A. Assume the preferred stock is noncumulative, calculate the amount of dividends per share for each share of stock for each year.

Year	Dividend Amount	Preferred	Common

B. Assume the preferred stock is cumulative, calculate the amount of dividends per share each year for each share of stock.

Year	Dividend Amount	Preferred	Common

SOLUTIONS

I. Matching

1. CC	5. Q	9. BB	13. N	17. X	21. L	25. H	29. W
2. V	6. K	10. S	14. B	18. Y	22. M	26. Z	
3. J	7. G	11. O	15. A	19. AA	23. C	27. F	
4. P	8. U	12. T	16. E	20. D	24. I	28. R	

II. Multiple Choice

1.   C   Each share of common stock usually gives the stockholder one vote in the election of the board of directors.

2.   D   Recall that mutual agency is a characteristic of partnerships not present in corporations. Transferability of ownership is a characteristic that the corporate form of organization simplifies as compared with partnerships. Limited agency has no meaning.

3.   B   Stated value, like par value, is an arbitrary value assigned to a share of stock.

4.   A   Additional paid-in capital is the excess of the price paid to the corporation over the par value of the stock.

5.   A   Dividends represent the distribution of the earnings of the corporation and are not guaranteed.

6.   D   The declaration of a dividend reduces Retained Earnings and increases the liability account, Dividends Payable.

7.   C   The payment of a cash dividend results in cash being paid to stockholders to settle the liability created by the declaration of the dividend.

8.   A   When capital stock is issued in exchange for non-cash assets, the transaction should be recorded at fair market value.

9.   B   The declaration of a dividend by the board of directors creates a current liability.

10.   D   Dividends in arrears is not a liability since a dividend must be declared to create a liability. However, dividends in arrears do impair the amount of capital available to common stockholders. Dividends in arrears are usually disclosed by a footnote.

III. Completion

1. common (Corporations may also issue preferred stock, but that is optional.)
2. bylaws
3. receiving dividends and in event of a liquidation
4. the board of directors
5. Income Tax Payable
6. common stockholders' equity
7. record
8. declaration
9. market
10. charter; state

IV. Daily Exercises

1.

    Preferred stock
    Paid-in capital in excess of par - preferred
    Common stock
    Paid-in capital in excess of par - common
    Donated capital
    Retained earnings

Study Tip: Paid-in (contributed) capital is always listed first, followed by Retained Earnings.

---

2. Either Revenue from Donations or Donated Capital will be credited when assets are donated to the company. Donated Capital is credited when the source of the donations is a governmental agency; otherwise, Revenue from Donations is credited. Donated Capital is a stockholders' equity account on the balance sheet while Revenues from Donations appears as Other Revenue on the Income Statement.

3.

a.	Cash		1,200,000	
		Common Stock		40,000
		Paid-in Capital in Excess of Par - Common		1,160,000
b.	Cash		1,200,000	
		Common Stock		40,000
		Paid-in Capital in Excess of Stated Value - Common		1,160,000
c.	Cash		1,200,000	
		Common Stock		1,200,000

4.

9/10	Retained Earnings		30,000	
	Dividends Payable			30,000
9/20	No entry			
10/30	Dividends Payable		30,000	
	Cash			30,000

Study Tip: Remember no entry is required on the record date. This simply determines who will receive the dividends when mailed.

5.

    Preferred: $50 × 4% = $2 per share × 4,000 shares = $8,000.
    Common: $30,000 - $8,000 = $22,000, or $2.20 per share.

Since the preferred stock is noncumulative, the preferred shareholders are only entitled to the current year's dividend ($8,000). The balance is distributed to the common stock.

6.

Preferred: $8,000 per year (see above) × 4 years = $32,000.

Since the board of directors only declared $30,000 for dividends, preferred shareholders receive the entire amount ($7.50 per share) and still have a $2,000 arrearage. The common stock receives nothing!

V. Exercises

1.

3/1	Cash		600,000	
	Common Stock			40,000
	Paid-in Capital in Excess of Par - Common			560,000
3/10	Cash		300,000	
	Preferred Stock			250,000
	Paid-in Capital in Excess of Par - Preferred			50,000
3/28	Inventory		25,000	
	Equipment		60,000	
	Common Stock			2,000
	Paid-in Capital in Excess of Par - Common			83,000

2.

Stockholders' Equity

Paid-in capital:

Preferred stock, 6%, no-par, $50 stated value, 25,000 shares authorized, 5,000 shares issued	250,000
Paid-in capital in excess of par – preferred stock	50,000
Common stock, $1 par, 300,000 shares authorized, 42,000 shares issued	42,000
Paid-in capital in excess of par – common stock	643,000
Total paid-in capital	985,000
Retained earnings	95,000
Total stockholders' equity	1,080,000

3.

A. Preferred: 3 years × 2,000 shares × $50 par × 8% = $24,000
   Common: $60,000 - $24,000 = $36,000

B. Preferred: 3 years × 2,000 shares × $50 par × 8% = $24,000
   Since $20,000 is less than the $24,000 preferred stockholders must receive before common stockholders receive anything, all $20,000 goes to the preferred stockholders.

4.

$$\text{Preferred book value} = \frac{\text{Total preferred equity} + \text{Dividends in arrears}}{\text{Number of preferred shares outstanding}}$$

$$\text{Preferred book value} = \frac{\$22,000 + \$0}{400} = \$55$$

$$\text{Common book value} = \frac{\text{Total equity} - (\text{Total preferred equity} + \text{Dividends arrears})}{\text{Number of common shares outstanding}}$$

$$\text{Common book value} = \frac{\$719,500 - (\$22,000 + \$0)}{15,500} = \$45.00$$

5.

Income Tax Expense	84,700	
Income Tax Payable		65,100
Deferred Income Tax		19,600

Income Tax Expense = $242,000 × 35% = $84,700
Income Tax Payable = $186,000 × 35% = $65,100
Deferred Income Tax = $84,700 - $65,100 = $19,600

VI. Beyond the Numbers

Here's the solution—see below for the explanation. This is more difficult than you might have thought.

Situation	Return on Assets	Return on Stockholders' Equity	Common Book Value
a. preferred stock is non-cumulative	increase	decrease	decrease
b. preferred stock is cumulative	increase	decrease	decrease

The formulas are:

$$\text{Rate of return on total assets} = \frac{\text{Net income} + \text{Interest expense}}{\text{Average total assets}}$$

$$\text{Rate of return on common stockholders' equity} = \frac{\text{Net income} - \text{Preferred dividends}}{\text{Average common stockholders' equity}}$$

$$\text{Common book value} = \frac{\text{Total equity} - (\text{Total preferred equity} + \text{Dividends arrears})}{\text{Number of common shares outstanding}}$$

For the return on assets, neither net income nor interest expense change because dividends of $20,000 were paid (regardless of who got how much.) However, average total assets will decrease because of the $30,000 reduction in cash. Therefore, return on assets will increase in both situations.

For return on stockholders' equity, the numerator (net income less preferred dividends) is smaller because of the dividend payment. The denominator (average stockholders' equity) is also decreasing because the total dividends are debited to Retained Earnings. In Exercise #5, the numerator is decreasing by $8,000 while the denominator is decreasing by $30,000. In Exercise #6, the numerator is decreasing by $30,000 while the denominator is decreasing by $32,000 (the $30,000 dividends recorded plus the $2,000 still in arrears to the preferred shareholders).

For common book value, the numerator in both exercises is decreasing while the denominator remains constant.

VII. Demonstration Problems

Demonstration Problem #1 Solved and Explained

Requirement 1

1/10	Cash	750,000	
	Common Stock (50,000 × $1)		50,000
	Paid-in Capital in Excess of Par -		
	Common Stock (50,000 × $14)		700,000
	Sold common stock at $14 per share.		

The payment of cash is recorded by debiting Cash and crediting Common Stock for the number of shares times the par value of the stock (50,000 × $1). The balance is recorded in the premium account, Paid-in Capital in Excess of Par - Common Stock.

1/11	Cash (6,000 × $25)	150,000	
	Preferred Stock (6,000 × $25)		150,000
	Issued preferred stock at par.		

Preferred Stock is credited for the shares times par (6,000 × $25).

1/17	Land	420,000	
	Common Stock (20,000 × $1)		20,000
	Paid-in Capital in Excess of Par -		
	Common Stock ($420,000 - $20,000)		400,000
	To issue common stock at a premium price.		

When a corporation issues stock in exchange for an asset other than cash, it debits the asset received (in this case, land) for its fair market value and credits the capital accounts as it would do if cash were the asset received.

1/24	Land	125,000	
	Donated Capital		125,000
	To record land received as a donation from the town.		

The donation of land by a town is a gift. Since the donor is a governmental entity, the donation is recorded by debiting the asset received at its current market value and by crediting Donated Capital. Since the building is worthless, the debit should be made to the Land account.

1/27	Cash	62,000	
	Preferred Stock (2,000 × $25)		50,000
	Paid-in Capital in excess of par -		
	Preferred ($62,000 - $50,000)		12,000

The amount received above the stock's par value is recorded in a premium account, Paid-in Capital in excess of par - Preferred Stock.

1/31	Income Summary	3,800	
	Retained Earnings		3,800

To close Income Summary by transferring net income into Retained Earnings.

At the end of each month or year, the balance of the Income Summary account is transferred to Retained Earnings. Video Productions, Inc. earned a small profit in January. The closing entry will debit Income Summary (to reduce it to zero) and credit Retained Earnings (increasing stockholders' equity to reflect profitable operations).

Requirement 2

Preferred Stock

	1/11 150,000
	1/27 50,000
	Bal. 200,000

Common Stock

	1/11 50,000
	1/17 20,000
	Bal. 70,000

Paid-in Capital in Excess of Par - Preferred Stock

	1/27 12,000
	Bal. 12,000

Paid-in Capital in Excess of Par – Common Stock

	1/11 700,000
	1/17 400,000
	Bal. 1,100,000

Retained Earnings

	1/31 3,800
	Bal. 3,800

Donated Capital

	1/24 125,000
	Bal. 125,000

Requirements 3

Video Productions, Inc.
Balance Sheet - Stockholders' Equity Section
January 31, 1999

Stockholders' equity:	
Preferred stock, 6%, $25 par, 100,000 shares authorized	$ 200,000
Paid-in capital in excess of par - Preferred stock	12,000
Common stock, $1 par, 1,000,000 shares authorized	70,000
Paid-in capital in excess of par - Common stock	1,100,000
Donated capital	125,000
Total paid-in capital	1,507,000
Retained earnings	3,800

Total stockholders' equity	$1,510,800

Requirement 4

Preferred:

Liquidation value (8,000 shares × $30)	$ 240,000
Dividends in arrears	0
Stockholders' equity allocated to preferred	240,000
Book value per share ($240,000 ÷ 8,000 shares)	$ 30.00

Common:

Total stockholders' equity	$1,510,800
Less: Stockholders' equity allocated to preferred	240,000
Stockholders' equity allocated to common	1,270,800
Book value per share ($1,270,800 ÷ 70,000 shares)	$18.15 (rounded)

Calculated as follows:

Date	No. of Shares	Transactions
1/10	50,000	Issued
1/17	20,000	Issued
	70,000 Shares	

Demonstration Problem #2 Solved and Explained

A. Preferred stock is noncumulative.

Year	Dividend Amount	Preferred	Common
X1	$0	$0	$0
X2	$2,000	$0.40 per share ($2,000 ÷ 5,000 shares)	$0
X3	$40,000	$1.00 per share 5,000 shares × $25 par × 4%	$1.75 per share $35,000 ÷ 20,000
X4	$120,000	$1.00 per share 5,000 shares × $25 par × 4%	$5.75 $115,000 ÷ 20,000

The preferred stock is noncumulative so the shareholders are only entitled to the current year's dividend, which is $1/share for a total of $5,000. Any (and all) excess goes to the common shareholders.

B. The preferred stock is cumulative.

Year	Dividend Amount	Preferred	Common
X1	$0	$0	$0

There are now $5,000 of preferred dividends in arrears.

Year	Dividend Amount	Preferred	Common
X2	$2,000	$0.40 per share ($2,000 ÷ 5,000 shares)	$0

There are now $8,000 of preferred dividends in arrears.

Year	Dividend Amount	Preferred	Common
X3	$40,000	$2.60 per share	$1.35 per share

First, the preferred shares get their arrearage which is $1 each from X1 and $.60 from X2 for a total of $1.60. Then they get their $1 for X3, so a total of $2.60. The balance $27,000 ($40,000 - $13,000) goes to common.

Year	Dividend Amount	Preferred	Common
X4	$120,000	$1.00 per share	$5.75

Preferred has no arrearage so they receive $1.00 per share with the remainder going to common.

Study Tip: Most preferred stock is cumulative. The term has no meaning when applied to common stock.